MEASURES of SUCCESS®

A Comprehensive Musicianship Band Method

DEBORAH A. SHELDON • BRIAN BALMAGES • TIMOTHY LOEST • ROBERT SHELDON
PERCUSSION WRITTEN AND EDITED BY DAVID COLLIER

Welcome to *Measures of Success* and the amazing world of instrumental music! You are about to begin an exciting musical journey full of rewards and challenges. As you practice, you will find yourself sharing the gift of music with family, friends, and audiences. So get ready—your path to success begins now!

HISTORY OF PERCUSSION

Percussion instruments predate any other instruments. They have been found in nearly every society on Earth with examples dating back thousands of years. Historically, percussion instruments have played an important role in ceremonies, communication, military exercises, and musical expression. Percussion instruments are any instruments that produce a sound when they are struck, shaken or scraped. They are categorized by the way they produce their sounds. Instruments that vibrate when struck, like cymbals and triangles, are known as idiophones. Instruments that have a drumhead which vibrates, like snare drum and bass drum, are known as membranophones. Early drums were constructed from tree logs covered with animal skins. In the 13th century, small bowl-shaped drums of Arabic origin (called nakers) came to Europe. The timpani, derived from nakers, were added to the European orchestra in 1675, followed by cymbals in 1680, and bass drum in 1779. The snare drum was added much later.

The orchestra bells originated in Germany and were called "glockenspiel" (many composers continue to call them that to this very day). They originally were a set of bells of varying sizes. In the late 16th century, a musical keyboard design was introduced to make them easier to play. Handel is credited as the first major composer to use an early version of orchestra bells in a composition.

The percussion family is very large and includes timpani, drums of all kinds, keyboard percussion, cymbals and gongs, accessory instruments, world percussion, effects instruments, and the modern drumset. Today percussion plays a key role in wind bands, marching bands, orchestras, movie soundtracks, and jazz, rock and world music ensembles.

ABOUT THIS BOOK

Your book is divided into two main sections. The first section includes snare drum, bass drum, accessory percussion and timpani. These pages are often divided into A and B pages because there are multiple instruments you will learn. The second section contains all of the keyboard percussion exercises. Be sure to work from both sides of the book so that you become a *complete percussionist!*

Production: Frank J. Hackinson
Production Coordinators: Ken Mattis, Brian Balmages, and Philip Groeber
Cover Design and Interior Line Drawings: Danielle Taylor and Adrianne Hirosky / Interior Layout and Design: Andi Whitmer
Engraving: Tempo Music Press, Inc. / Printer: Tempo Music Press, Inc.

THE F·J·H MUSIC COMPANY INC.
Frank J. Hackinson

ISBN-13: 978-1-56939-819-7

SNARE DRUM ASSEMBLY

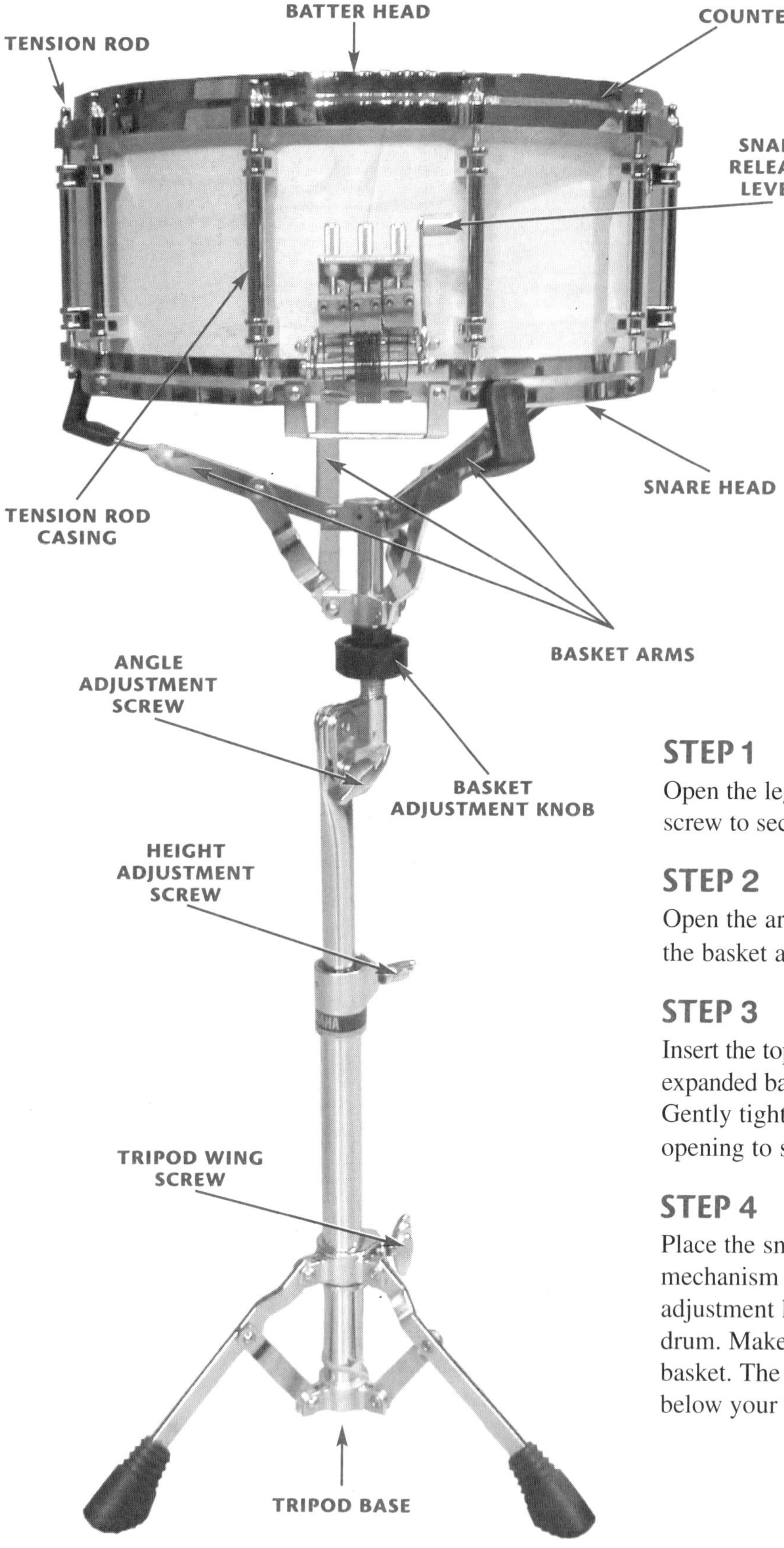

STEP 1

Open the legs of the tripod base. Gently tighten the wing screw to secure the legs.

STEP 2

Open the arms of the top basket. You may need to loosen the basket adjustment knob to fully expand the arms.

STEP 3

Insert the top part of the stand into the tripod base so that the expanded basket arms are several inches below your waist. Gently tighten the height adjustment screw at the base opening to secure both parts.

STEP 4

Place the snare drum in the basket with the snare release mechanism facing your stomach. Tighten the basket adjustment knob so that the arms securely cradle the snare drum. Make sure the snare drum does not move in the basket. The drumhead should be level and positioned just below your waist.

PARTS OF THE DRUM STICK

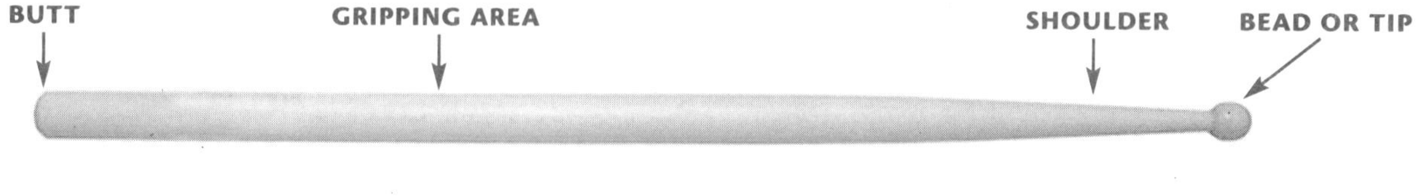

CHECK IT OUT!

OSTURE CHECKLIST

- Stand straight, tall and relaxed
- Height of drum is just below your waist
- Snare release mechanism faces your body
- Elbows comfortably away from your sides
- Arms are relaxed in front of body with a very slight downward angle

MATCHED GRIP CHECKLIST

- The grip is the same in both hands
- **Grip point** is 1/3 the way up from the butt of the stick between thumb and first finger
- Thumb stays inline with the stick
- Remaining fingers gently wrap around the stick
- Palms are facing down

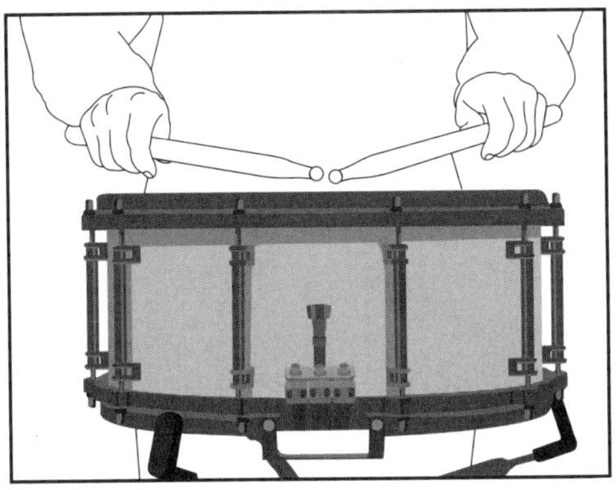

STICK POSITION CHECKLIST (THE REST POSITION)

- Stick tips rest 2 inches above the center of the drum head or practice pad
- Sticks are held at an angle similar to a pizza slice
- Striking area is within a circle the size of a quarter

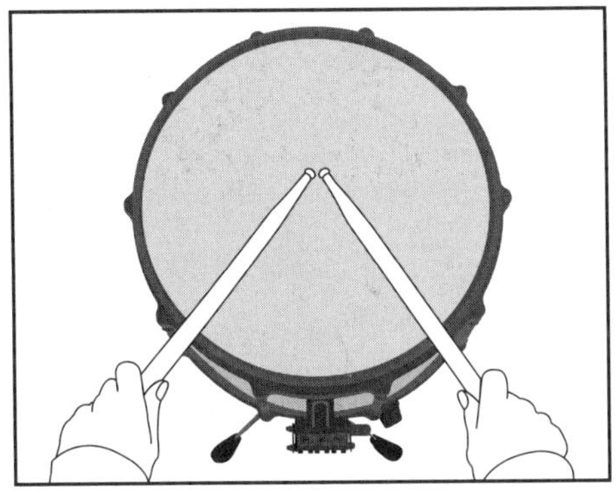

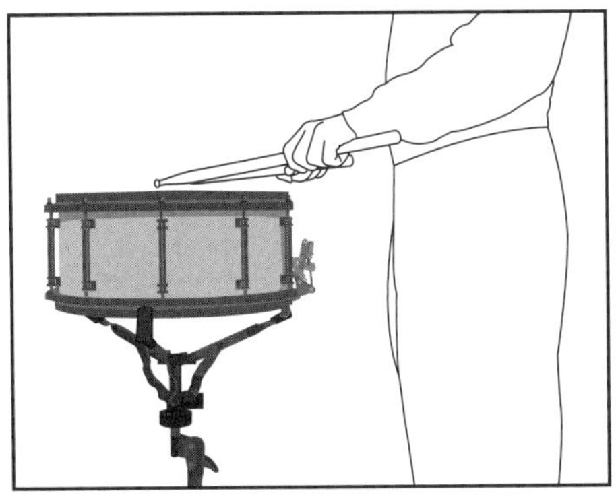

RECOMMENDED STICKS AND MALLETS

- 1 pair of general or 2B snare drum sticks
- 1 pair of hard rubber xylophone mallets
- 1 pair of hard rubber or plastic bell mallets
- 1 pair of general or medium timpani mallets
- 1 pair of medium rubber xylophone mallets (for wood block)
- 1 pair of medium vibraphone mallets (for suspended cymbal)
- 1 pair of medium metal triangle beaters
- 1 medium bass drum mallet

SNARE DRUM CARE

DAILY

- Check that the stand is assembled correctly and the wing screws are tightened before placing the drum in the snare basket
- Exercise caution when placing your snare drum on its stand
- Wipe away fingerprints with a soft cloth from all metal surfaces including the stand
- Always store your snare drum in its case when not in use

WEEKLY

- Check that all tension rods are secure
- Adjust the snare tension as needed to maintain the desired sound

NEVER

- Never place any objects on the batter head (top head)
- Never let any objects make contact with the fragile snare head (bottom head)
- Never keep any objects that can damage the drum inside its case

TYPES OF STROKES

Primary Stroke: This is the basic stroke on snare drum and keyboard percussion instruments. It is a tossing motion to the instrument with a relaxed rebound or follow-through back to the up position. For each hand motion, there is only one sound on the drum. When done smoothly, it is also known as a **legato stroke.**

Bounce Stroke: This stroke has the same motion as a primary stroke, but the tip of the stick is allowed to bounce on the drum head to produce a buzzing sound. For each hand motion, there is more than one sound.

Grace or Tap Stroke: This is a small stroke that has a very small up stroke and then returns to the rest position.

STROKE PRODUCTION

Step 1: Place the sticks in the rest position.

Step 2: In one motion, use your wrist to raise the tip of the right stick from the rest position to a height of 10–12 inches (the **up position**) and toss it toward the drum head. Keep all fingers in contact with the stick.

Step 3: Let the stick rebound back to the up position.

Step 4: Repeat the process with the left stick.

Step 5: When alternating hands, the stick that is not moving waits in the rest position.

For Practice: Hold a tennis ball in one hand. Toss it to the floor and catch it as it bounces back. Switch hands. This is the type of motion you will use when you make a primary stroke..

PRACTICE ROUTINE

- Start with both sticks in the rest position.
- Play each pattern at a steady speed using relaxed primary strokes
- Watch to see that your stick tips strike in the center of the drum head or practice pad
- Watch to see that your sticks come up to the same height and listen to see if they sound the same
- Be sure to use only your wrists

Percussionists use **R** and **L** to refer to right and left hands. Throughout this book, you will see these **stickings** as a guide.

LET'S PLAY!

R R R R | R R R R | L L L L | L L L L |
1 2 3 4   1 2 3 4   1 2 3 4   1 2 3 4

(rest)
R R R R | - - - - | L L L L | - - - - |
1 2 3 4   1 2 3 4   1 2 3 4   1 2 3 4

R - R - | R - R - | L - L - | L - L - |
1 2 3 4   1 2 3 4   1 2 3 4   1 2 3 4

R R R - | L L L - | R R R - | L L L - |
1 2 3 4   1 2 3 4   1 2 3 4   1 2 3 4

R L R - | L R L - | R L R - | L R L - |
1 2 3 4   1 2 3 4   1 2 3 4   1 2 3 4

L R L - | R L R - | L R L - | R L R - |
1 2 3 4   1 2 3 4   1 2 3 4   1 2 3 4

PRELUDE: SOUNDS BEFORE SYMBOLS

EORY

PITCH, BEAT, AND RHYTHM

Pitch is the highness or lowness of a note or tone. The **beat** is the pulse of the music. **Rhythm** is a pattern of short or long sounds (or silences) that fit within a steady beat.

ARTICULATION

Articulation is the result of a stroke and how you strike the drum.

Play some of the familiar songs below. Since you are playing snare drum, the ***pitch*** will stay the same, while the ***rhythm*** will identify the song.

Bingo
Mary Had a Little Lamb

Jingle Bells
Old MacDonald

London Bridge
Twinkle, Twinkle Little Star

MAKING MUSIC

With your director's help, assemble your snare drum carefully. You are now ready to play with the winds! Remember to focus on posture, grip and stroke production.

ND WE'RE OFF!

(rest)
R R R R|– – – –|L L L L|– – – –|
1 2 3 4 1 2 3 4 1 2 3 4 1 2 3 4

U CLAIRE DE LA LUNE

R R R R|L L L L|R R R R|L L L L|
1 2 3 4 1 2 3 4 1 2 3 4 1 2 3 4

IOT CROSS BUNS

R – R –|R R R R|L – L –|L L L L|R R R R|L L L L|R – L –|R L R L|
1 2 3 4 1 2 3 4 1 2 3 4 1 2 3 4 1 2 3 4 1 2 3 4 1 2 3 4 1 2 3 4

MARY HAD A LITTLE LAMB

R R R R|L L L –|R R R –|L L L –|R R R R|L L L L|R R L L|R – – –|
1 2 3 4 1 2 3 4 1 2 3 4 1 2 3 4 1 2 3 4 1 2 3 4 1 2 3 4 1 2 3 4

COMPOSER'S CORNER

It is your turn to compose your *own* piece of music! Use any combination of R, L and dashes to complete this piece. Give it a title and perform it for a friend or family member!

Title:______________________ Composer (your name):______________________

R ___ ___ ___|___ ___ ___ –|___ ___ ___ ___|___ ___ ___ ___|

OPUS 1

THEORY

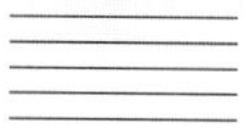

MUSIC STAFF
The **music staff** is where notes and rests are written. It has 5 lines and 4 spaces.

LONG TONE
A **long tone** is a held note. The fermata (𝄐) indicates to hold the note until your teacher tells you to rest.

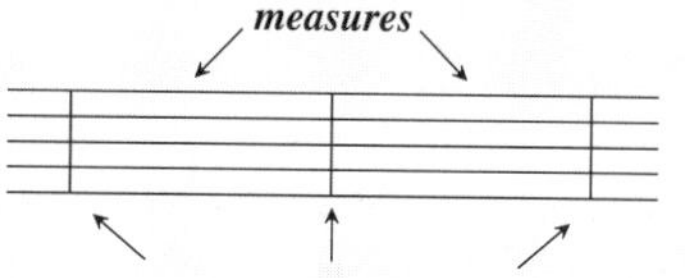

BAR LINES
Bar lines divide the music staff into measures.

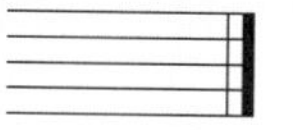

FINAL BAR LINE
A **final bar** line indicates the end of a piece.

1.1 FIRST NOTE *Unlike the bells, the snare drum sound will decay immediately during a long tone. Watch your teacher carefully so you are ready for your next entrance.*

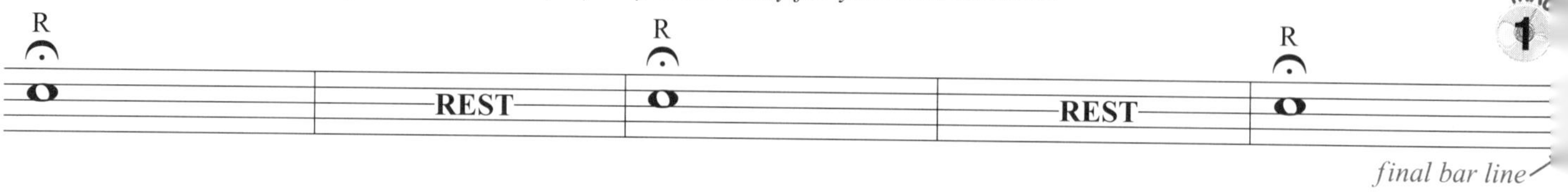

RHYTHM

BEAT
The **beat** is the pulse of the music.
Tap your foot to keep a steady beat!

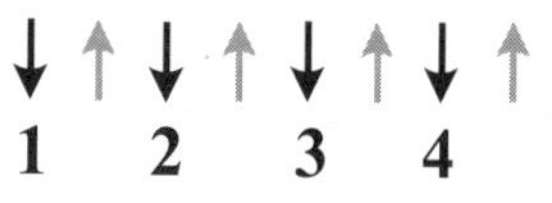

NOTES AND RESTS
Notes represent sound. **Rests** represent silence.

Quarter Note = 1 beat of sound

Quarter Rest = 1 beat of silence

FOUR ON A HAND
Playing four consecutive notes with the same hand is called **four on a hand.**

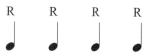

1.2 FOUR IN A ROW *This piece has four beats in each measure. Remember to tap your foot.*

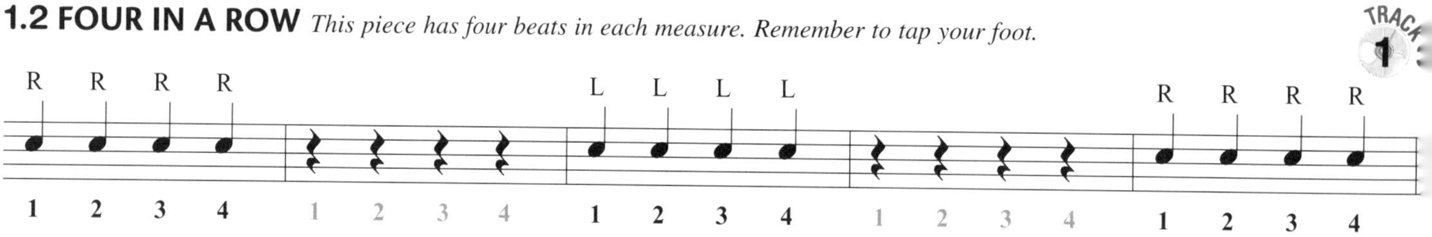

1.3 SECOND NOTE

1.4 FOUR MORE *How many measures do you see?*

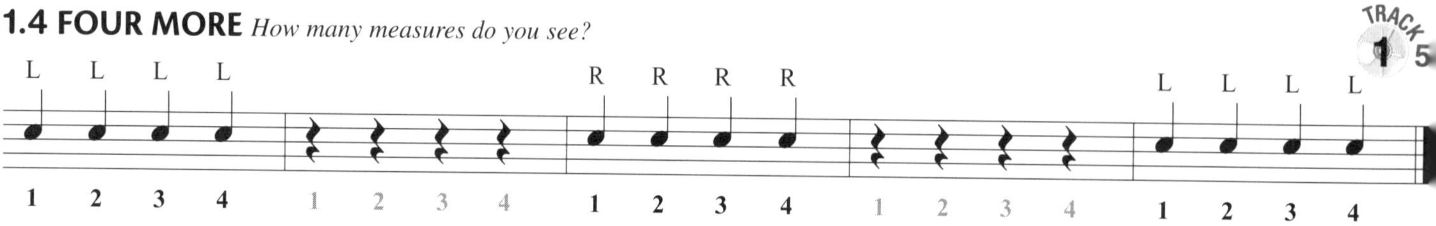

DOUBLE STICKING

Double sticking or **doubling** means that you play two consecutive notes with the same hand.

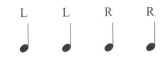

.5 UP AND DOWN

TRACK 1 6

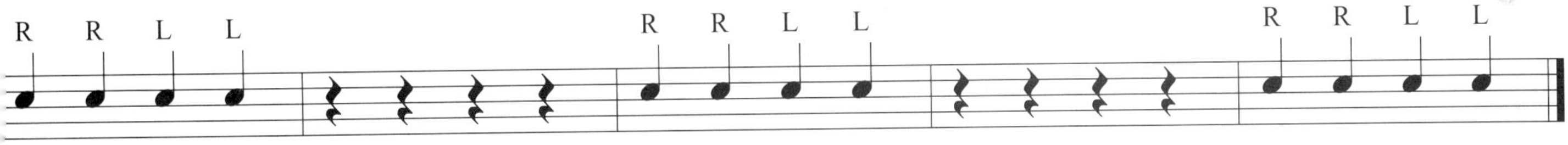

1.6 ALL MIXED UP

TRACK 1 7

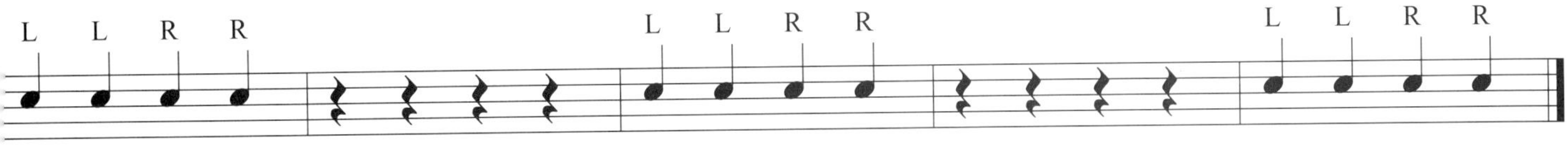

FOR PERCUSSION ONLY

These exercises reinforce **four on a hand** and **double sticking.** Raise the tip of each stick to the same height and strike the head in the same spot to produce a uniform sound. Count each line carefully and steadily as you play. Follow the printed stickings and watch for pattern changes.

Once you have mastered each exercise, try playing all four lines without stopping!

A

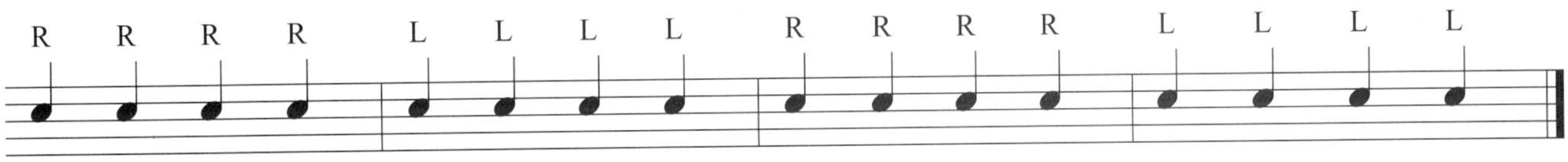

B

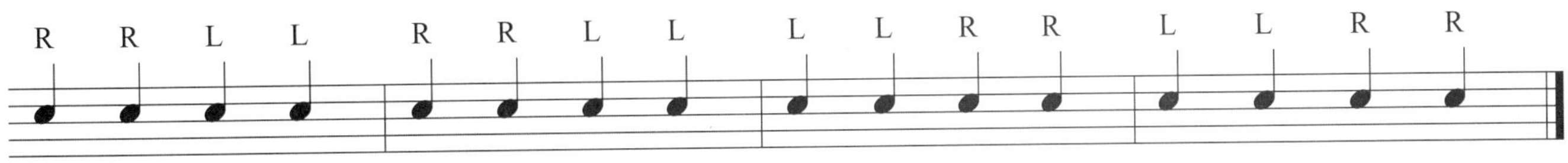

C

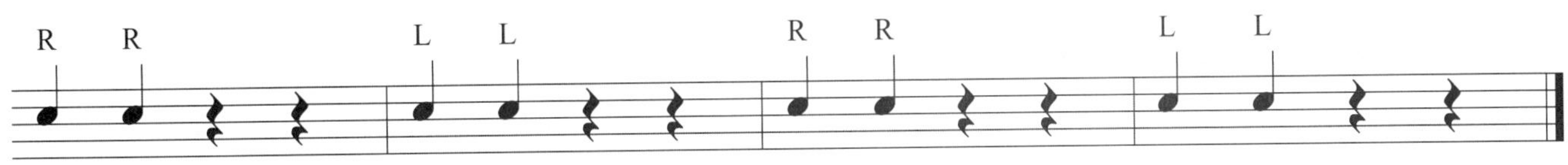

D

THEORY

ACCIDENTALS

Accidentals are signs that alter a note's pitch. They are explained in the keyboard percussion side of your book on page 6.

ALTERNATE STICKING

Alternate sticking means that your hands take turns playing each succeeessive note.

1.7 THIRD NOTE'S A CHARM

1.8 ALL TOGETHER

1.9 WHAT GOES UP...

1.10 RHYTHM RENDEZVOUS

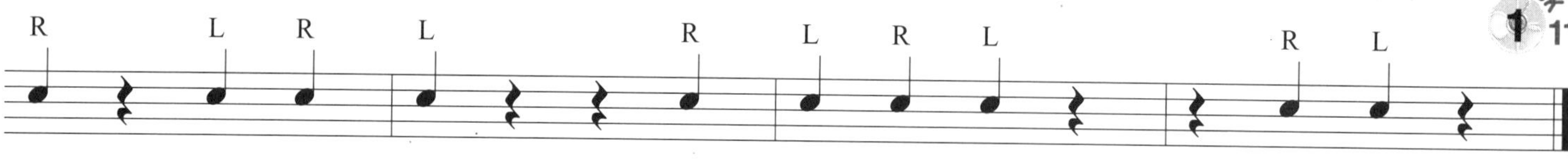

FOR PERCUSSION ONLY

Use alternate sticking with primary strokes. Pay careful attention to grip. Be sure each stick comes up to the same height and strike the drum head in the center. Listen to be sure each stroke sounds the same.

A

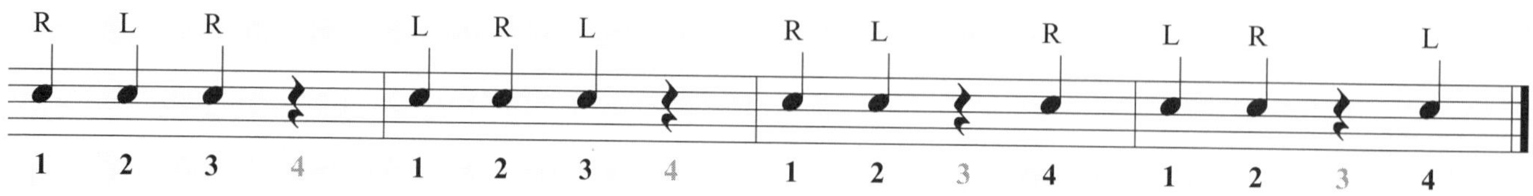

B

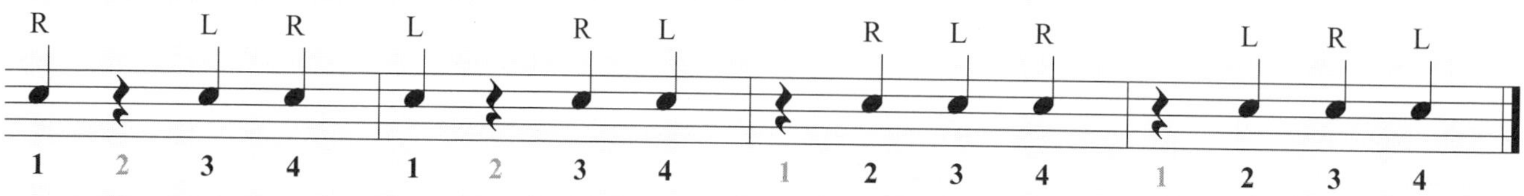

EORY

CLEFS

Clefs are signs that help name notes or designate different instruments on a staff.

The **neutral clef** is used for a variety of percussion instruments with each line and space assigned to a specific instrument. Snare drum is often assigned to the third space from the bottom while bass drum is often assigned to the first space. Crash cymbals may appear below the staff. These assignments can change based on the preferences of the composer.

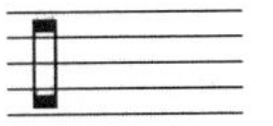

The **treble clef** is used for keyboard percussion and is explained on page 6 of the keyboard percussion section.

The **bass clef** is used for timpani and sometimes marimba. It is explained on page 42b. The bass clef was often used for battery percussion in older publications.

The musical alphabet uses A B C D E F and G. Each line and space of the staff has a note name. To find a treble clef note, move up or down by lines and spaces in the musical alphabet sequence.

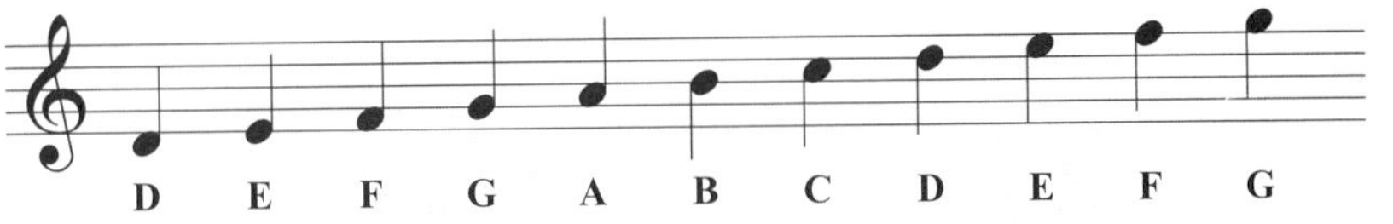

LEDGER LINES

Ledger Lines extend the staff. Notes written above or below the staff appear with ledger lines.

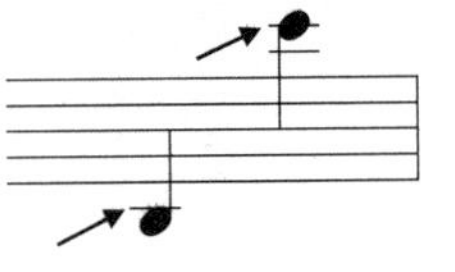

NAME THAT NOTE... *Use your knowledge of the musical alphabet to fill in the Bonus Boxes!*

ONUS BOX

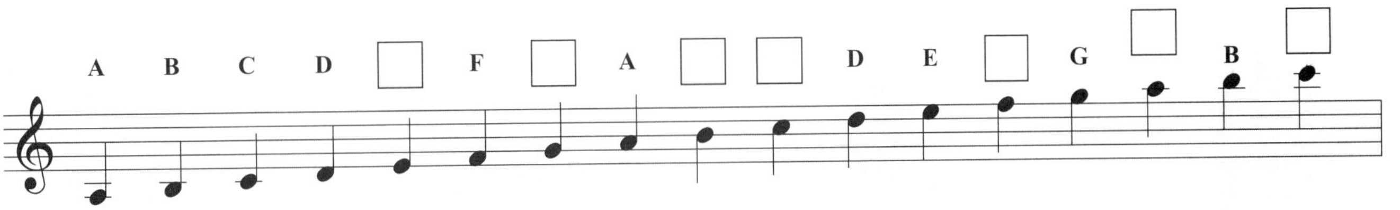

1.10a STICK SHIFT – Snare Drum Solo

David Collier

TRACK 1 77

RHYTHM

HALF NOTES AND WHOLE NOTES

Half Note
2 beats of sound

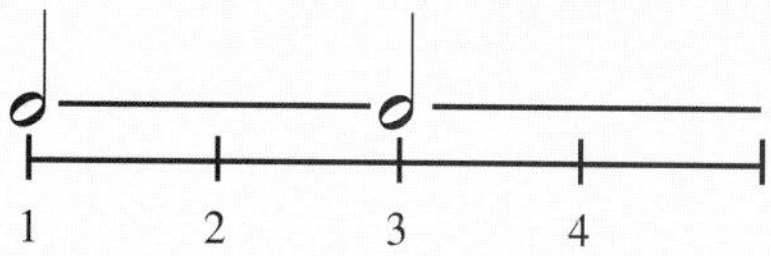

Whole Note
4 beats of sound

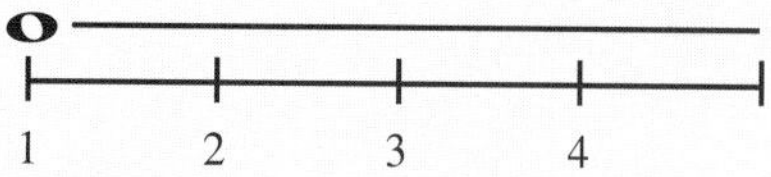

HALF RESTS AND WHOLE RESTS

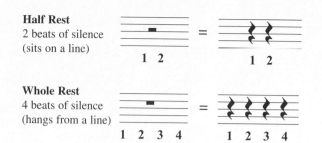

Half Rest
2 beats of silence
(sits on a line)

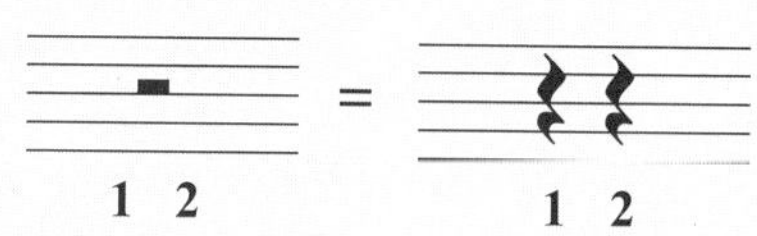

Whole Rest
4 beats of silence
(hangs from a line)

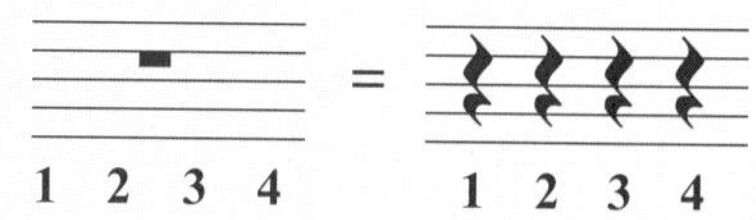

TIME SIGNATURE

The top number shows the number of beats in each measure.
The bottom number shows the type of note that receives one beat.
Hint: Replace the top number with a "1" and you will get a fraction that equals the type of note that gets one beat!

Number of beats in a measure.
Type of note that gets one beat.

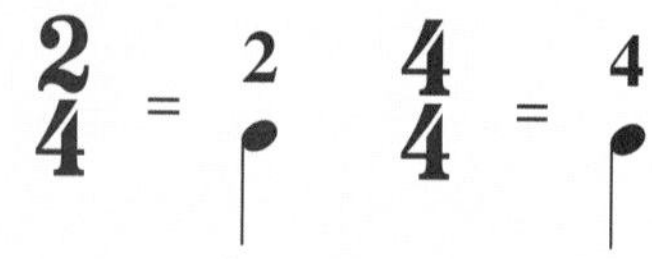

BASS DRUM

Bass drum is a primary instrument in the percussion section. It is played with a mallet that has a large, heavy end. Hold the mallet in your right hand like a snare drum stick and turn the wrist so that your thumb is up (toward the ceiling). The stroke is like drawing a backwards 'C' in the air and striking the bass drum in the center of the head. **B.D.** is the abbreviation for bass drum.

RIGHT HAND LEAD

Right hand lead occurs when the right hand starts and falls on primary counts (in this case, beats 1 and 3). Right hand lead feels natural to right-handed players. For left-handed percussionists, using **RHL** will strengthen your weaker hand.

1.11 GOING PLACES *Circle the half rests.*

TRACK 1

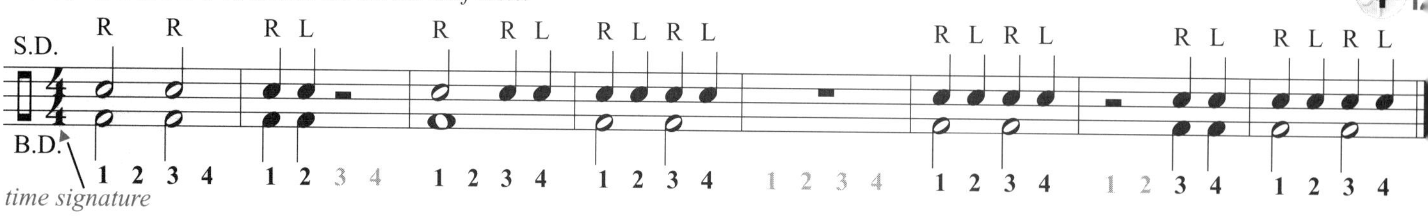

FOR PERCUSSION ONLY

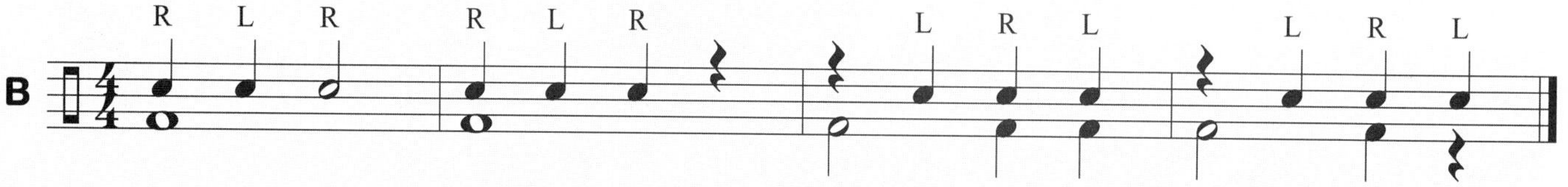

HEORY

FERMATA

When playing on your own, hold a note or rest with a **fermata** longer than its assigned value.

.12 COUNTDOWN *Hold the note with a fermata longer than its assigned value.*

TRACK 1 13

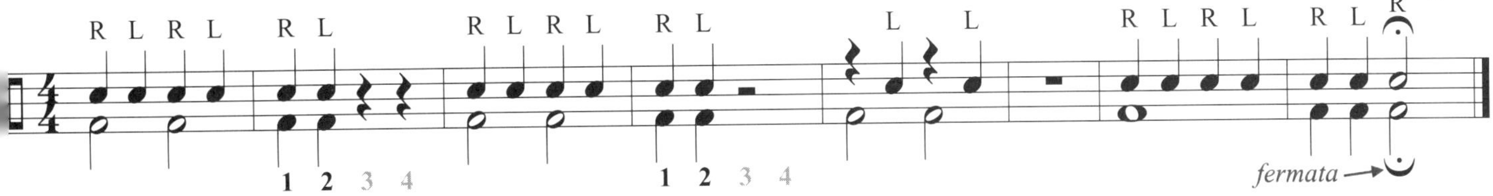

HEORY

REPEAT SIGN

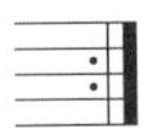

A **repeat sign** is a final bar line with two dots. Without stopping, go back to the beginning and play the music a second time.

.13 TURN AROUND

TRACK 1 14

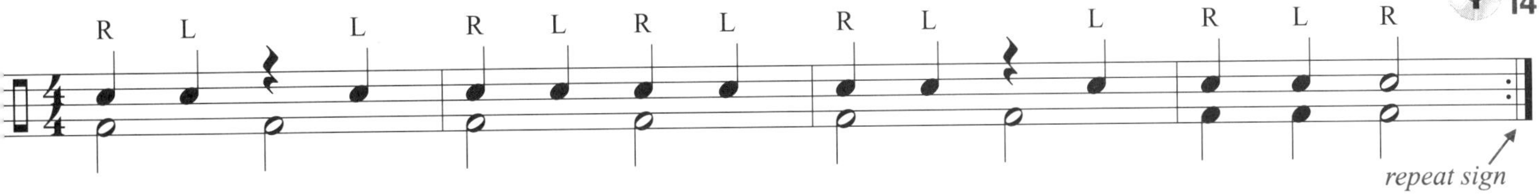

1.14 HOT CROSS BUNS

English Folk Song

TRACK 1 15

1.15 HERE WE GO! *Draw in the bar lines, then play!*

TRACK 1 16

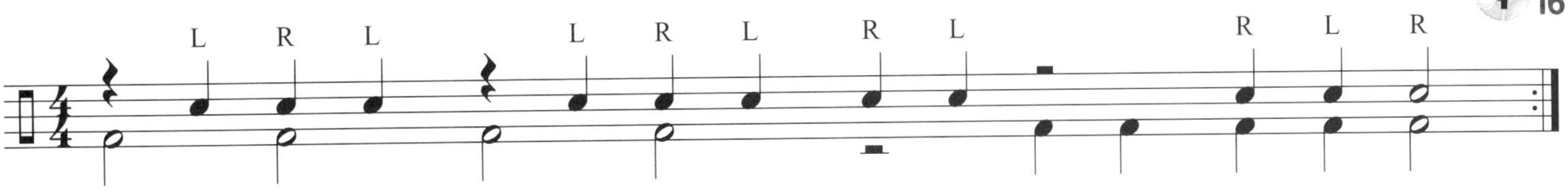

FOR PERCUSSION ONLY

Add the missing stickings using Right Hand Lead (RHL).

A

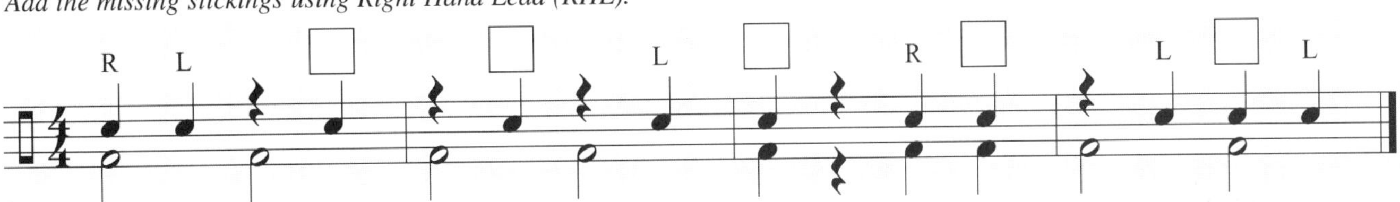

Add stickings using RHL.

B

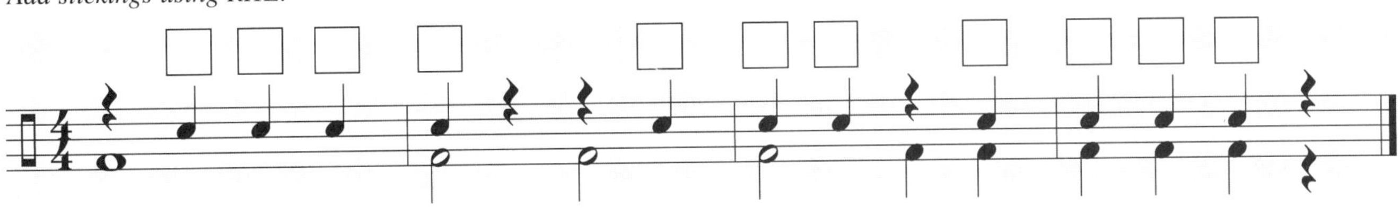

1.16 AU CLAIRE DE LA LUNE *Musicianship Challenge! – Without the CD, play 1st time quietly, 2nd time loudly.*

Add missing stickings using RHL.

French Folk Song

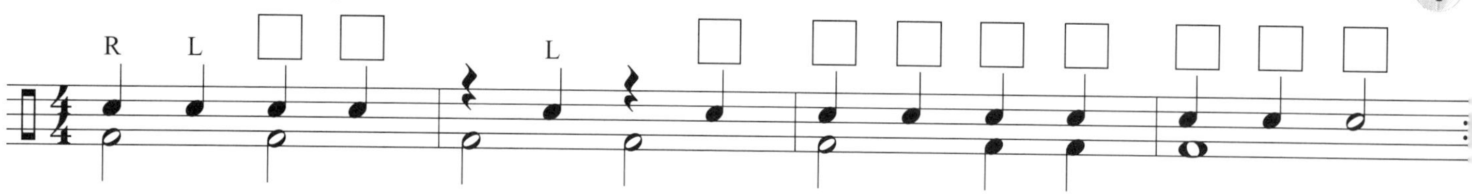

MUFFLING

Muffling means to stop the sound and control the vibrations of a percussion instrument. This is most often done on a rest. In order to play rests on bass drum, use the left hand to muffle the drum. Do this by placing the fingertips of the left hand on the head 6 inches from the rim during the rest. Take the fingertips off the head when you play the next note. Sometimes you can muffle the bass drum while playing to make the rhythm clearer.

1.17 MARY HAD A LITTLE LAMB *Muffle the bass drum on the rests.*

Traditional

1.18 MARY HAD A COOL LAMB

Traditional Melody

THEORY

STYLE AND FORM: DUET

A **duet** has two different parts performed simultaneously by two individuals or groups.

1.19 BEAT STREET — Duet *A Beat Street exercise indicates to clap the rhythm.*

CLAP

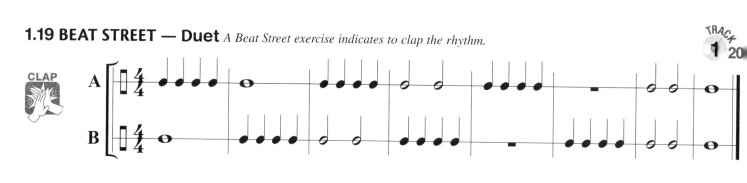

1.20 DUET LIKE THIS

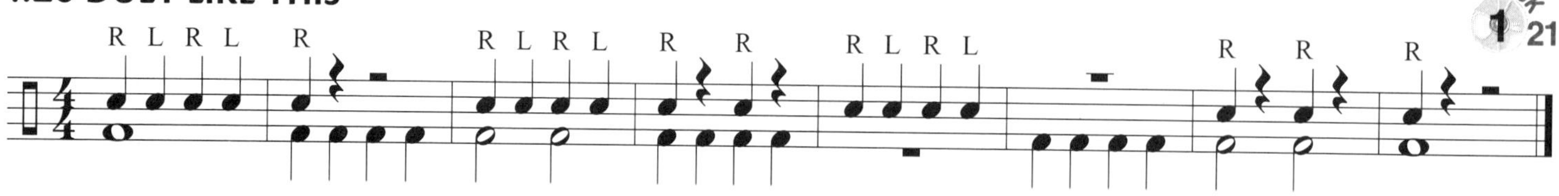

MULTIPLE BOUNCE STROKE

A **roll** is the percussionist's means of sustaining a note. The **multiple bounce stroke** is the first step to produce a roll. To play this stroke, toss the tip of the drum stick to the drum and let it bounce on the head as many times as possible. Keep you fingers attached to the stick!

FOR PERCUSSION ONLY

A

B

C
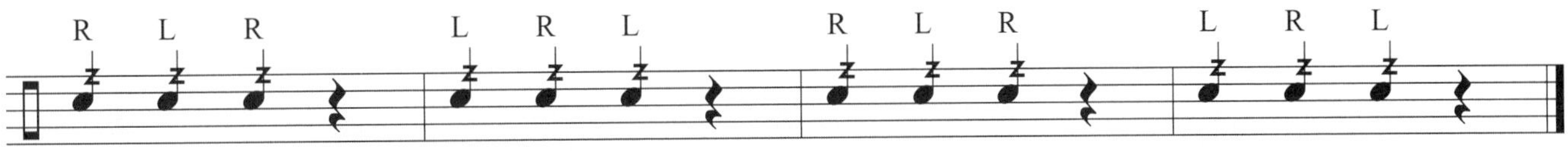

D
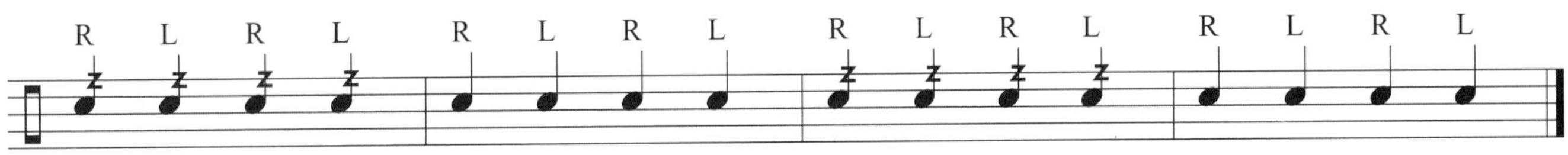

1.21 CLIMBING HIGHER

TRACK 1 22

1.22 HOME BASE

TRACK 1 23

1.23 EVEN HIGHER! *Trace the clef!*

TRACK 1 24

THEORY

PHRASING

A **phrase** in music is similar to a sentence in speech. It should continue uninterrupted until the music indicates a breath. Always listen for the phrasing in the winds.

1.24 DOWN BY THE STATION

American Folk Song

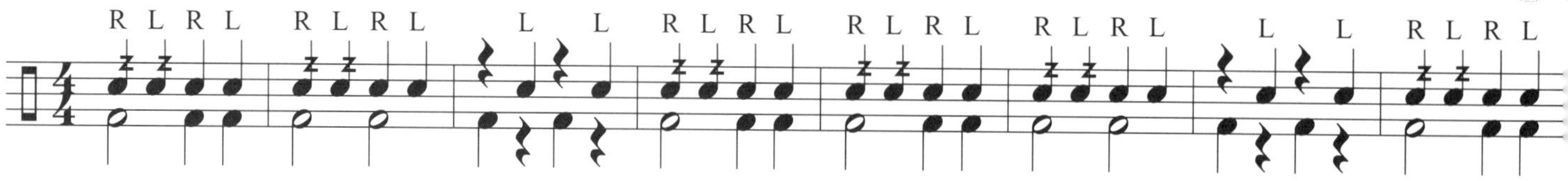

HISTORY

MUSIC

Stephen Collins Foster (1826 – 1864) was an American songwriter born in Pennsylvania. He published his first piece when he was 18 years old. Some of his most famous songs are *Oh! Susanna, Camptown Races,* and *Some Folks Do.* His compositions capture the spirit of American folk music during the 1800s.

ART

During this time in history, artists of the Hudson River School were hard at work in the United States. Frederic Church painted *Morning, Looking East Over the Hudson Valley from the Catskill Mountains* about the same time that *Camptown Races* was written.

WORLD

The world was introduced to Ebenezer Scrooge (the famous character in Charles Dickens' *A Christmas Carol*), Abraham Lincoln delivered the Gettysburg Address, and the stapler was patented.

1.25 SOME FOLKS DO

Before you play, draw these symbols where they belong: Neutral Clef, Time Signature, Final Bar Line.

Stephen C. Foster

1.26 SCALING THE WALL *Work with another student to learn this piece.*

ON THE PODIUM

CONDUCTING IN $\frac{4}{4}$ TIME

Your band director has been conducting a four-beat pattern. Now it is your turn to conduct! Place your right hand in a "handshake" position and follow the diagram to conduct in $\frac{4}{4}$ time.

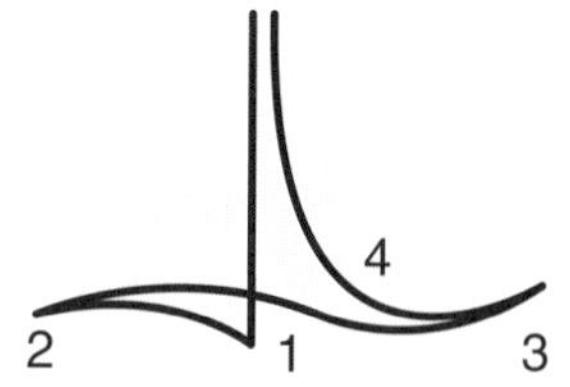

1.27 GOOD KING WENCESLAS *Conduct a partner, your section, or the entire class!*

ON THE PODIUM

English Carol

TRACK 28

1.28 STOMP ROCK

TRACK 29

OPUS 1 ENCORE!

INTERPRETATION STATION

TRACK 1 30

Listen to CD 1 Track 30. Describe the music and how it makes you feel.

SIMON "SEZ"

Listen to the rhythms your director plays and echo them back. Listen carefully!

COMPOSER'S CORNER

A composer is someone who creates original music. It is YOUR turn to be a composer!
Using the notes or rests you already know, complete this composition. Guide rhythms have been provided for you in parentheses.

le:______________________________ Name:______________________

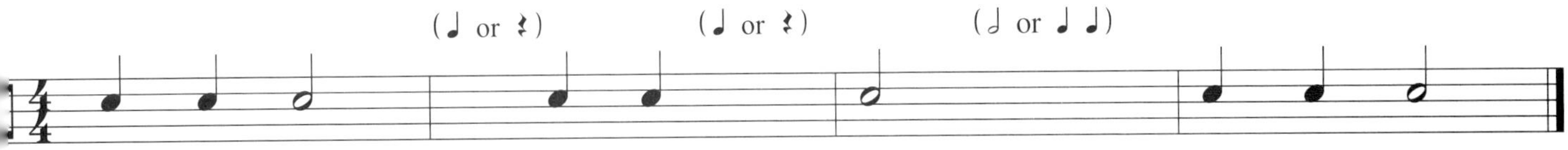

PENCIL POWER

Match the following terms with their symbols.

1. _____ Clef	6. _____ Quarter Note
2. _____ Time Signature	7. _____ Whole Note
3. _____ Repeat Sign	8. _____ Whole Rest
4. _____ Fermata	9. _____ Half Rest
5. _____ Half Note	10. _____ Quarter Rest

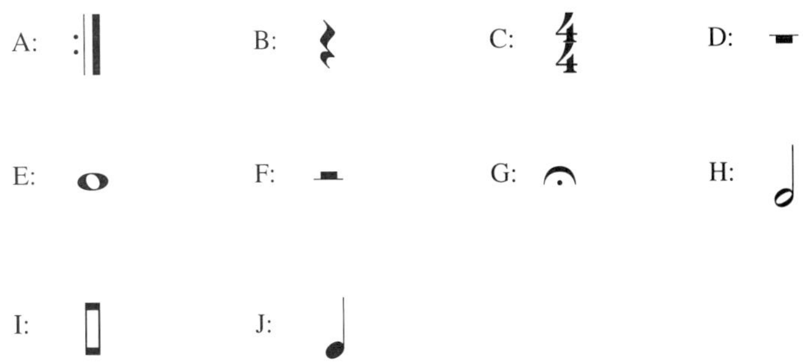

CURTAIN UP!

Time to perform! Practice these pieces and play them for friends or family members. Introduce each piece by its title.
Remember to bow when you are finished!

1.29 GO TELL AUNT RHODY *Teach your audience to conduct a four-beat pattern!*

American Folk Song — TRACK 1 31

N THE ODIUM

1.30 CUCKOO SAMBA

TRACK 1 32

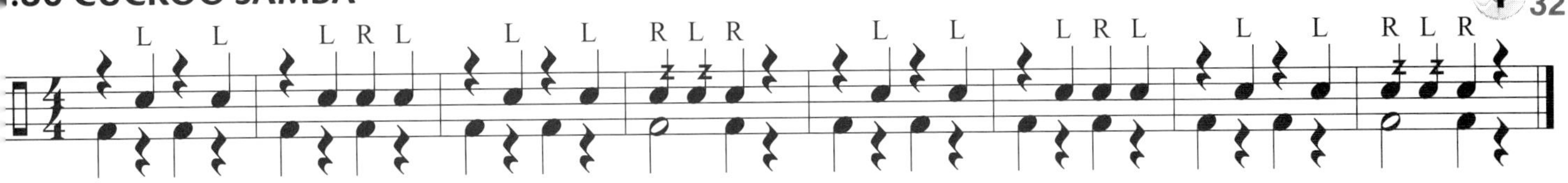

1.31 LIGHTLY ROW — Duet *Pair up with a friend to perform this piece for your audience.*

Traditional — TRACK 1 33

OPUS 2

HISTORY

MUSIC

Ludwig van Beethoven (1770 – 1827) lived most of his life in Vienna, Austria. His music became a bridge between Classical and Romantic music. When *Symphony No. 9* and its *Ode to Joy* were performed for the first time, Beethoven was completely deaf!

ART

Romanticism in art was an important movement in Europe and themes often included nationalism. Eugene Delacroix was one of the most important French artists. His *Liberty Leading the People* commemorates the French Revolution of 1830 and the overthrow of King Charles X.

WORLD

Around this time in history, Mexico became a republic, trains first carried passengers in England, the first photograph was taken, and ice cream was first sold in the United States!

2.1 ODE TO JOY *Musicianship Challenge! – Without the CD, play the 1st phrase gently, the 2nd phrase majestically. Hint: This piece uses 4-measure phrases.*

TRAC 1

Ludwig van Beethoven

RUDIMENT

RUDIMENTS

Rudiments are rhythmic patterns that use different types of strokes with a specific sticking. They are the building blocks of snare drumming.

FLAMS

Flam

The **flam** is a rudiment composed of a small tap stroke and a primary stroke. The small note, or grace note, has no rhythmic value. It is played with a tap stroke and precedes the beat. The large note, or main note, is played with a primary stroke that sounds on the beat. When played correctly, the flam will sound longer than a primary stroke.

Right Flam

LR

Right flam – Begin by holding the left stick in the *tap position* (about 2 inches above the drum head) and the right stick in the *up position* of the primary stroke. Toss both sticks toward the drum head at the same speed. The left stick will hit the drum head just before the right stick.

Left Flam

RL

Left flam – Hold the right stick in the *tap position* and the left stick in the *up position.* Toss both sticks toward the drum head at the same speed. The right stick will hit the drum head just before the left stick.

FOR PERCUSSION ONLY

A

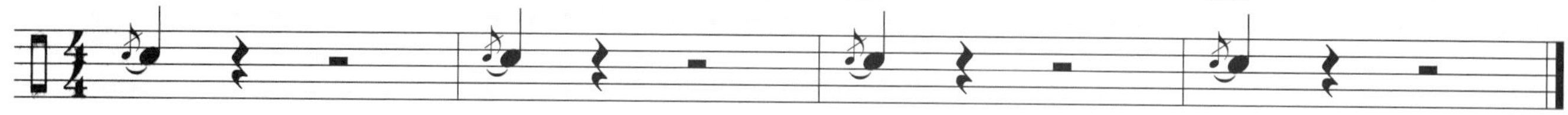

B

2.2 OUTER LIMITS *Use appropriate stick heights for each flam.*

TRACK 1 3

3 OLD MACDONALD *This exercise uses both left and right flams.*

American Folk Song

TRACK 1 36

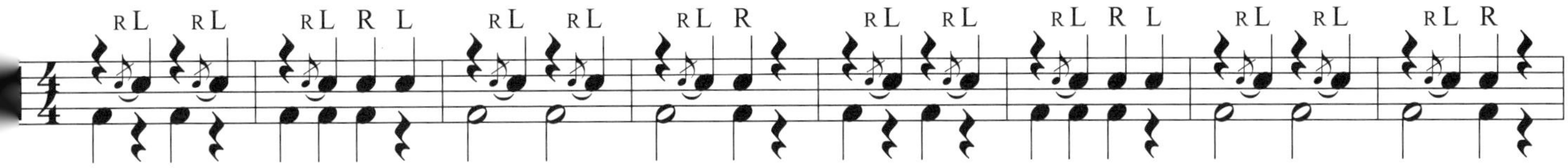

4 SHARK! *Musicianship Challenge! – Without the CD, play this like you are being chased. Play steady notes with multiple bounce strokes during the fermata.*

TRACK 1 37

5 CRUSADER'S HYMN *This exercise uses RHL. Use right flams on beats 1 and 3, and left flams on beats 2 and 4.*

Silesian Folk Song

TRACK 1 38

KEY SIGNATURE

THEORY

The **key signature** indicates which notes to play sharp or flat. It appears at the beginning of each staff. It is also explained in the keyboard percussion side of your book on page 11.

- There can be up to 7 sharps in a key signature. **Sharps** (♯) follow this order: F, C, G, D, A, E, B
- There can be up to 7 flats in a key signature. **Flats** (♭) follow this order: B, E, A, D, G, C, F

6 KEYNOTE MARCH *Musicianship Challenge! – Play this piece like you would hear it in a parade.*

TRACK 1 39

FOR PERCUSSION ONLY

Keep tap strokes at 2 inches and primary strokes at 10 inches.

A

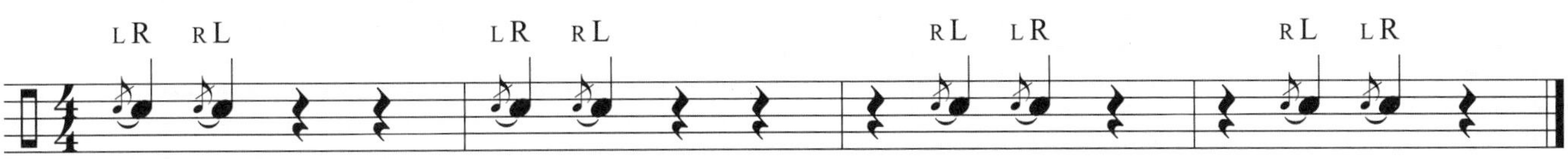

B

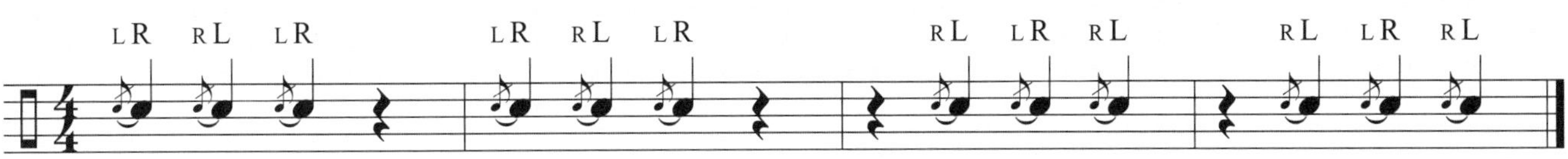

TRIANGLE

The **triangle** is a 3-sided piece of metal that is open in one corner. It should be suspended from a triangle clip that has a loop of very thin, strong cord. Form your hand as if holding a glass. Rest the tip of the clip on your middle finger and the back of the clip on your thumb. The triangle will hang between your fingers. Gently strike the triangle with a thin metal triangle beater near one of the closed corners. To stop the sound or muffle the triangle, gently grasp the triangle with your fingertips. **Tri.** is the abbreviation for triangle.

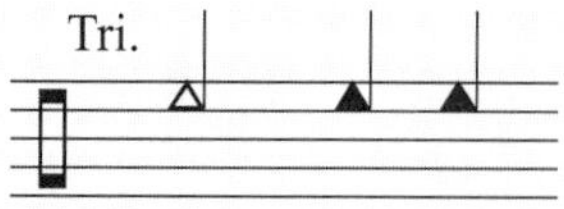

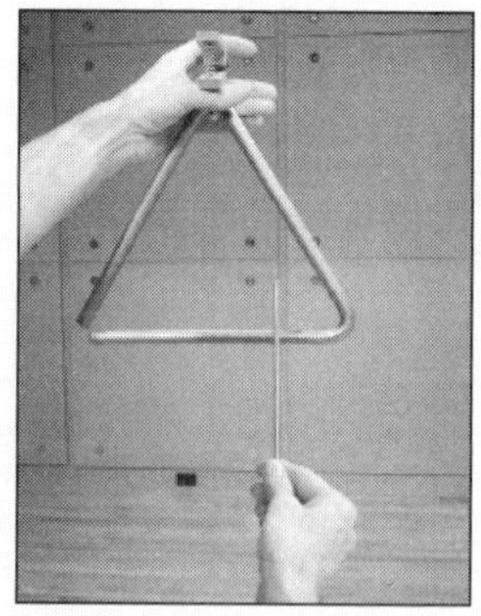

HISTORY

MUSIC

Wolfgang Amadeus Mozart (1756 – 1791) was born in Salzburg, Austria. He was a child genius and composed his first minuet when he was just five years old! During his short life of 35 years, he wrote over 600 musical compositions. Many of his works continue to be performed today.

ART

As Mozart wrote in the Classical style, Neoclassicism in visual art was being explored by artists such as Jacques-Louis David, a French painter. This style can be seen in his painting, *The Death of Socrates,* which was completed in 1787.

WORLD

The thirteen American Colonies broke away from the British Empire in the American Revolutionary War, the *Declaration of Independence* was signed, and Johnny Appleseed was born.

2.7 STAR SEARCH *Muffle the triangle on the rests.*

French Melody
adapted by Wolfgang A. Mozart

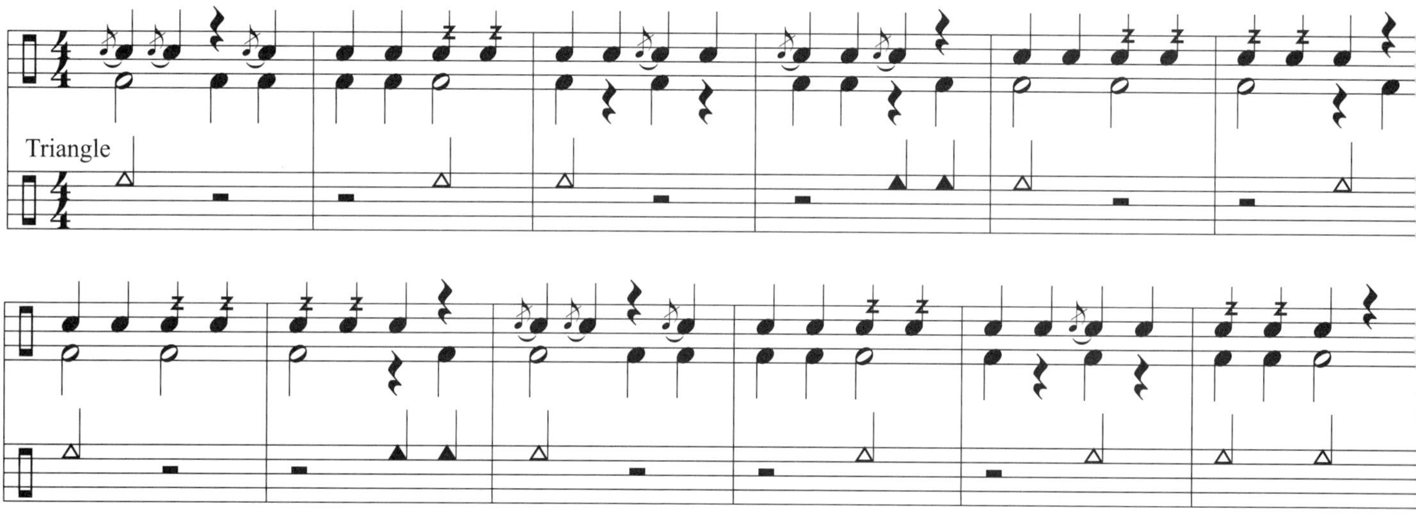

THEORY

DYNAMICS

Dynamics indicate how loudly or softly to play. Italian terms are often used in music to indicate volume.

p (*piano*) – play softly

f (*forte*) – play loudly

DYNAMICS AND STICK HEIGHTS

On percussion instruments, change dynamics by changing the height and striking location of your sticks or mallets. For snare drum, ***f*** = 10" above the center of the head. ***p*** = 2" above the edge of the head near the counterhoop.

2.8 BEAT STREET *Clap the rhythm with dynamics!*

CLAP

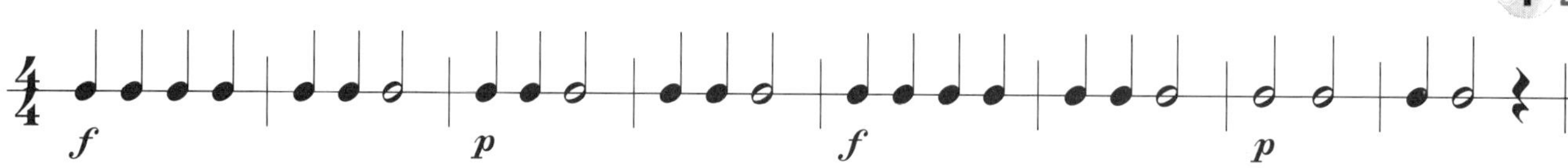

9 LONDON BRIDGE

English Folk Song

TRACK 1 42

EIGHTH NOTES

Eighth Note = half beat of sound

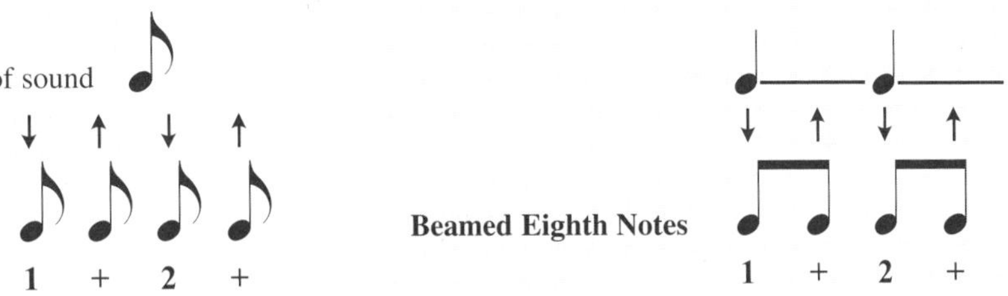

BEAM GROUPS

10 JINGLE BELLS – Duet *Remember to adjust your stick height and stick location when playing dynamics.*

James Pierpont

TRACK 1 43

ON THE PODIUM

When dynamics indicate *loud*, a conductor's gestures are bigger.
When dynamics indicate *soft*, gestures are smaller.
Practice conducting a four-beat pattern with dynamics!

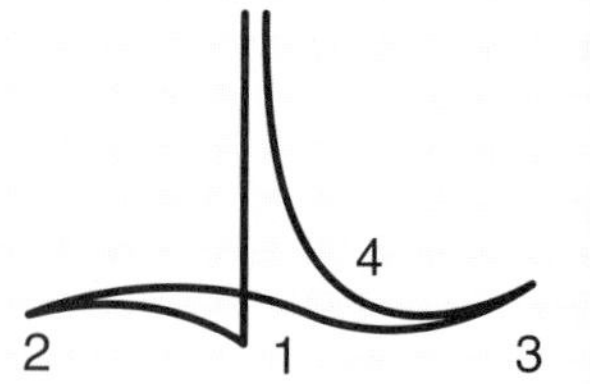

2.11 DREIDEL SONG

Traditional Hannukah Song

TRACK 1

ON THE PODIUM

THEORY

DYNAMICS

Mezzo is an Italian term that means "medium" or "moderately." The letter *m* is an abbreviation used in dynamics.

mp (*mezzo piano*) – play moderately soft

mf (*mezzo forte*) – play moderately loud

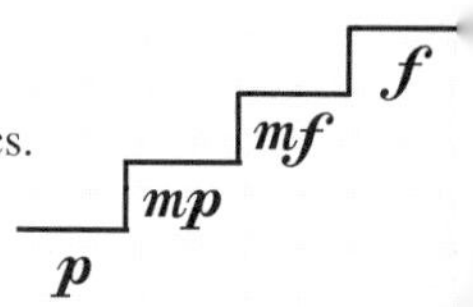

DYNAMICS AND STICK HEIGHTS

For snare drum, ***mf*** = 6–8" above the center of the head. ***mp*** = 4" above the head, half way between the center and edge (near the counterhoop).

2.12 BEAT STREET *Clap the dynamics!*

TRACK 1

CLAP

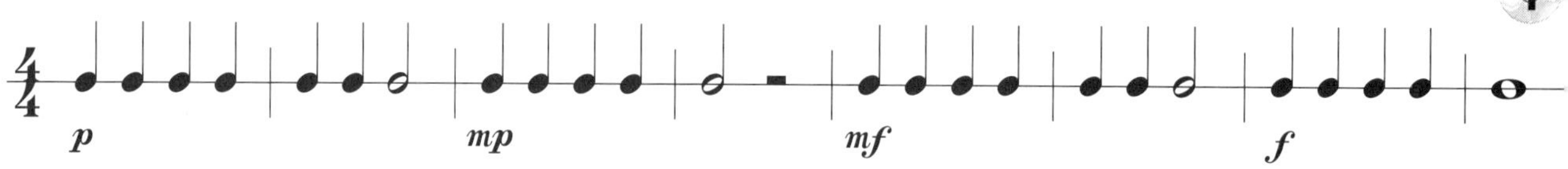

RUDIMENT

PARADIDDLE

The **paradiddle** is a rudiment that uses single and double sticking.

Right Paradiddle

Left Paradiddle

2.13 DYNAMIC DOODLE ALL DAY

American Folk Melody

TRACK 1

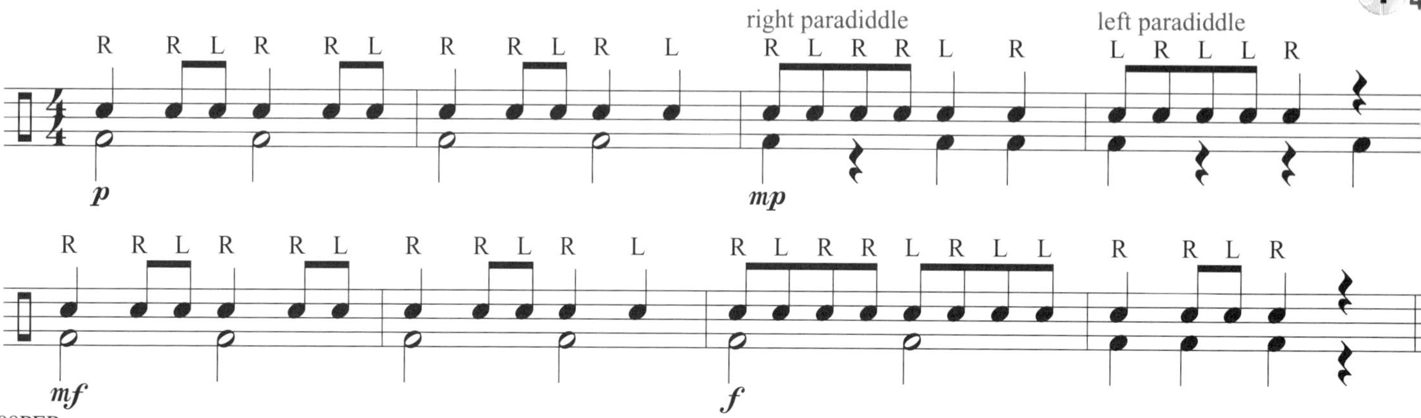

SUSPENDED CYMBAL

A **suspended cymbal** is a single cymbal placed or "suspended" on a cymbal stand. Use medium yarn or cord mallets on the cymbal. Snare drum sticks may also be used. Play 1–2 inches from the edge when using mallets, and 3 inches from the edge when using sticks. To muffle the suspended cymbal, grasp the edge of the cymbal with the fingers. **Sus. Cym.** is the abbreviation for suspended cymbal.

HEORY

PICK-UP NOTES

Pick-up notes lead into the first full measure of a phrase.
When pick-up notes are used to begin a piece, their combined rhythmic value is often subtracted from the last measure.

.14 A–TISKET, A–TASKET *Muffle the suspended cymbal on the rests.*

American Folk Song — TRACK 1 47

2.15 OH! SUSANNA – Duet

Stephen C. Foster — TRACK 1 48

WOOD BLOCK

A **wood block** is a rectangular piece of wood with a deep slot near the top. It produces a hollow sound. Hold the wood block in the palm of your curved hand to form a resonating chamber. Strike the top with an unwrapped medium hard rubber mallet. The best sound is produced close to the edge of the top near the open slot. **W.B.** is the abbreviation for wood block.

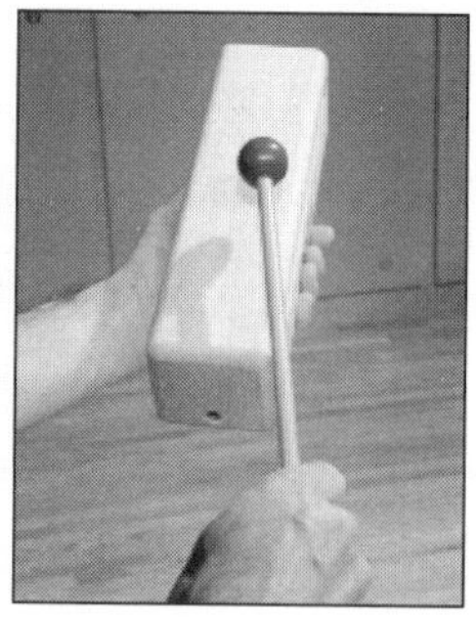

MARACAS

Maracas are instruments that are hollow with beads, pellets or seeds inside. They make a rattle sound when played. Hold them with the bulb facing forward, your thumb, 3rd and 4th fingers holding the handle, and your 1st and 2nd finger on top of the bulb. Snap your wrists to produce a short, crisp sound. **Mrcs.** is the abbreviation for maracas.

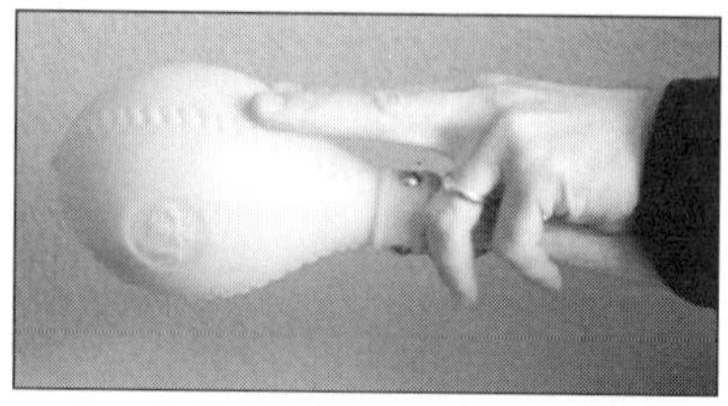

MULTIPLE BOUNCE STROKES ON EIGHTH NOTES

Remember to keep the eighth notes steady with an equal bounce or "buzz" in each hand. Work to connect the bounces between the eighth notes.

FOR PERCUSSION ONLY

2.16 AFRICAN SAFARI

TRACK 14

THEORY

ARTICULATION: ACCENT

> An **accent** indicates to emphasize a note by playing one dynamic louder. Be sure to use the correct stick height!

2.17 LEAN ON IT *Notice that an accent has been added to the first note of a single paradiddle.*

TRACK 1 50

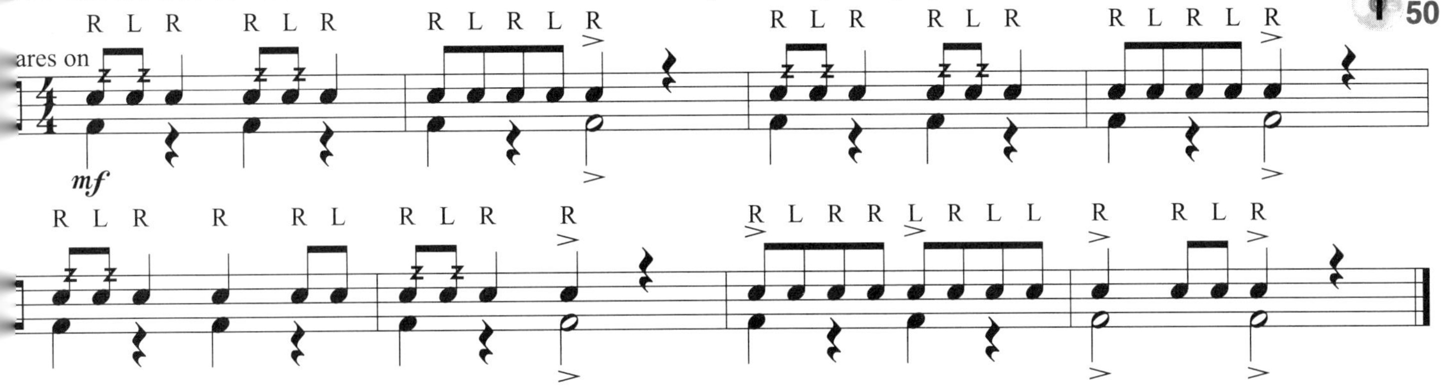

TAMBOURINE

A **tambourine** is a small hand drum with a skin head on top and rows of metal discs called jingles. It is held at the spot that doesn't have jingles. Have the fingers of your left hand curved under with your thumb on top. Hold the tambourine at a 45° angle and strike it with the bunched fingers of your other hand. ***mf–f*** dynamics are played in the center, ***p*** is played at the edge and ***mp*** is played half way between the center and the edge. **Tamb.** is the abbreviation for tambourine.

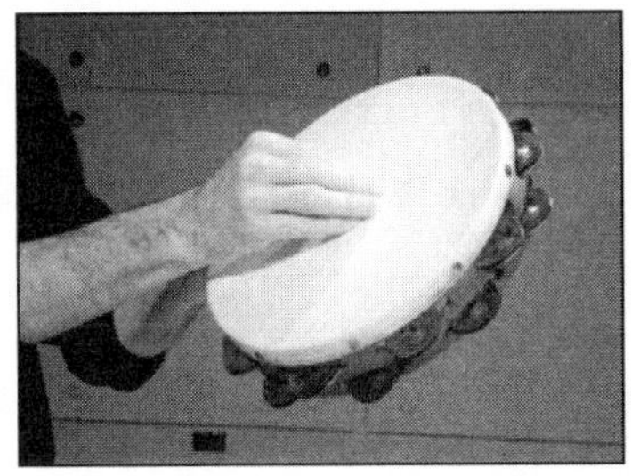

RHYTHM

EIGHTH RESTS

The **eighth rest** receives one-half beat in $\frac{4}{4}$ time. Eight of them can fit into each measure.

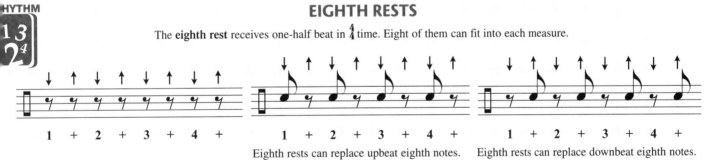

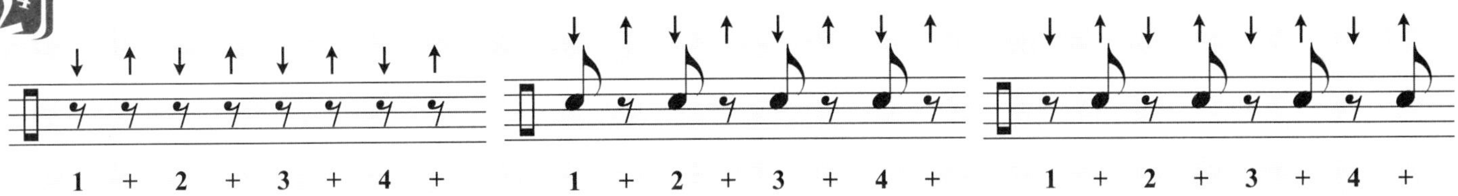

Eighth rests can replace upbeat eighth notes. Eighth rests can replace downbeat eighth notes.

2.18 WALK TO MY LOU

American Folk Melody

TRACK 1 51

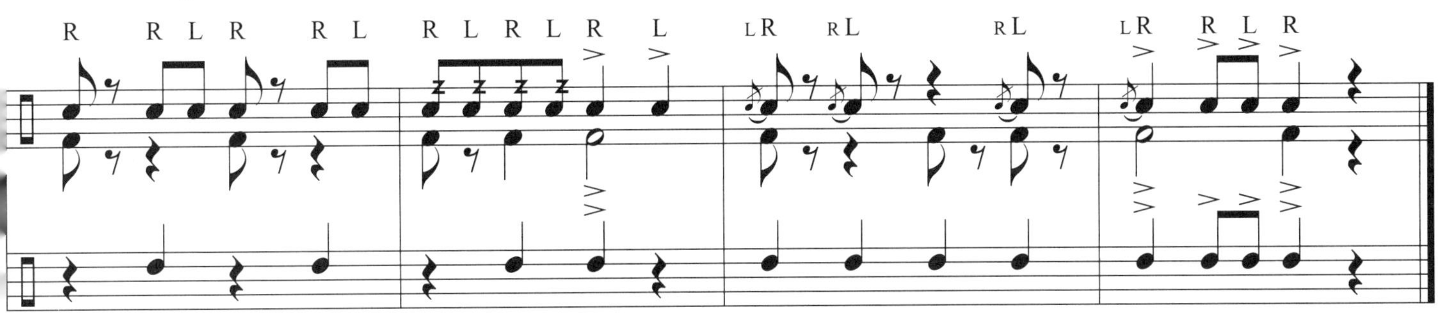

RHYTHM

SYNCOPATION

Music has strong beats and weak beats. Most of the time, we stress strong beats (**1** 2 **3** 4).
Sometimes, we shift the stress onto weak beats (1 **2** 3 **4**).
This is known as **syncopation**. Longer, accented notes that occur on weak beats often identify syncopation.

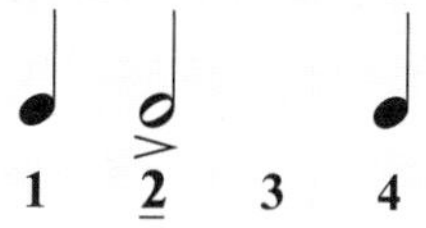

2.19 BEAT STREET

CLAP

CRASH CYMBALS

Crash cymbals are a pair of cymbals that are played by striking them together. Grasp the strap between your thumb and first finger in each hand. Wrap the rest of the fingers around the strap and hold the cymbals about 2 inches apart at a 45° angle in front of you. Strike the cymbals together making sure that they hit off center and one edge before the other. To muffle, pull the cymbals into your stomach on the rests. **Cr. Cym.** is the abbreviation for crash cymbals.

2.20 SHOO FLY

American Folk Song

21 CHANT

TRACK 1 54

.21a SOME ACCESSORIES REQUIRED – Accessory Percussion Ensemble

David Collier

TRACK 1 78

OPUS 2 ENCORE!

INTERPRETATION STATION

Listen to CD 1 Track 55. You will hear two performances of the same piece. Which one is more musical and why?

SIMON "SEZ"

Listen to CD 1 Track 56. You will hear a well-known song. Listen first, sing it, then find the pitches on your keyboard percussion instrument. You can then play along with the accompaniment track that follows. Can you match the initial recording?

COMPOSER'S CORNER

Use the notes and rhythms you have learned to complete the composition. Be sure to give it a title!

Title:____ Name:____________________

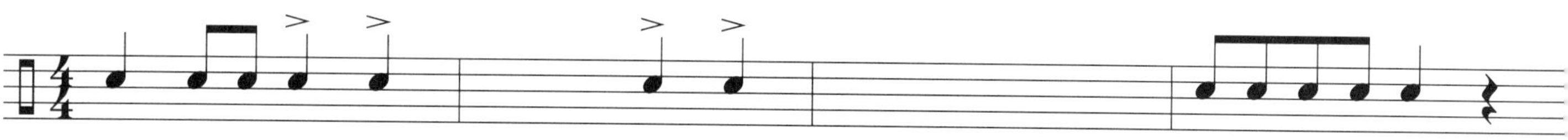

PENCIL POWER

The Secret Decoder: Using your knowledge of keyboard percussion, name the notes and solve the puzzles!

1. 

Beethoven went ___ ___ ___ ___ towards the end of his life.

2. 

The ___ ___ ___ ___ in the ___ ___ ___ ___ photo h___ ___ ___ ___ ___ ___ ___ with time.

3. 

H___ h___ ___ to pay an extra ___ ___ ___ for the ___ i ___ ___ ___ ___ ___ ___ ___ ___ ___ .

4. 

He ___ ___ ___ ___ ___ ___ when he mistakenly ate ___ ___ ___ corned ___ ___ ___ ___ and ___ ___ ___ ___ ___ ___ ___ !

CURTAIN UP!

2.22 TOKECANG

Traditional Indonesian

TRACK 1 57

.D.: Use a mallet with a small head to have a cleaner, more articulate sound.
Play the quarter and eighth notes in the center of the head, but play the half notes about 6 inches off center.

CURTAIN UP! FIRST CONCERT

2.23 CONCERT WARM-UP NO. 1

TRACK 1

2.24 CONCERT WARM-UP NO. 2

TRACK 15

2.25 THE SYNCOPATED ROW BOAT – Duet

Traditional Melody

TRACK 16

26 CROWN OF MAJESTY – Full Band

Robert Sheldon

TRACK 1 61

2.27 OBWISANA – Duet or Full Band with Percussion

Ghanian Folk Song

TRACK 1 62

2.28 FANFARE FOR A WINTER CELEBRATION – Full Band

arr. Brian Balmages

29 THE SECTION BATTLE RAG – Full Band

Brian Balmages

TRACK 1 64

2.30 ON CARIBBEAN SHORES (MARY ANN) – Full Band

Jamaican Folk Song
arr. Robert Sheldon

.31 ROCK THE HOUSE – Full Band

Brian Balmages

TRACK 1 66

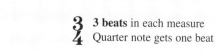

OPUS 3

RHYTHM

MORE TIME SIGNATURES

3/4 **3 beats** in each measure
Quarter note gets one beat

2/4 **2 beats** in each measure
Quarter note gets one beat

3.1 BEAT STREET

CLAP

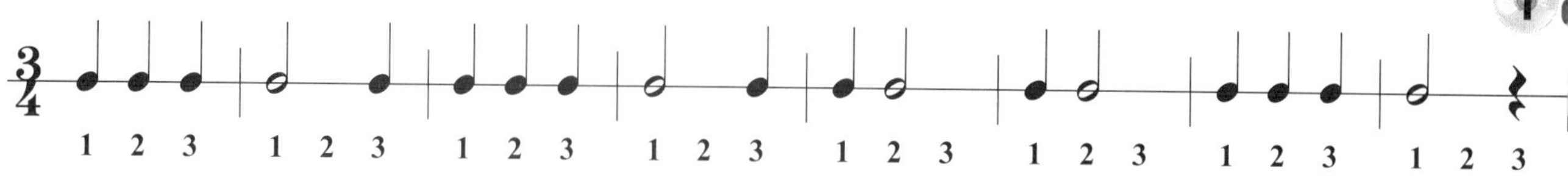

3.1a STREET BEAT— For Percussion Only

Each Street Beat exercise can be played alone or with the Beat Street that precedes it.

RUDIMENT

FLAM ACCENT

The **flam accent** is a rudiment made of a flam followed by two primary strokes.

3.2 THREE'S A CROWD

3.3 THREE POINTER

3.4 BEAT STREET

CLAP

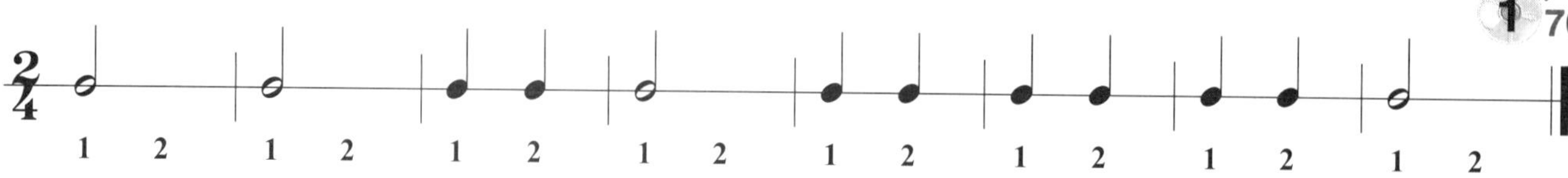

3.4a STREET BEAT — For Percussion Only

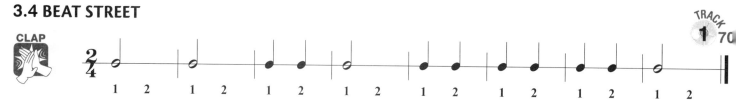

RUDIMENT

FLAM TAP

The **flam tap** is a rudiment made of a flam followed by a primary stroke. The two primary strokes are doubled.

FOR PERCUSSION ONLY

3.5 RAIN, RAIN, GO AWAY

Traditional

TRACK 1 71

ON THE PODIUM

CONDUCTING IN 2/4 TIME

It is your turn to conduct a two-beat pattern. With your right hand in a "handshake" position, follow the diagram to conduct in 2/4 time.

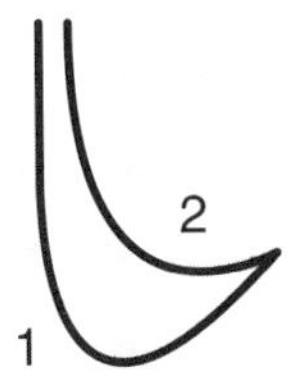

3.6 TWO FOR YOU

TRACK 1 72

ON THE PODIUM

3.7 TERRIBLE TWOS

TRACK 1 73

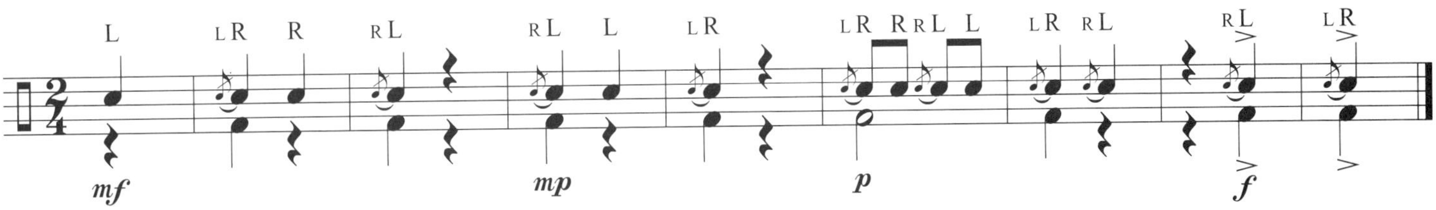

3.7a FLAM CHOWDER — Snare Drum Solo

TRACK 1 79

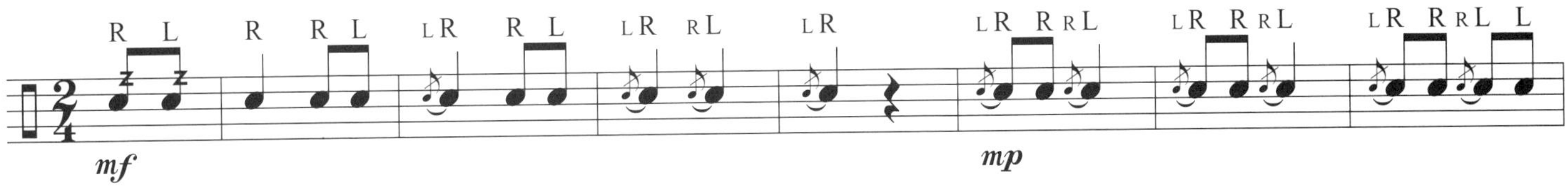

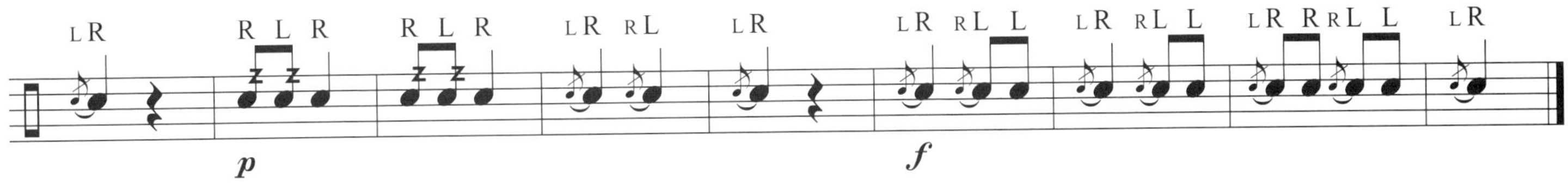

THEORY

REVISITING ACCIDENTALS

Accidentals include **flat** (♭), **sharp** (♯), and **natural** (♮) signs found in front of notes, but not in the key signature. A flat sign (♭) lowers the pitch one half-step. It remains in effect for the rest of the measure. It is further explained in the keyboard percussion side of your book on page 19.

LET RING

Let ring (or **let vibrate**) means to allow the sound of instruments like triangle, cymbals, or bass drum to continue until the next attack. It is represented by a small curved line.

3.8 CANYONS

THEORY

NEW KEY SIGNATURE

This is the key of E♭ **Major.**

This key signature indicates that all Bs, Es, and As should be played as B-flats, E-flats, and A-flats. It is further explained in the keyboard percussion section of your book on page 19.

3.9 ROYAL SCEPTER *Musicianship Challenge! – Play this piece in a noble style.*

3.10 THINGS ARE LOOKING UP

TRACK 1 76

YTHM

THE RULE OF THE DOT

Adding a dot after a note increases the length of the note ***by half its value.***
When adding a dot to a half note, it becomes a **dotted half note.**

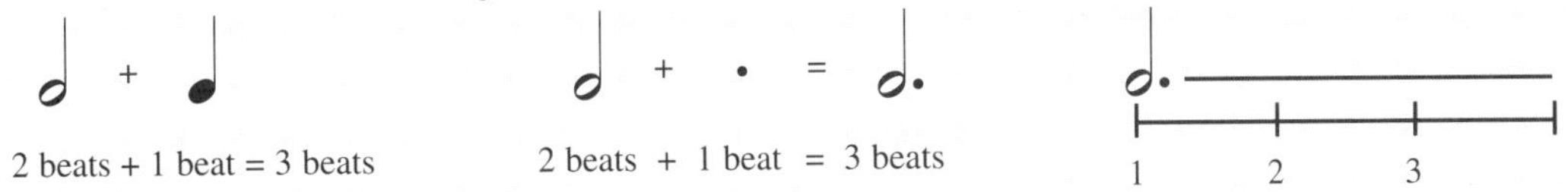

.11 BEAT STREET

Begin CD 2 TRACK 2 1

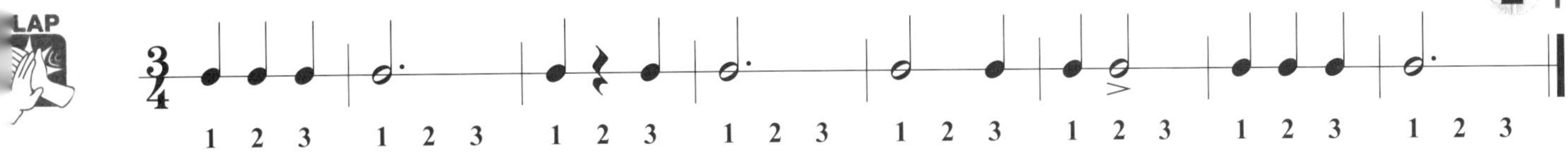

.11a STREET BEAT— For Percussion Only

TRACK 2 1

.12 TRIPLE CROWN *Strive for an even sound throughout.*

TRACK 2 2

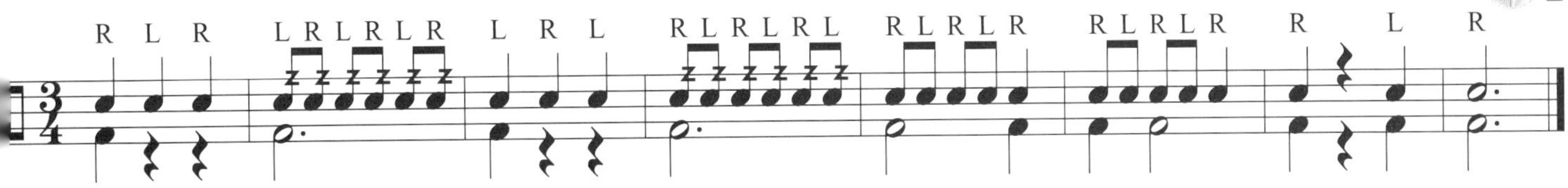

.13 MINUET

Daniel G. Türk

TRACK 2 3

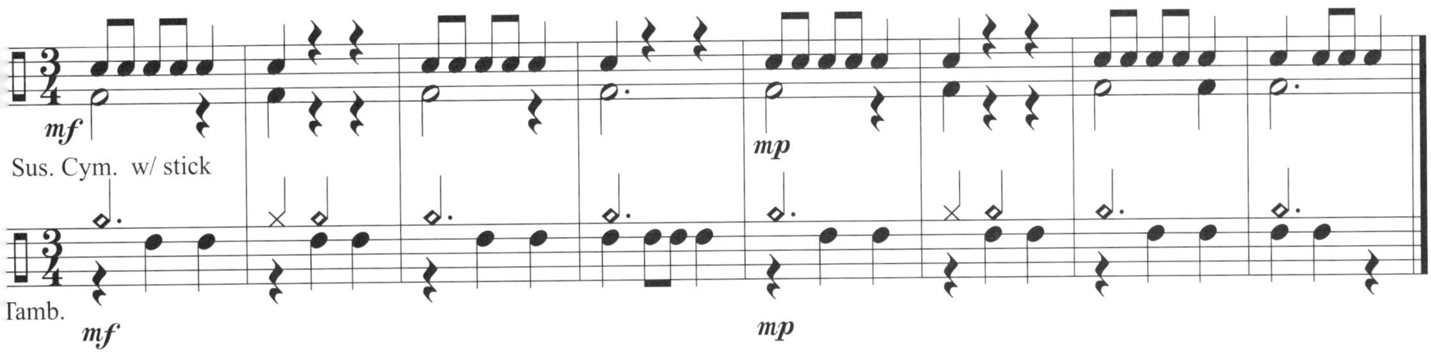

Start Page 20a

3.14 JUNGLE RITUAL

TRACK 2 4

3.15 VOLGA BOATMEN *p–f* Play *piano* the first time and *forte* the second time.

Russian Folk Song

3.16 SHE WORE A YELLOW RIBBON

Traditional American

RUDIMENT

DOUBLE PARADIDDLE

A **double paradiddle** is a rudiment made of four single strokes followed by a double stroke.
Notice there is an accent on the first note.

3.17 CAMPTOWN RACES – Duet

Stephen C. Foster

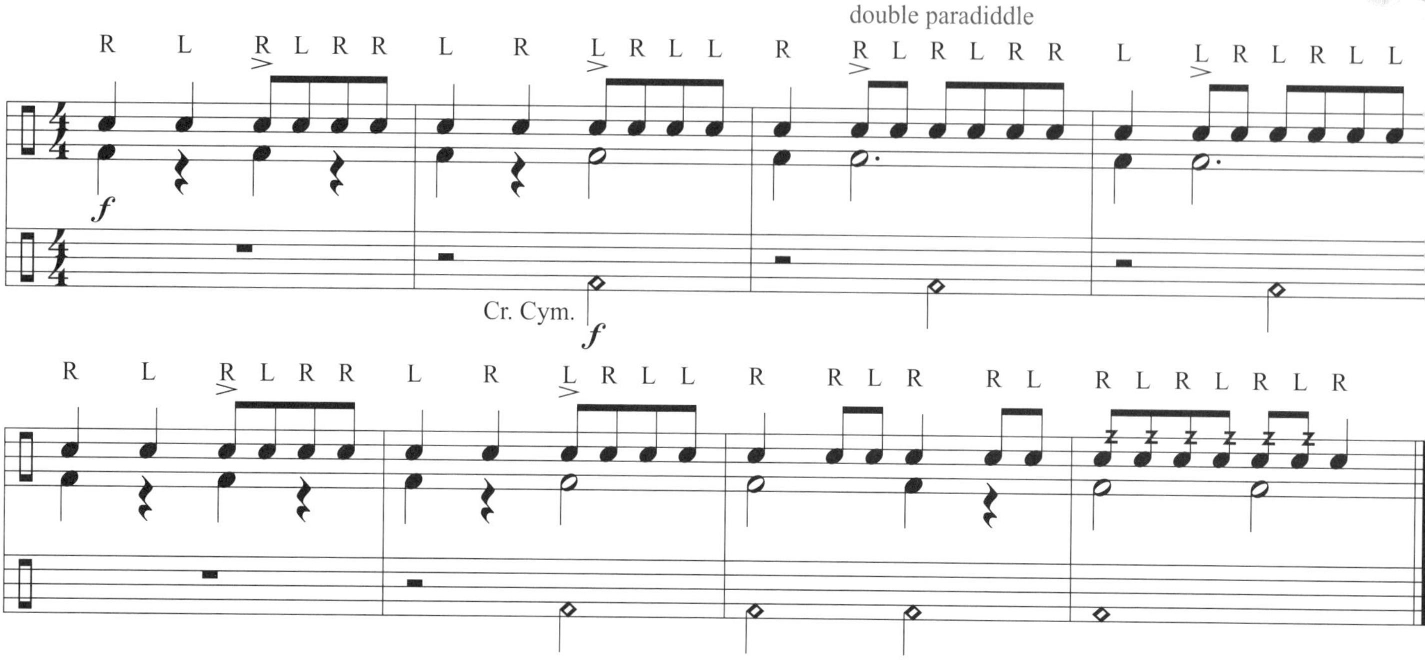

.18 BEAT STREET *Tap your foot to keep a steady beat!*

TRACK 2 8

CLAP

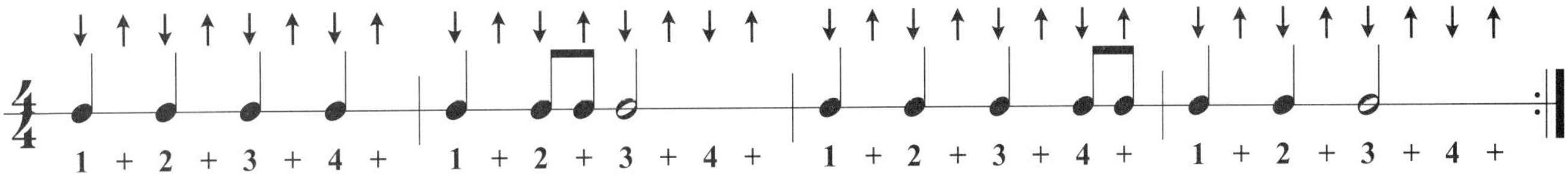

.18a STREET BEAT— For Percussion Only

TRACK 2 8

.19 EIGHTH NOTE EXPRESS

TRACK 2 9

THEORY

COMMON TIME

C The **common time** symbol means the same thing as $\frac{4}{4}$ time.

3.20 GRANDMA GRUNTS

Traditional American

TRACK 2 10

Start Page 21a

3.21 SKIP TO MY LOU

American Folk Song

TRACK 2 11

RHYTHM

WHOLE MEASURE REST

Rest for the entire measure. Check the time signature!

3.22 WALTZING LOU *How should you play these dynamics?*

TRACK 2

American Folk Melody

RHYTHM

SIXTEENTH NOTES

Sixteenth Note = quarter beat of sound 

Beamed Sixteenth Notes 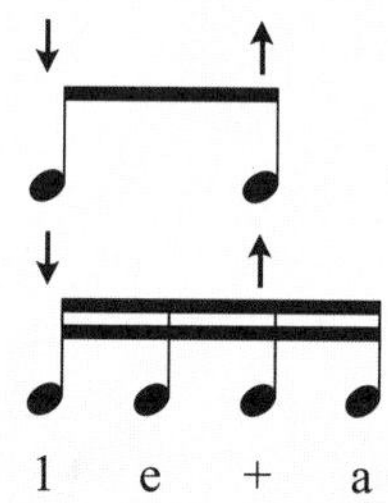

Turn to page 25d for a series of preparatory exercises and sixteenth note studies.

THEORY

ENCLOSED REPEAT SIGNS

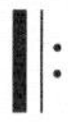  Repeat the music between the two signs.

3.23 TWO BY FOUR

TRACK 2 13

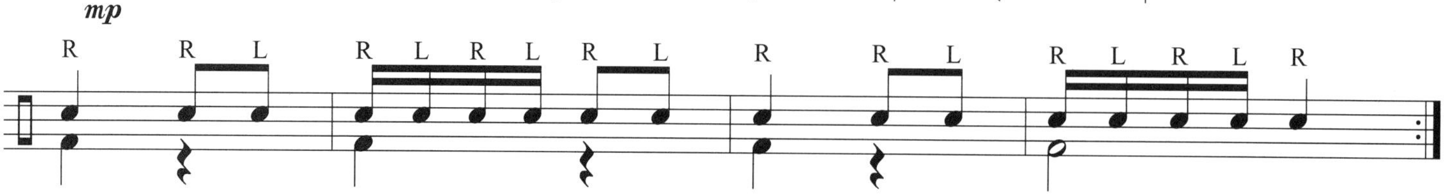

THEORY

STYLE AND FORM: ROUND

In a **round**, each musician plays the same part, but enters at a different time.

3.24 FRÉRE JACQUES – Round *As each musician reaches ②, the next musician should begin playing at ①.*

French Folk Song

TRACK 2 14

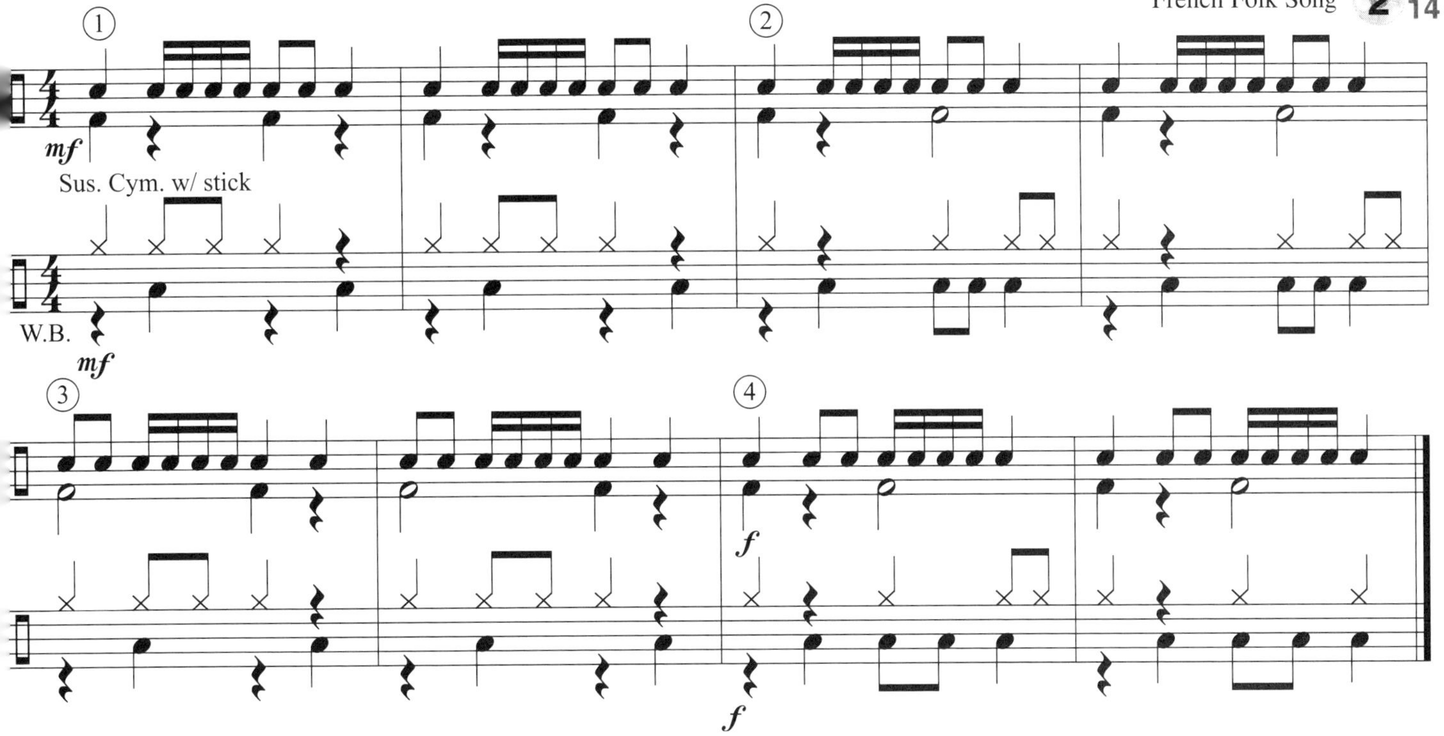

THEORY

STYLE AND FORM: THEME AND VARIATIONS

Composers create a **variation** when they change a melody in some way. Changes can be made to the notes, rhythm, key, and even the time signature! While you will notice the differences in each variation, you will still be able to recognize the original theme.

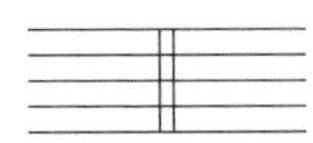

A **double bar line** indicates the end of one section and the beginning of another.

3.25 VARIATIONS ON A FRENCH MELODY

TRACK 2 15

THEORY

DYNAMICS

Crescendo means to gradually play louder. **Decrescendo** means to gradually play softer.

Remember to gradually change the height and striking location of your sticks!

3.26 IT'S SWELL *Clap first, then play!*

SUSPENDED CYMBAL ROLL

A **suspended cymbal roll** is played using alternating single strokes. Place one mallet at 9 o'clock and the other at 3 o'clock near the edge of the cymbal. End the roll with one strike on the release beat. Multiple notes in a roll are connected by a **tie,** which is a curved line that "ties" the notes together. Muffle the cymbal on the rest unless the music indicates to let the sound ring. Use medium cord vibraphone or medium yarn marimba mallets.

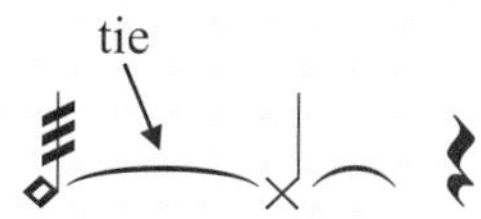

3.27 OUTTA MY WAY

3.28 REGAL FANFARE *Use RHL.*

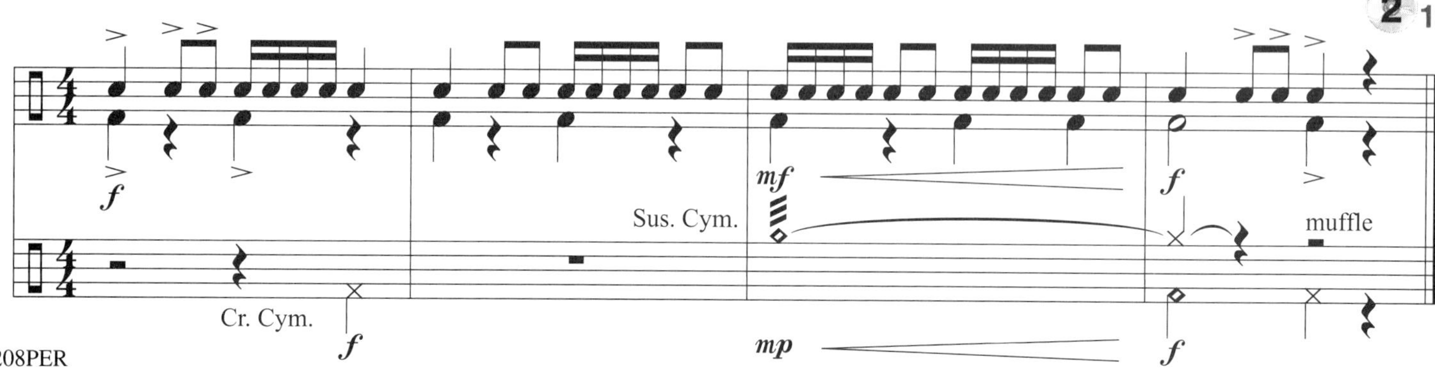

TORY

MUSIC

German born **George Frideric Handel** (1685 – 1759) composed many types of music including oratorios, operas, and orchestral works. *Music for the Royal Fireworks* was written when George II of Great Britain hired him to write music to accompany fireworks in London. The event commemorated the signing of the Treaty of Aix-la-Chapelle in 1749.

ART

During colonial times, American painting and drawing focused on portraiture. Joseph Badger painted portraits of prominent figures and children in colonial Boston. His style can be seen in the portrait of *Jeremiah Belknap*, painted in 1758.

WORLD

Sir Isaac Newton stated the three universal laws of motion. In the same publication he used the Latin word *gravitas* that would become known as gravity. Also, America founded its first hospital in Pennsylvania.

29 MUSIC FOR THE ROYAL FIREWORKS

George F. Handel

TRACK 2 19

.30 SCALE THE WALL

TRACK 2 20

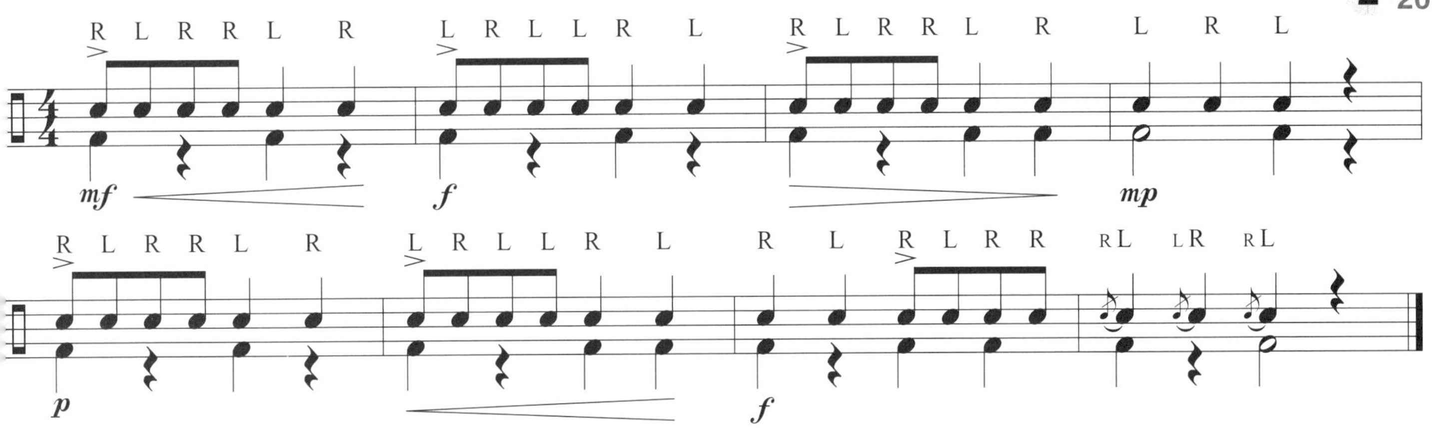

3.31 NEW FRONTIERS

3.32 THE SAINTS GO MARCHING IN *Pick-up notes lead into measure 1.*

Traditional Spiritual

ON THE PODIUM

CONDUCTING IN $\frac{3}{4}$ TIME

It is your turn to conduct a three-beat pattern. With your right hand in a "handshake" position, follow the diagram to conduct in $\frac{3}{4}$ time.

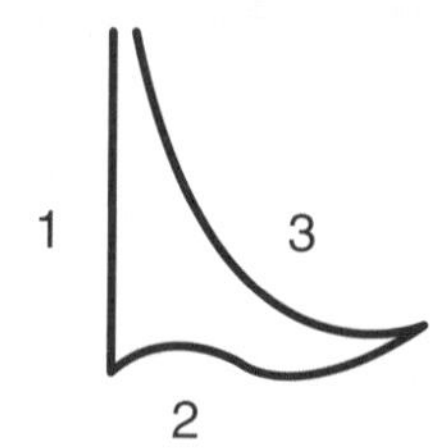

3.33 ROLLING ALONG

ON THE PODIUM

HEORY

FIRST AND SECOND ENDINGS

At the **first ending**, play through it to the repeat sign. Go back to the beginning or the previous repeat sign and play again. Skip the first ending – play the **second ending** instead.

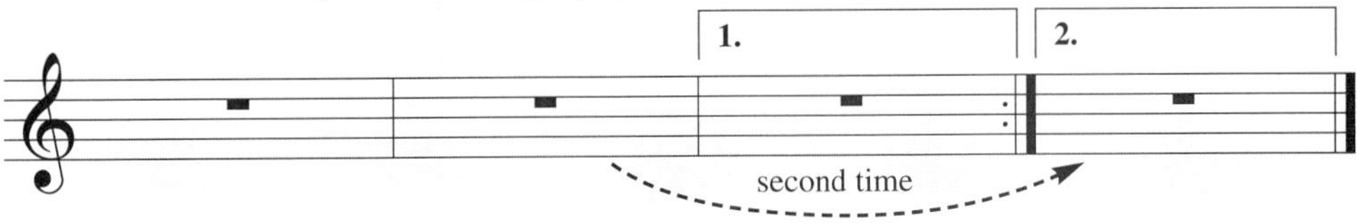

3.34 LONG, LONG AGO

Traditional 2 24

SLEIGH BELLS

Sleigh bells have small bells attached to a stick or on a strap. To play, hold them parallel to the floor with both hands and shake with a short, snappy wrist motion.

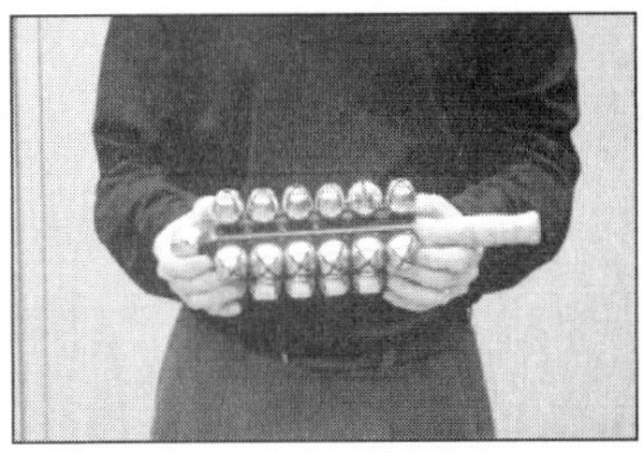

3.35 JOLLY OLD SAINT NICHOLAS – Duet

American Carol 2 25

OPUS 3 ENCORE!

INTERPRETATION STATION

TRACK 2

Listen to CD 2 Track 26. You will hear four musical examples, all composed using a different time signature. As you listen, pay close attention to how rhythmic ideas are grouped. Circle the correct time signature for each example.

1. $\frac{3}{4}$ $\frac{4}{4}$ 2. $\frac{2}{4}$ $\frac{3}{4}$ 3. $\frac{3}{4}$ $\frac{4}{4}$ 4. $\frac{2}{4}$ $\frac{3}{4}$

SIMON "SEZ"

TRACK 2

Listen to CD 2 Track 27. You are going to hear a piece called *One Note Wonder.* It gets its title because it uses only one pitch! You will hear dynamics that make it very interesting. Play along with the accompaniment track that follows, imitating the dynamics and rhythm of the initial recording to make it musical.

COMPOSER'S CORNER

It is your turn to be a composer again! Use rhythms you have learned to complete each measure (remember to look at the time signature). Then give your piece a title and perform it for a friend or family member!

Title:____ **Name:**____________________

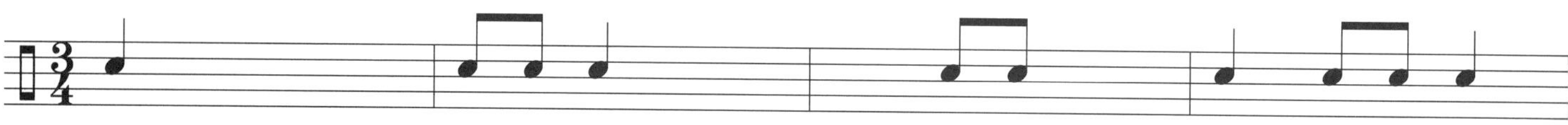

PENCIL POWER

Each measure below is rhythmically incomplete! For each example, add *one note* to complete the measure and make it correct.

1. 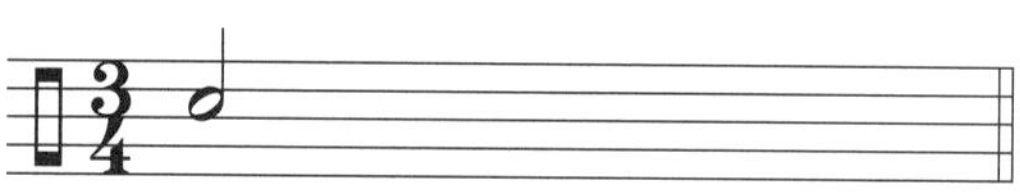

2. 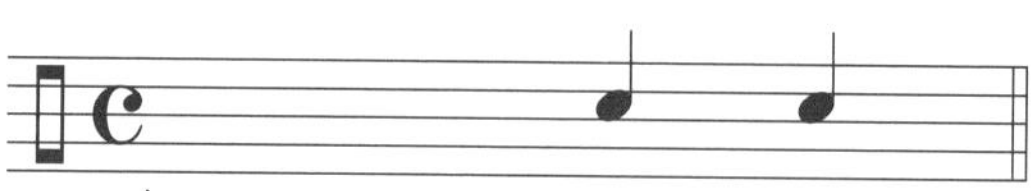

3. 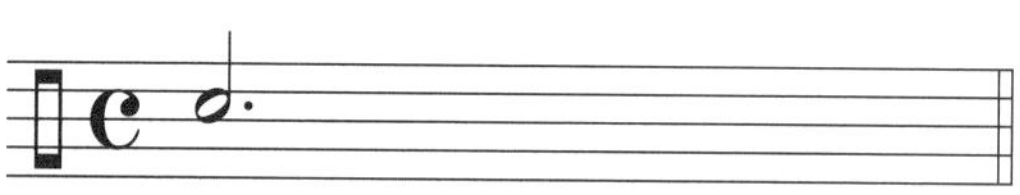

4. 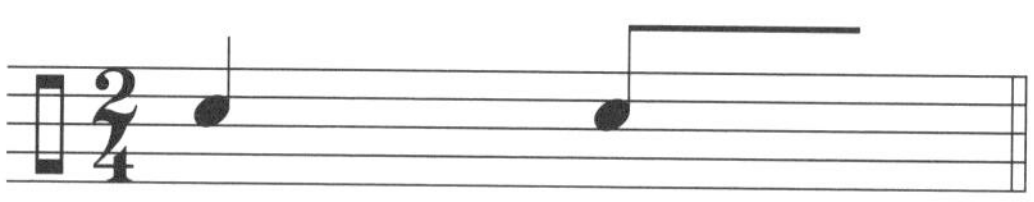

PENCIL POWER — For Percussion Only

Match the following terms with their symbols.

1. _____ Right flam
2. _____ Flam tap
3. _____ Double paradiddle
4. _____ Left flam
5. _____ Flam accent
6. _____ Paradiddle

A: 

B: 

C: 

D: 

E: 

F: 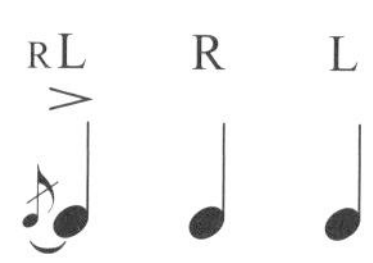

CURTAIN UP!

.36 ZUM GALI GALI – Round

Traditional Hebrew Song

TRACK 2 28

3.37 DRY BONES

Spiritual

TRACK 2 29

3.37a IT'S RUDIMENTAL, WATSON! — Snare Drum Solo

David Collier

TRACK 2 68

CURTAIN UP! FULL BAND

THEORY

MULTIPLE MEASURE REST

In some pieces, there will be instances when you rest for a few measures at a time. When this happens, you will see the **multiple measure rest** symbol. The number above the symbol tells you how many measures of rest to count.

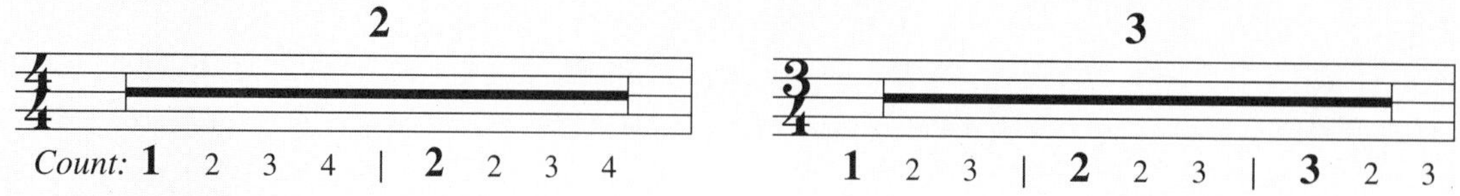

This symbol tells you to rest for two measures in 4/4 time. This symbol tells you to rest for three measures in 3/4 time.

3.38 WILLIAM TELL OVERTURE (Snare Drum, Bass Drum)

Gioachino Rossini
arr. Brian Balmages

38 WILLIAM TELL OVERTURE (Wood Block, Crash Cymbals)

Gioachino Rossini
arr. Brian Balmages

TRACK 2 30

3.39 ABOVE THE CLOUDS (Snare Drum, Bass Drum)

Robert Sheldon

With motion

3.39 ABOVE THE CLOUDS (Triangle, Tambourine)

Robert Sheldon

With motion

SIXTEENTH NOTE STUDIES

These exercises will help reinforce sixteenth notes. Focus on playing evenly and with a steady tempo.

EPARTORY EXERCISE

npare this exercise to the one above. Are there similarities?

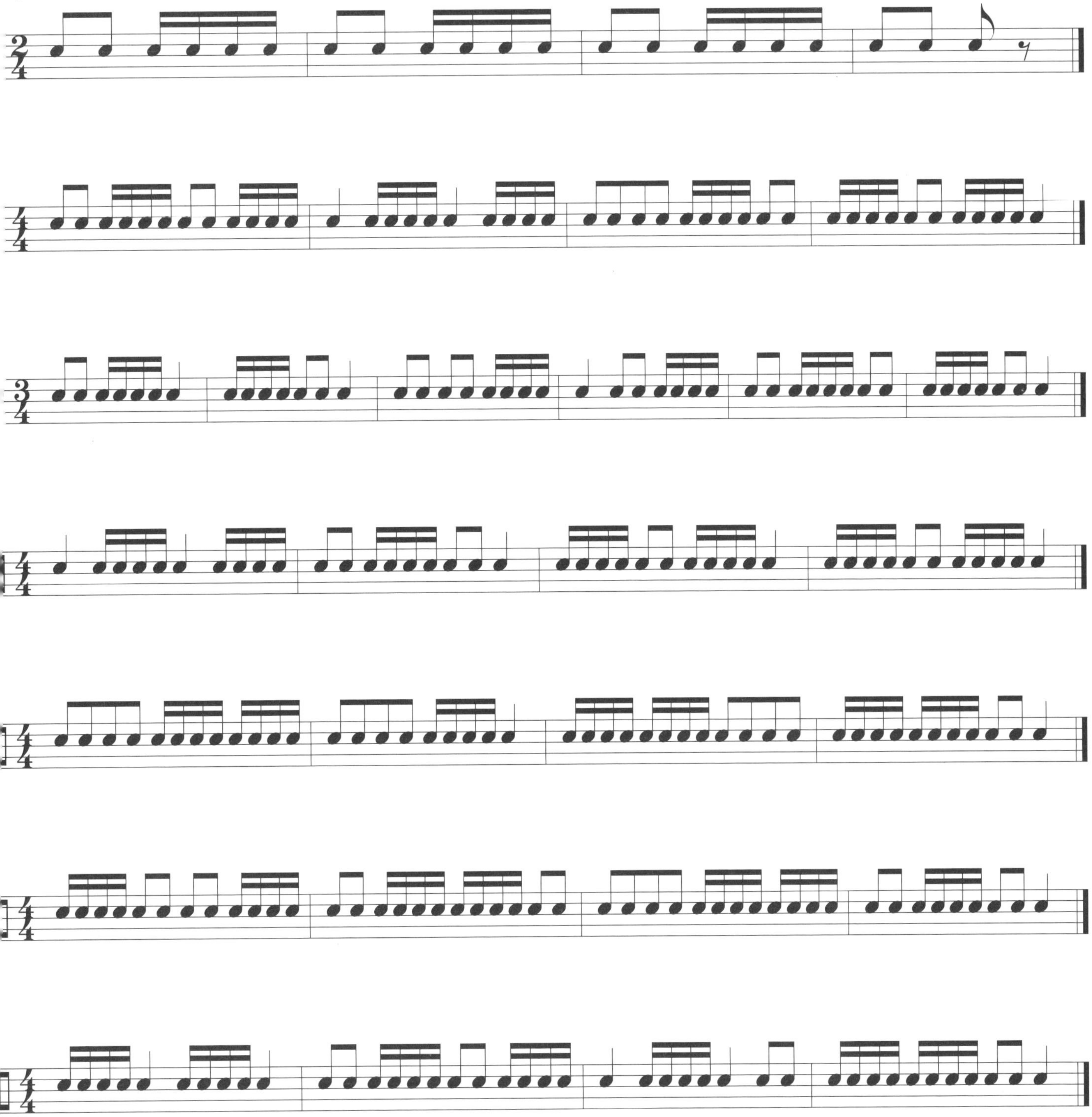

OPUS 4

RHYTHM

EIGHTH NOTE/TWO SIXTEENTH NOTE GROUP

An eighth note can replace the first two sixteenth notes in a group of four sixteenth notes. This creates an **eighth note/two sixteenth note group.**

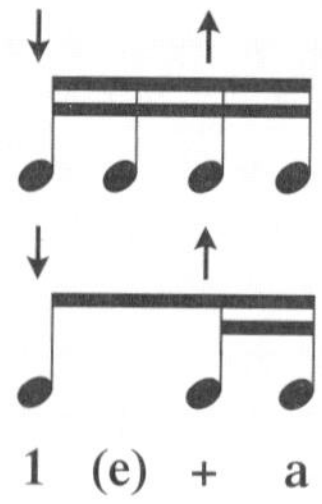

FOR PERCUSSION ONLY

4.1 CIRCUS ACT

TRACK 2

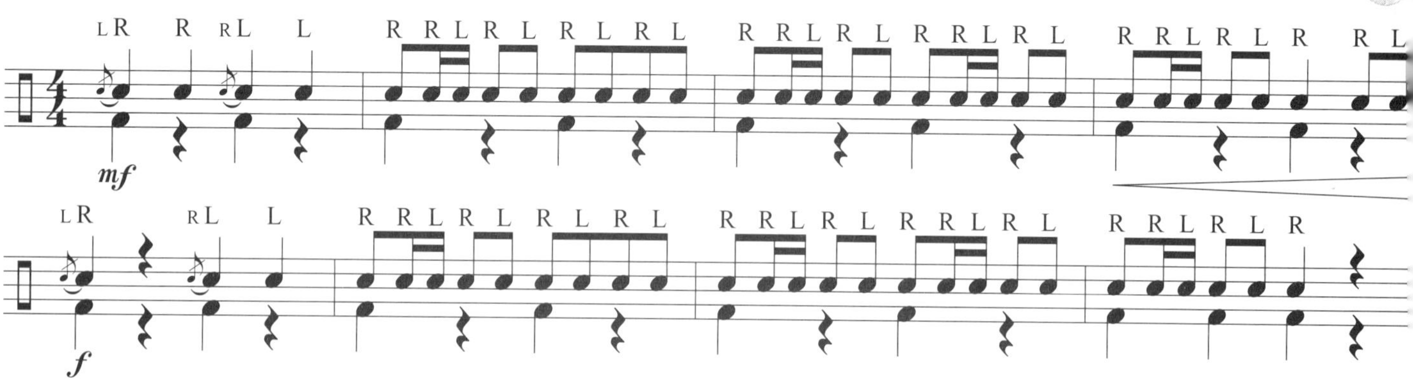

4.2 DAYBREAK

TRACK 2

ON THE PODIUM

Legato *(smooth and flowing)*

.3 CHIAPANECAS

Mexican Folk Song

TRACK 2 34

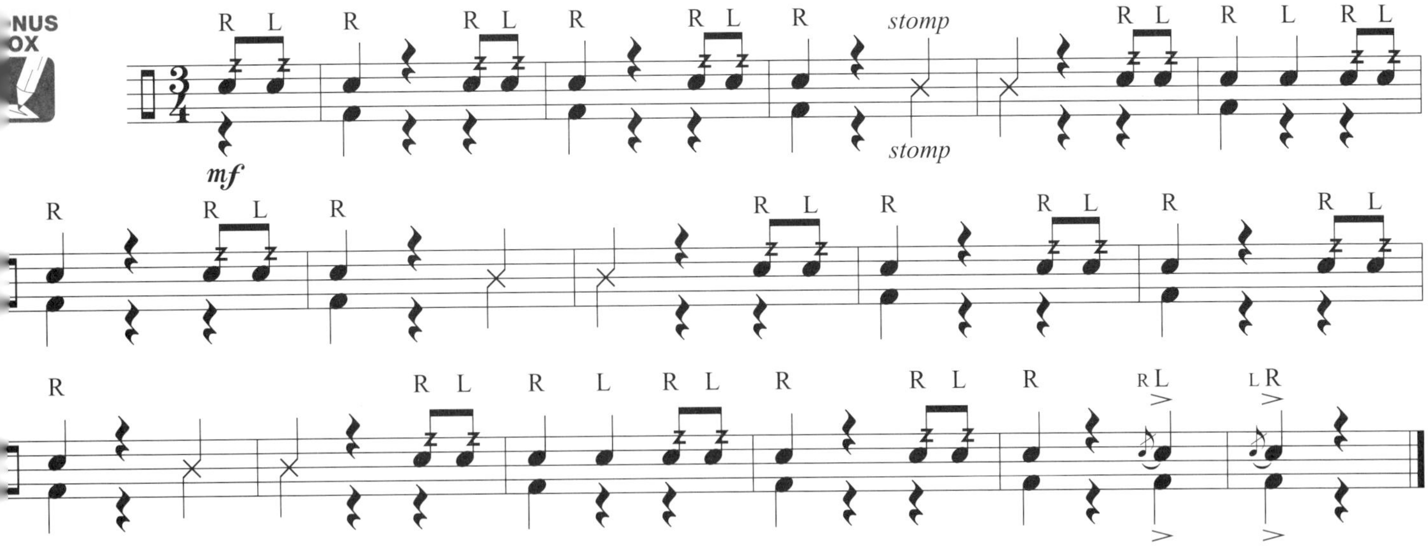

.4 SLURRED NOT SHAKEN *This exercise focuses on single paradiddles with sixteenth notes.*

TRACK 2 35

EIGHTH REST/TWO SIXTEENTH NOTE GROUP

An eighth rest can replace the eighth note to create an **eighth rest/two sixteenth note group.**

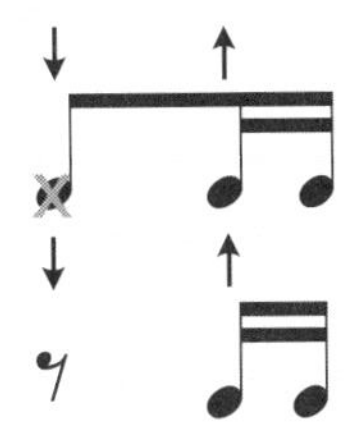

4.5 SLIP 'N' SLIDE

TRACK 2 36

THEORY

TEMPO

Tempo is the speed of the beat. Music can move at different rates of speed.

Largo – a slow tempo **Moderato** – a medium tempo **Allegro** – a fast tempo

4.6 MUSETTE

J.S. Bach TRACK 2

CROSS STICK

Place the shoulder of the left hand stick across the counterhoop and rest the butt in the center of the drum head. Raise the tip of the stick and click the rim. Keep the butt of the stick in contact with the drum head. Cross stick is often notated with an × notehead.

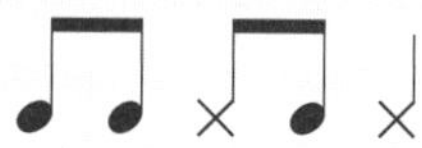

4.7 CIELITO LINDO

Mexican Folk Song TRACK 2

ON THE PODIUM

STORY

MUSIC

Gustav Mahler (1860 – 1911) was a noted composer and conductor of the late Romantic era. He spent time in New York conducting the Metropolitan Opera and the New York Philharmonic Orchestra. He is mainly known for his large symphonies (his *Symphony No. 8* uses over a thousand performers!).

ART

French artist Georges Seurat painted *A Sunday Afternoon on the Island of La Grande Jatte*. This large painting, depicting a scene of recreation in Paris, was created using a technique called pointillism. Composed entirely of painted dots, it took him nearly two years to finish.

WORLD

Mark Twain published *The Adventures of Tom Sawyer*, Sir Arthur Conan Doyle introduced the world to Sherlock Holmes, and the coin-operated telephone was invented.

8 THEME FROM SYMPHONY NO. 1 – Round

TRACK 2 39

Gustav Mahler

argo

HYTHM

TIES REVISITED

A **tie** is a curved line that connects two or more notes. These notes are "tied" together and played to sound like one longer note.

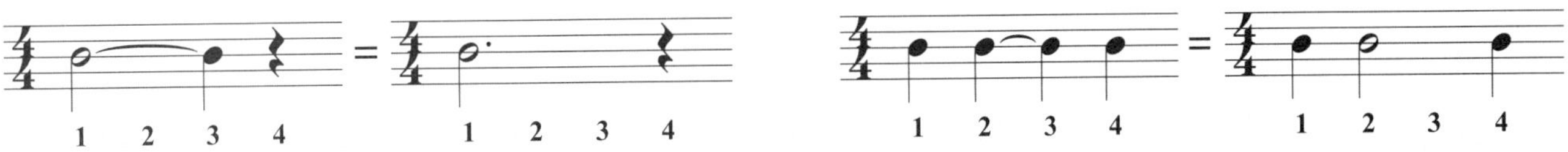

DIMENT

MULTIPLE BOUNCE ROLL

A **multiple bounce roll** is created by adding multiple bounce strokes to consecutive sixteenth notes. This is also called a **concert roll** or a **buzz roll.** Be sure to keep the sixteenth notes steady, the hands even, and the bounces consistent.

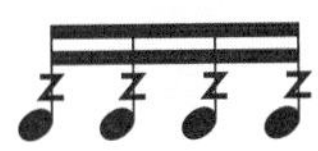

4.9 MAKING CONNECTIONS

TRACK 2 40

4.10 ALL TIED UP *Use RHL and keep the sixteenth notes steady as you work on longer multiple bounce rolls.*

TRACK 2 41

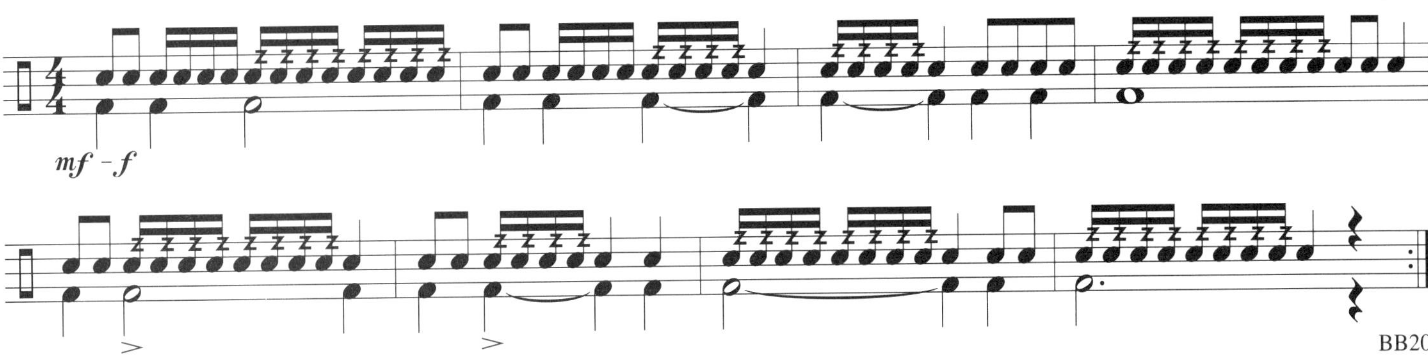

HISTORY

MUSIC

Pyotr Ilyich Tchaikovsky (1840 – 1893) was a Russian composer who studied music at a very young age. His most famous works include the ballet *The Nutcracker* and the exciting *1812 Overture*. He composed *Capriccio Italien* after a visit to Italy during Carnivale season.

ART

In 1880, the Arts and Crafts Movement was going strong in England. This style is reflected in art, architecture, and interior design. Works by British architect Herbert Tudor Buckland and American architect Frank Lloyd Wright are typical of the Arts and Crafts style.

WORLD

Wabash, Indiana became the first town to be completely illuminated using electric light and the Statue of Liberty was presented to the United States by the people of France.

4.11 CAPRICCIO ITALIEN

TRACK 2

Pyotr I. Tchaikovsky

Allegro

RUDIMENT

ROLLS

A **quarter note roll** is made up of four sixteenth notes using multiple bounce strokes.
A **half note roll** is made up of eight sixteenth notes using multiple bounce strokes.
A roll is often tied to the next beat which is struck. This note is called the **release.**

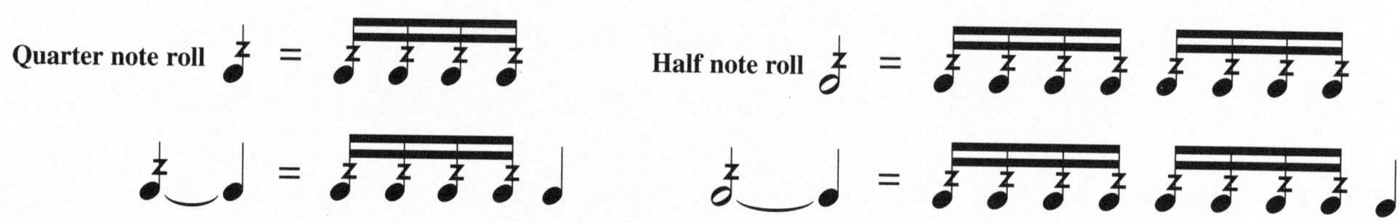

FOR PERCUSSION ONLY

4.12 BARCAROLLE *Though notated differently, the rolls in measures 2, 3, 5 and 6 all sound the same.*

TRACK 24

Jacques Offenbach

Moderato

THEORY

NEW KEY SIGNATURE

This is the key of A♭ **Major.**

This key signature indicates that all Bs, Es, As, and Ds should be played as B-flats, E-flats, A-flats, and D-flats. It is further explained in the keyboard percussion section of your book on page 28.

.13 THE BLUE BELLS OF SCOTLAND

Scottish Folk Song TRACK 2 44

Maestoso *(majestically)*

HISTORY

MUSIC

John Philip Sousa (1854 – 1932) was a violinist, composer, and conductor born in Washington, D.C. He conducted the United States Marine Band from 1880 until 1892. His marches, such as *The Stars and Stripes Forever, Semper Fidelis*, and the *Liberty Bell*, are well known and important to American culture.

ART

In the early 20th century, artist Salvador Dali of Spain was mostly known as a surrealist and emphasized visions of the subconcious. *The Persistence of Memory* (1931), a scene with melting clocks, is perhaps one of his best known works.

WORLD

Elsewhere in 1917, the Russian revolution began, World War I was still raging, and the first commercial recordings of jazz music were available to the public.

4.14 HIGH SCHOOL CADETS *Use RHL in this exercise.*

John Philip Sousa TRACK 2 45

March Tempo

RHYTHM

TWO SIXTEENTH/EIGHTH NOTE GROUP

An eighth note can replace the last two sixteenth notes in a group of four sixteenth notes.
This creates a **two sixteenth/eighth note group.**

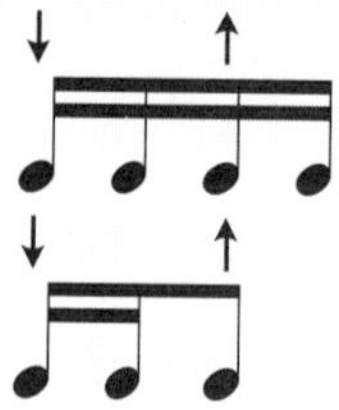

1 e + (a)

THEORY

ONE-MEASURE REPEAT

Repeat the music written in the previous measure.

4.15 IT'S ONLY NATURAL *For soft playing, hold the tambourine at a 45° angle and tap with finger tips at the edge.*

TRACK 2

Dolce *(sweetly)*

4.16 ACCIDENTAL BLUES – Duet

TRACK 24

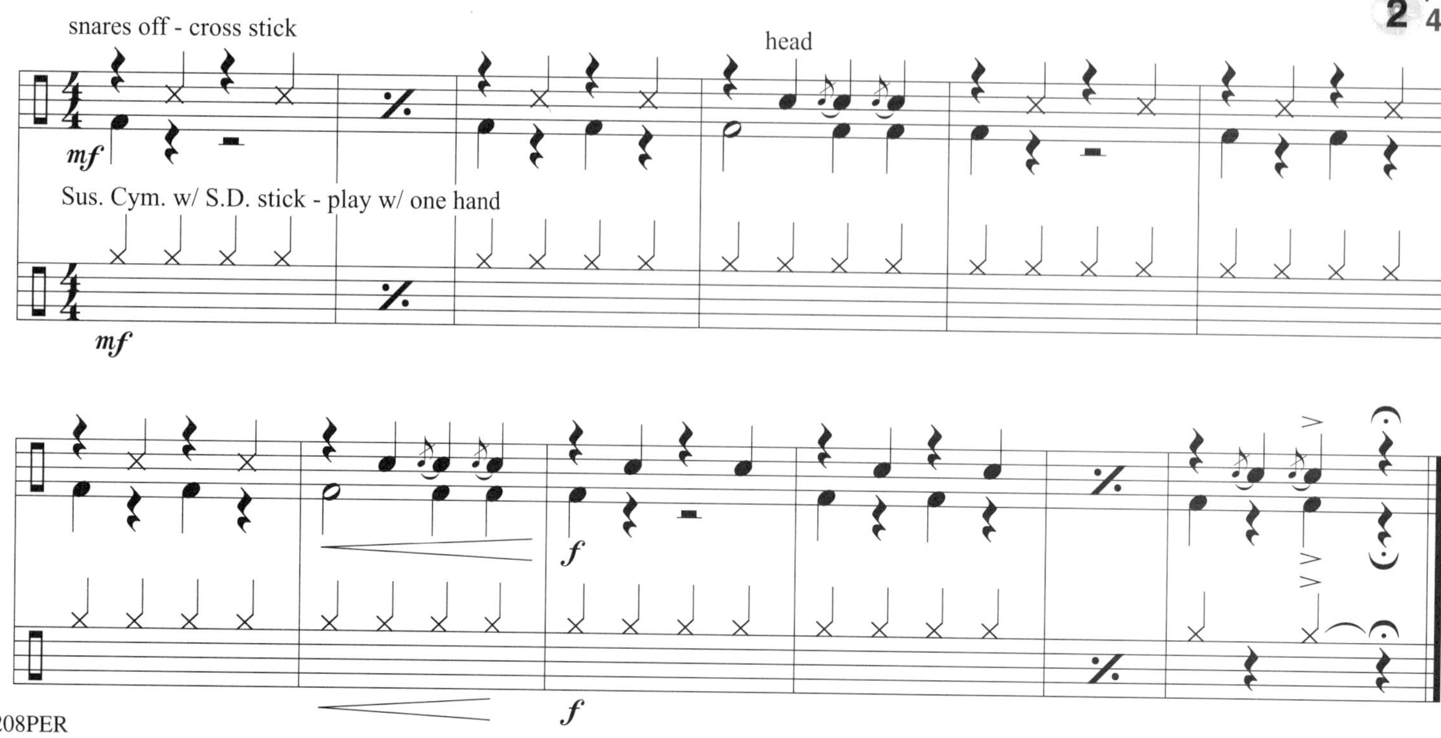

RHYTHM

RETURN OF THE DOT RULE

Adding a dot after a note increases the length of the note by half its value. Here, the dot is used with a quarter note to create a **dotted quarter note.**

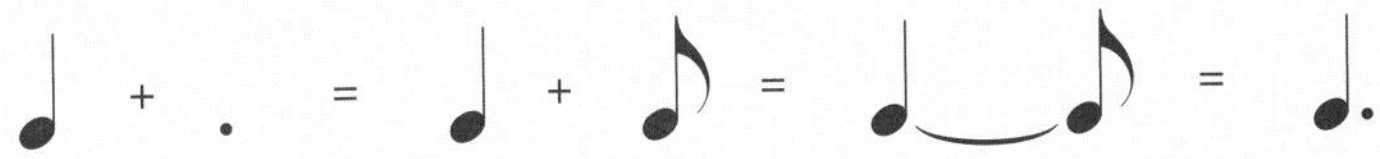

4.17 BEAT STREET *Tap your foot to keep a steady beat.*

TRACK 2 48

CLAP

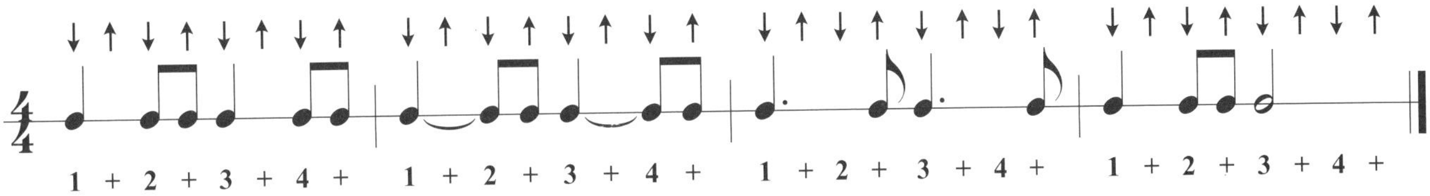

4.17a STREET BEAT — For Percussion Only

TRACK 2 48

4.18 DOTS A LOT

TRACK 2 49

THEORY

RITARDANDO

Ritardando – abbreviated "*rit.*" – means to make the tempo gradually slower.

DOTTED QUARTER NOTE ROLL

As always, strike the note at the end of the tie.

FOR PERCUSSION ONLY

4.19 ALL THROUGH THE NIGHT

Welsh Folk Song

TRACK 2 50

4.20 AMERICA

TRACK 2

Traditional

Maestoso

THEORY

D.C. AL FINE

D.C. is an abbreviation for *da capo*, an Italian term that refers to the beginning. At the **D.C. al Fine**, return to the beginning and play again until the **Fine**.

4.21 ALOUETTE

TRACK 2 5

French-Canadian Folk Song

Moderato

CLAVES

The **clave** is a Latin American instrument. Rest one clave on the finger tips and heal of the palm in the left hand. Strike this clave in the center with the other clave held loosely in the right hand.

22 BANANA BOAT SONG *Calypso is a blend of African and Caribbean music.*

Caribbean Folk Song — TRACK 2 53

Calypso

Play with the stick on the counterhoop for a rim click.

ISTORY

MUSIC

Antonín Dvořák (1841 – 1904) was from a small town near Prague, in the Czech Republic. He eventually moved to the United States and became the director of the New York Conservatory of Music. In 1888, the Conservatory welcomed African-Americans while other schools were still practicing segregation. His *Symphony No. 9 ("From the New World")* was composed during his brief time in America. It is influenced by Native American music and African-American spirituals.

ART

The art world experienced Cubism, a style in which objects were broken up, then reassembled in abstract forms. Pablo Picasso was perhaps the foremost Cubist ever. His *Guernica* (1937) depicts the German bombing of Guernica during the Spanish Civil War.

WORLD

Congress abolished slavery in the U.S. Territories, Albert Einstein was born, the World's Columbian Exposition was held in Chicago, and New York became the first state to require license plates on cars.

4.23 THEME FROM THE NEW WORLD SYMPHONY *Focus on your dotted quarter and quarter note rolls.*

Antonín Dvořák — TRACK 2 54

Largo

RHYTHM

MORE ABOUT THE DOT

While a dotted quarter note is usually followed by an eighth note, the eighth note sometimes appears *before* the dotted quarter note.

4.24 BEAT STREET

TRACK 2

CLAP

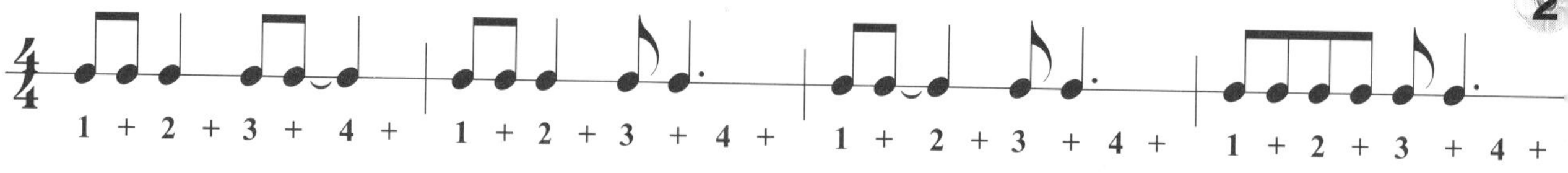

4.24a STREET BEAT — For Percussion Only

TRACK 2

4.25 CARIBBEAN CARNIVAL *This exercise uses left double paradiddles. Follow the stickings carefully.*

TRACK 2

Calypso

4.26 GOOD NIGHT LADIES *This exercise focuses on double strokes and double paradiddles. Follow the stickings carefully.*

Traditional

TRACK 2

Brightly

ON THE PODIUM

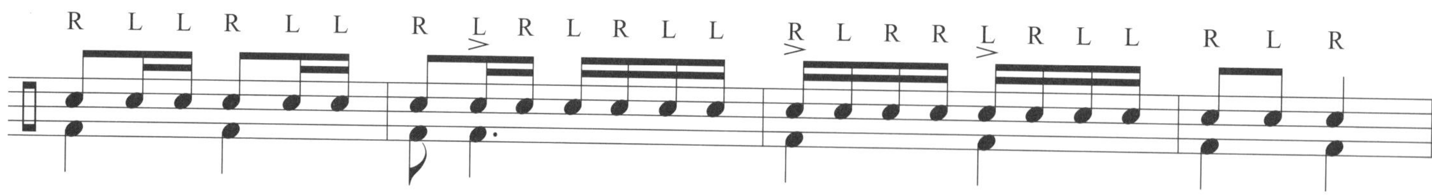

4.27 GOING TO KENTUCKY

American Folk Song

TRACK 2

Allegro

128 FILL 'ER UP

TRACK 2 59

129 MARCHE MILITAIRE

Franz Schubert

TRACK 2 60

Marziale *(in a march style)*

OPUS 4 ENCORE!

INTERPRETATION STATION

TRA 2

Listen to CD 2 Track 61. For each example, decide if the tempo is ***L**argo*, ***M**oderato*, or ***A**llegro*. Circle the correct answer.

1. L M A 2. L M A 3. L M A 4. L M A

SIMON "SEZ"

TRA 2

Listen to CD 2 Track 62. You are going to hear four examples. Match the performance to its correctly notated example. The first one has been done for you!

No. 1 = B No. 2 = ____ No. 3 = ____ No. 4 = ____

A.

B.

C.

D.

COMPOSER'S CORNER

Sometimes a composer takes an existing melody and presents it in a new way. This is called **arranging**. Change the rhythms of the music in *Alouette in Four* so it is playable in $\frac{2}{4}$ time. *Hint: Cut the rhythmic value of each note in half!* The arrangement has been started for you.

ALOUETTE IN FOUR

ALOUETTE IN TWO

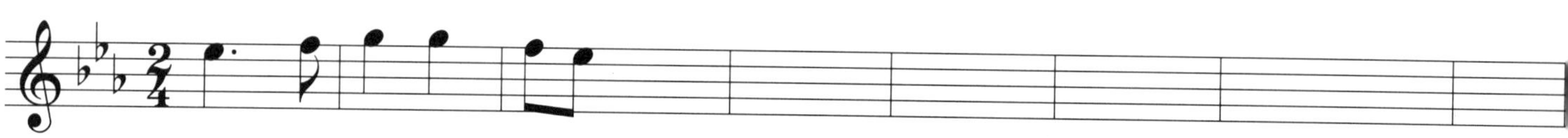

PENCIL POWER – MATCH THE COMPOSER

Match the composer with the correct fact by writing in the appropriate letter.

_____ Wolfgang Amadeus Mozart	A. Russian composer who wrote the famous ballet, *The Nutcracker*
_____ Antonín Dvořák	B. U.S. Marine Band conductor and composer known for his marches
_____ Gustav Mahler	C. His *Symphony No. 9* reveals the influence of African-American spirituals
_____ John Philip Sousa	D. Child genius who composed over 600 works in a short life of 35 years
_____ Ludwig van Beethoven	E. Continued to compose music after becoming completely deaf
_____ Pyotr Ilyich Tchaikovsky	F. Composer of the late Romantic era known for his large symphonies

CURTAIN UP!

4.30 HAVA NASHIRA – Round

Israeli Folk Song

TRACK 2 63

SNARE DRUM TECHNIQUE *Challenge yourself with these special snare drum studies!*

CURTAIN UP! FULL BAND

4.31 LITTLE SWALLOW (Suspended Cymbal, Triangle)

Chinese Folk Song
arr. Robert Sheldon

TRACK 2

.32 FURY (Snare Drum, Bass Drum)

Brian Balmages

TRACK 2 65

Allegro

4.32 FURY (Crash Cymbals, Suspended Cymbal, Triangle)

Brian Balmages

TRACK 2 65

Allegro

4.33 HAIL THE CONQUERING HERO

Instrumental Solo – Keyboard Percussion

George F. Handel
arr. Brian Balmages

TRACK 2

Piano Accompaniment

TRACK 2 6

(Piano accompaniment only)

33a IMAGINE THAT— Percussion Ensemble

nare Drum, Bass Drum)

David Collier &
Brian Balmages

TRACK 2 69

4.33a IMAGINE THAT— Percussion Ensemble

(Maracas, Tambourine)

David Collier &
Brian Balmages

33a IMAGINE THAT— Percussion Ensemble

ells)

David Collier &
Brian Balmages

TRACK 2 69

OPUS 5

RUDIMENT

FLAMACUE

The **flamacue** is a rudiment composed of a flam, 3 strokes and another flam. It always has an accent on the stroke after the first flam.

5.1 CATAPULT!

Begin CD 3

TRACK 3

5.2 UP AND OVER

TRACK 3

5.3 SMOOTH HORIZONS

TRACK 3

5.4 UP, UP AND AWAY!

TRACK 34

5 CLIMB ON *Practice your flam taps, flam accents, and flamacues. Pay careful attention to stickings.*

TRACK 3 5

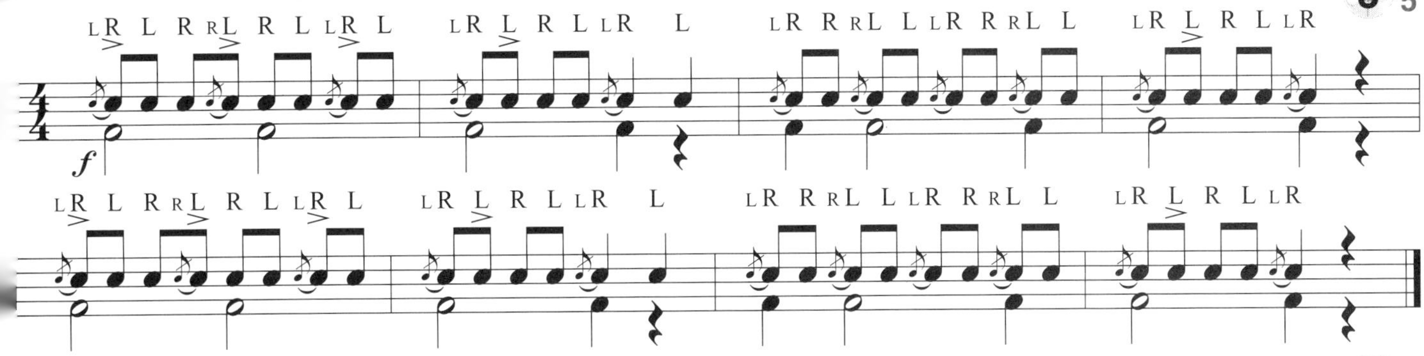

6 OVER EASY

TRACK 3 6

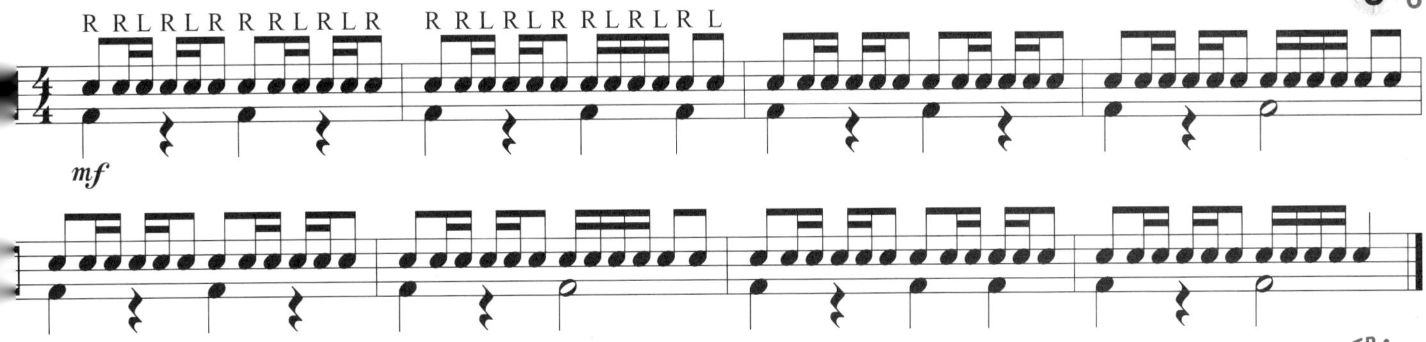

.7 ZERO GRAVITY

TRACK 3 7

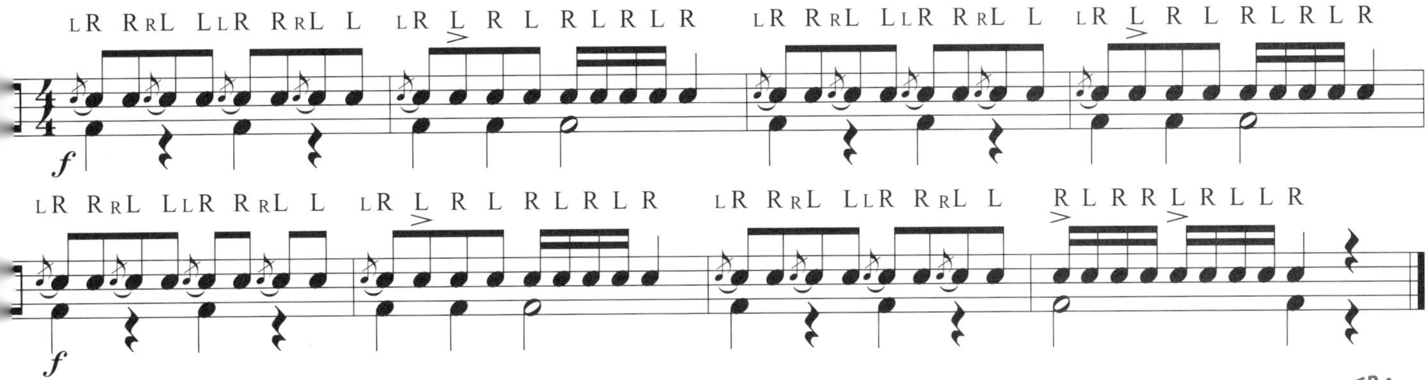

.8 BREAKING THROUGH

TRACK 3 8

.9 THE MOON TURNS DARK

French Folk Melody

TRACK 3 9

Misterioso *(mysteriously)*

EIGHTH NOTE ROLL

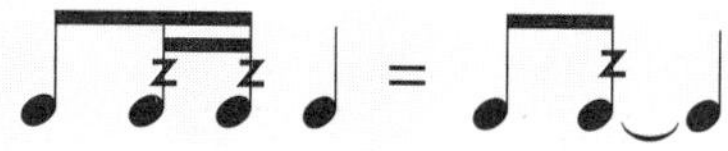

An **eighth note roll** is made up of two sixteenth notes using multiple bounce strokes.

5.10 IN ORBIT

5.11 CLEAR SKIES

5.12 SPIRIT!

5.13 BREAK IT DOWN

14 SHALOM, CHAVERIM

Hebrew Folk Song — TRACK 3 14

Allegro

15 THE UNDISCOVERED PLANET

TRACK 3 15

Aggressively

THEORY

TEMPO

Andante is a tempo between *Largo* and *Moderato*.

slow ← → fast

Largo – Andante – Moderato – Allegro

16 SAKURA, SAKURA

Japanese Folk Song — TRACK 3 16

Andante

HISTORY

MUSIC

German composer **Johannes Brahms** (1833 – 1897) was also an accomplished pianist and gave the first performance of many of his own works. *Lullaby (Wiegenlied)* was composed in 1868 to celebrate the birth of his friend's son.

ART

In the mid 1800s, Realists were concerned with objectivity. American artist James Whistler titled many of his works "harmonies" or "arrangements." An example is his *Arrangement in Grey and Black No. 1: Portrait of the Artist's Mother.*

WORLD

In 1868, floats appeared in New Orleans' Mardi Gras parade for the first time and the first Memori Day was celebrated in the United States.

5.17 LULLABY – Duet

Johannes Brahms

Cantabile *(in a singing style)*

5.18 BEAT STREET

CLAP

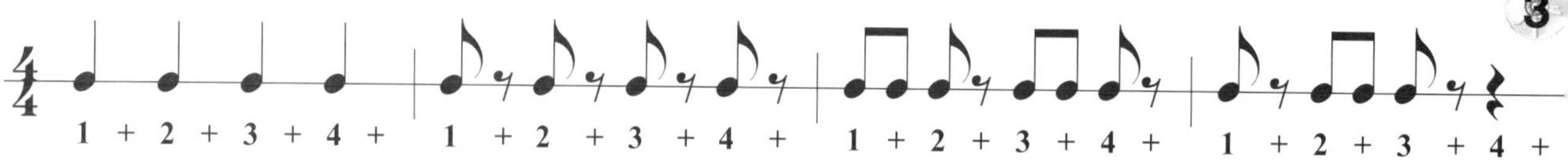

EIGHTH NOTE ROLLS REVISITED

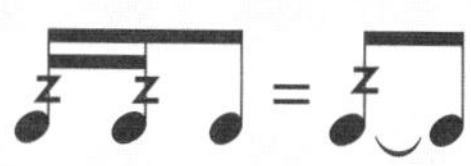

An **eighth note roll** can occur on the beat.

5.18a STREET BEAT– For Percussion Only

5.19 SCALING WITH EIGHTH RESTS

TORY

MUSIC

German composer **Johann Sebastian Bach** (1685 – 1750) began learning music as a young boy, studying violin and organ. He is thought to be one of the greatest composers who ever lived. His work is the model of the Baroque style.

ART

Peter Paul Rubens painted a series of works in the Baroque Style for Marie de Medici at the Luxembourg Palace in Paris, France. These works are now on display at the Louvre, one of the most famous art museums in the world.

WORLD

The tuning fork was invented by Englishman John Shore, the first folding umbrella was manufactured in France, and infamous pirate Edward Teach (Blackbeard) terrorized people along the Atlantic coast.

.20 MINUET NO. 1

TRACK 3 20

J. S. Bach

Moderato

SNARE DRUM WARM-UPS

TRACK 3 6

Play these warm-ups at different tempi and dynamics. Focus on your grip, stroke, quality of sound, and a steady beat. You can use the accompaniment track from 5.6 to keep a steady tempo.

5.21 BEAT STREET

CLAP

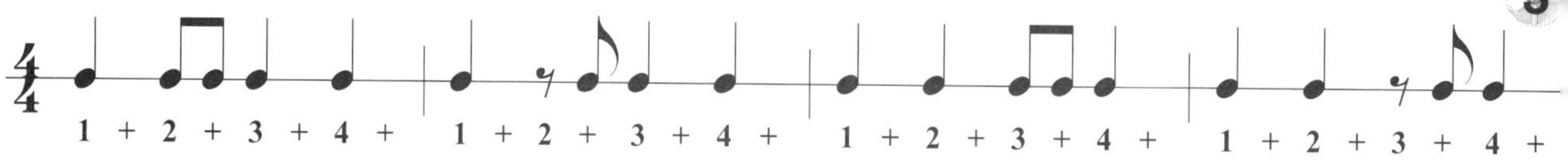

5.21a STREET BEAT – For Percussion Only

5.22 STEPPIN' OFF THE EIGHTH

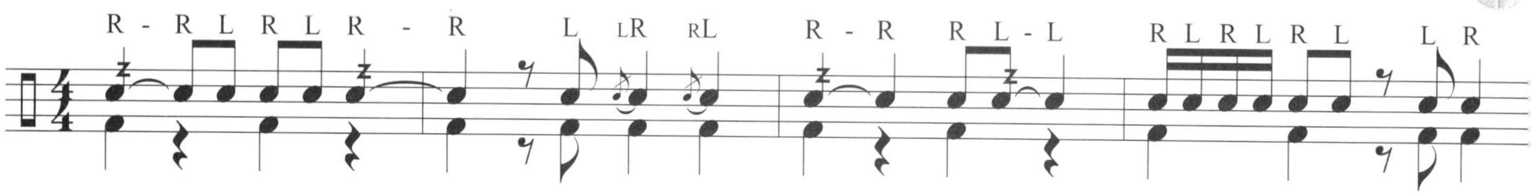

5.23 TIPTOE TANGO *Tango is a type of music and dance that originated in Buenos Aires, Argentina.*

ON THE PODIUM

TAMBOURINE TECHNIQUE

A **shake roll** is played by holding the tambourine perpendicular to the floor and quickly twisting the wrist to create a smooth sound. The roll begins and ends by striking the tambourine in the center with the bunched fingers of the opposite hand. Shake rolls are typically used when the dynamics are *mf* and louder.

.24 ROCK ON, ROCK OFF – Duet

TRACK 3 24

Driving

THEORY

ARTICULATION: TENUTO AND STACCATO

Tenuto
Play with full value.

Staccato
Play light and separated.

While these concepts are primarily addressed in the winds, they involve special techniques that you will learn as you become more advanced.

5.25 LONG AND SHORT OF IT

HISTORY

MUSIC

Austrian composer **Franz Joseph Haydn** (1732 – 1809) is often referred to as the father of the symphony (He wrote 108 of them!). *Symphony No. 94* is often called the *Surprise Symphony*. Haydn surprised listeners with an unexpected loud chord that came after some very quiet music.

ART

Americans saw paintings by countryman John Trumbull (his historical painting *Declaration of Independence* is on the back of the $2 bill). In England, young artist Joseph Turner was setting the tone for Impressionism.

WORLD

The United States Bill of Rights was ratified, the world's first Sunday newspaper (*The Observer*) was published in England, and Benjamin Franklin invented bifocals!

5.26 SURPRISE SYMPHONY

Franz J. Haydn

Andante

TORY

MUSIC

Paul Abraham Dukas (1865 – 1935) was a French composer who wrote in the Romantic style. His most famous work, *The Sorcerer's Apprentice,* is based on a poem by Johann Wolfgang von Goethe. The poem describes an apprentice who loses control of an enchanted broomstick.

ART

Edvard Munch, from Norway, painted in the Expressionist style which uses symbolism to portray many different themes. One of his best-known works is *The Scream* (1893).

WORLD

The 19th Amendment gave women the right to vote, author Madeleine L'Engle was born, and the first underground metro railway opened in Boston.

27 THE SORCERER'S APPRENTICE

Paul A. Dukas TRACK 3 27

Misterioso

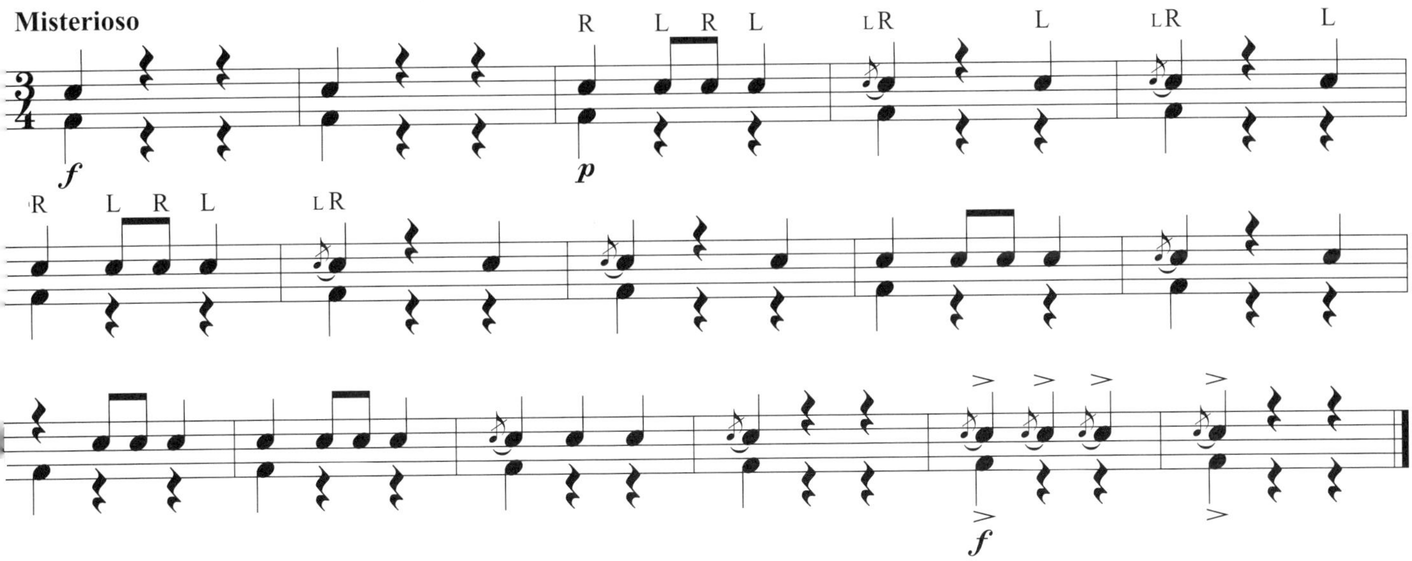

28 GO DOWN MOSES

Spiritual TRACK 3 28

TEMPLE BLOCKS

Originally from China, **temple blocks** are a set of 5 graduated, hollow wooden blocks. They produce a sound lower and rounder than wood blocks. They are played with medium to medium-hard rubber mallets close to the opening of the block. Their abbreviation is **T.B.**

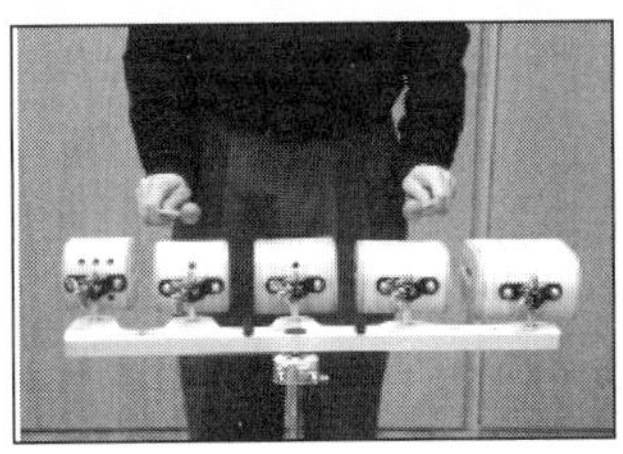

.29 JITTERS, CRITTERS

TRACK 3 29

Misterioso

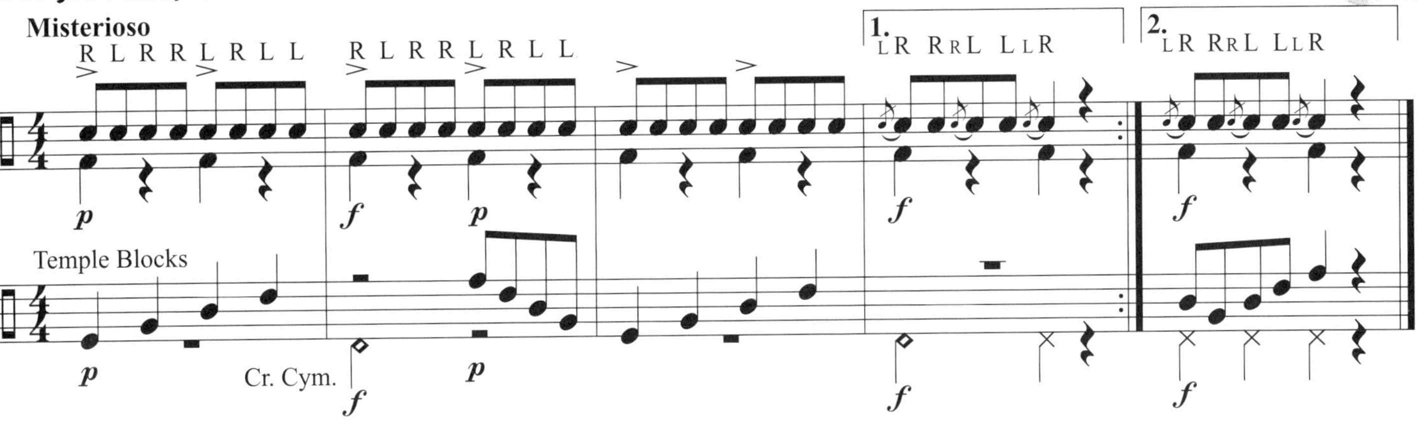

OPUS 5 ENCORE!

INTERPRETATION STATION

Listen to CD 3 Track 30. For each example, decide if the articulation is ***L**egato* or ***S**taccato.*
Circle the letter that corresponds with your answer.

1. L S 2. L S 3. L S 4. L S

SIMON "SEZ"

Listen to CD 3 Track 31. You will hear a well-known song. Listen first, sing it, then find the pitches on your keyboard instrument. You can then play along with the accompaniment track that follows. Can you match the notes and style of the initial recording?

COMPOSER'S CORNER

Writing a theme is just one part of a composer's process. Composers also use dynamics to make their music more expressive. Add your own dynamics and then play the piece expressively. Choose from the following:

p mp mf f < >

PENCIL POWER – MATCH THE STYLE TERMS

Match the style term with the correct definition by writing in the appropriate letter.

_____ Legato	A. In a singing style
_____ Maestoso	B. In a march style
_____ Dolce	C. Smooth and flowing
_____ Marziale	D. Sweetly
_____ Cantabile	E. Blend of African and Caribbean music
_____ Calypso	F. Majestically

CURTAIN UP!

5.30 LOCH LOMOND

Scottish Folk Song

Cantabile

30a TRIANGULATION— Accessory Percussion Ensemble

riangle, Claves)

David Collier &
Brian Balmages

TRACK 3 68

.30a TRIANGULATION— Accessory Percussion Ensemble

Tambourine, Wood Block)

David Collier &
Brian Balmages

TRACK 3 68

5.31 LA MORISQUE (RENAISSANCE DANCE)

(Snare Drum, Bass Drum)

Tielman Susato
arr. Brian Balmages

TRACK 3

5.31 LA MORISQUE (RENAISSANCE DANCE)

(Crash Cymbals, Triangle, Tambourine)

Tielman Susato
arr. Brian Balmages

TRACK 3

32 COSSACK'S MARCHING SONG

(Snare Drum, Bass Drum)

Russian Folk Song
arr. Robert Sheldon

TRACK 3 34

32 COSSACK'S MARCHING SONG

(Temple Blocks, Crash Cymbals)

Russian Folk Song
arr. Robert Sheldon

TRACK 3 34

OPUS 6

THEORY

ENHARMONICS

Two notes that have the same pitch but different names are called **enharmonics.** An example would be G♭ and F♯. They have different names but share the same bar on a keyboard instrument. They are further explained in the keyboard percussion side of your book on page 42.

RUDIMENT

FLAM PARADIDDLE

The **flam paradiddle** is a rudiment that is a single paradiddle with a flam on the first note. Remember to keep the tap stroke at 2 inches and the accent on the first primary note.

6.1 ENHARMONIC ZONE

6.2 THE SPHINX

6.3 THE SPY

TIMPANI

Timpani are large drums with a single head that is stretched across a copper bowl. They can be tuned to specific notes by moving the pedal up or down. Timpani are played using matched grip with general or medium timpani mallets. Strike the timpani in the beating spot, which is 3–4 inches from the counterhoop. Be sure to let the mallet rebound and follow through off the head. To muffle the sound, touch the head in the beating spot with the last 3 fingers of the hand.

CLEFS

The **bass clef**, also called the **F clef**, names F on the bass staff. The two dots appear on both sides of 4th line F. The musical alphabet uses A B C D E F and G. Each line and space of the staff has a note name. To find a bass clef note, move up or down by lines and spaces in the musical alphabet sequence.

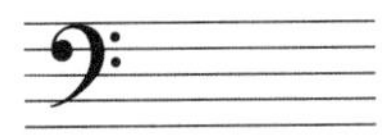

LEDGER LINES

Ledger lines extend the staff. Notes written above or below the staff appear with ledger lines.

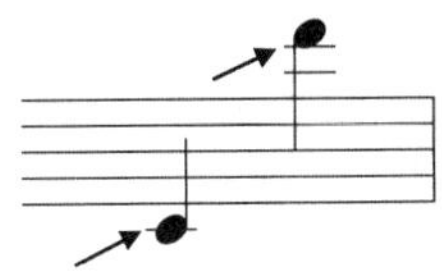

NAME THAT NOTE... *Use your knowledge of the musical alphabet to fill in the Bonus Boxes!*

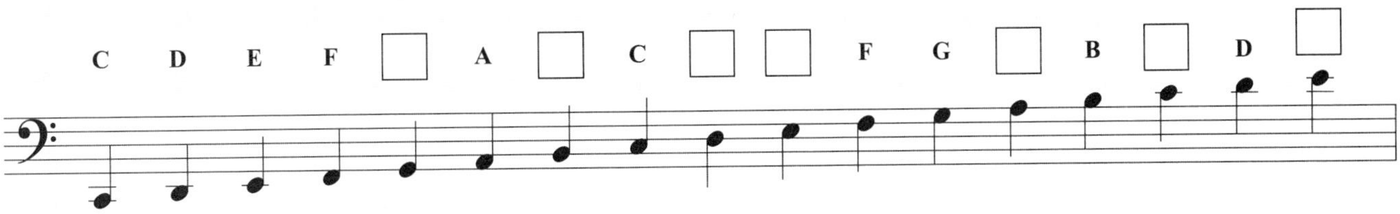

TRACK 3 38

.4 FINAL FRONTIER *This exercise uses double sticking.*

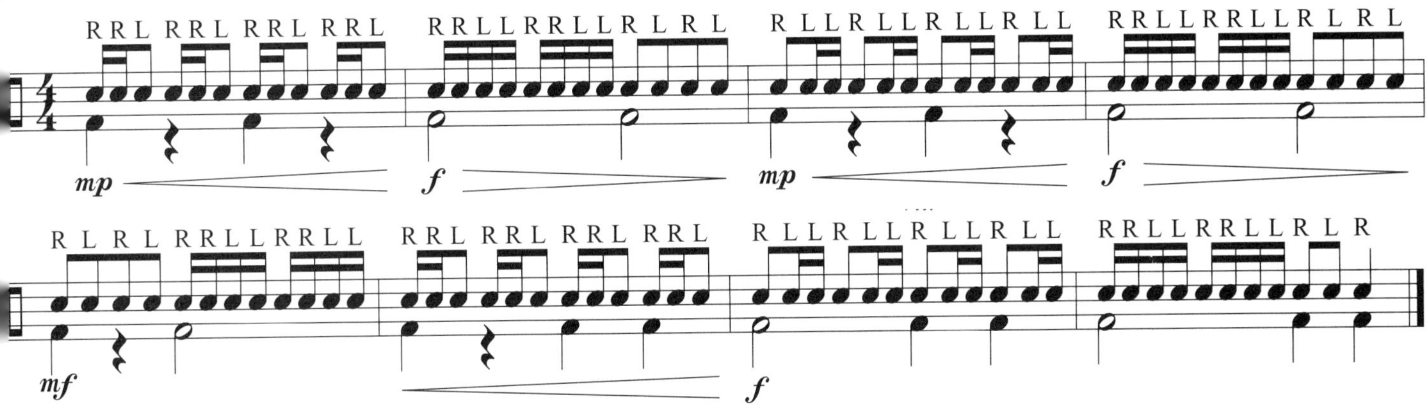

KEY SIGNATURES REVISITED

The **key signature** indicates which notes to play sharp or flat. It appears at the beginning of each staff.

- There can be up to 7 sharps in a key signature. **Sharps** (♯) follow this order: F, C, G, D, A, E, B
- There can be up to 7 flats in a key signature. **Flats** (♭) follow this order: B, E, A, D, G, C, F
- Your key signature in 2.6, *Keynote March,* indicates that all Bs, Es, As, and Ds should be played as B-flats, E-flats, A-flats, and D-flats.

This is the key of A♭ **Major.**

TRACK 3 38

6.4 FINAL FRONTIER – Timpani

6.5 MARCH SLAV

Maestoso

Pyotr I. Tchaikovsky

TRA 3

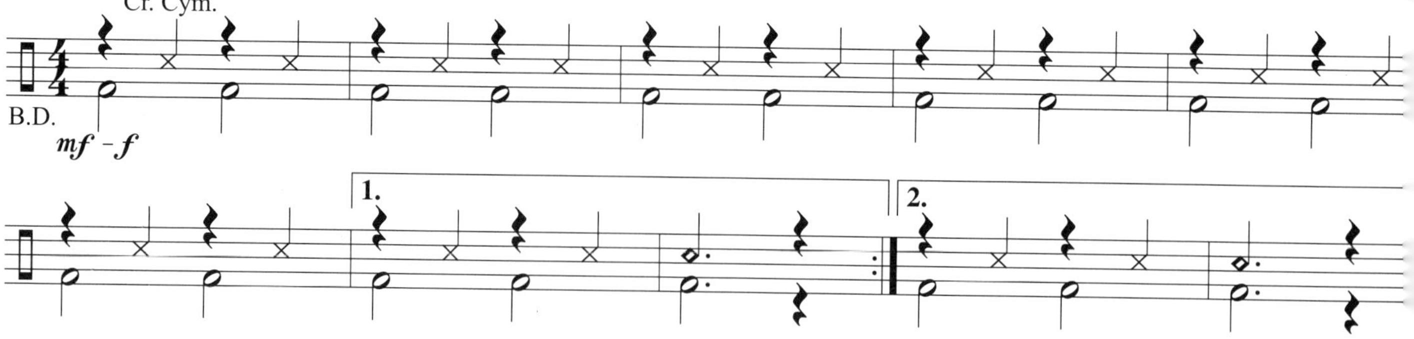

6.5 MARCH SLAV – Timpani

Maestoso

Pyotr I. Tchaikovsky

TRA 3

THEORY

DYNAMICS

pp (*pianissimo*) – play very soft

ff (*fortissimo*) – play very loud

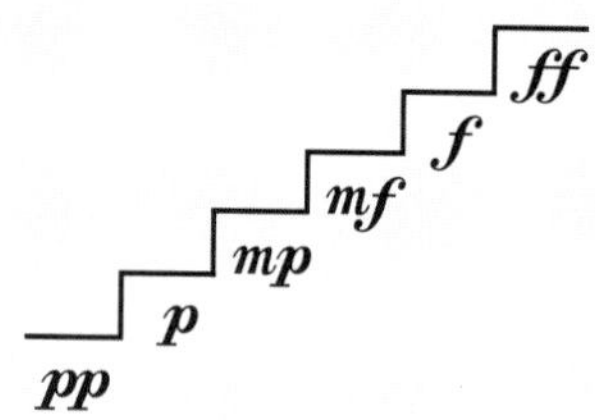

DYNAMICS AND STICK HEIGHTS

For snare drum, ***ff*** = 12" above the center of the head. ***pp*** = 1" above the edge of the head near the counterhoop. Remember, louder does not mean harder!

6.6 ARIRANG

Andante

Korean Folk Song

TRA 3

ON THE PODIUM

6a TIMPANZEE – Timpani Solo

TRACK 3 69

David Collier

TECHNIQUE CHECKLIST

- Keep mallet heads the same distance from the counterhoop
- Keep the mallet heights the same
- Maintain the correct grip
- Use primary strokes (also called legato strokes) with a good follow through
- Muffle on the rests

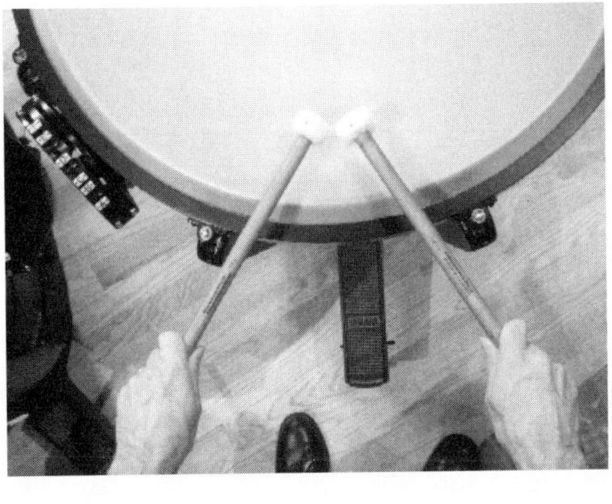

TIMPANI TUNING

- Lower the pedal
- Sound the pitch on the bells, a piano, or a pitch pipe
- Sing the pitch
- Strike the head one time
- Push the pedal up to the correct pitch

HISTORY

MUSIC

Italian born **Giuseppe Verdi** (1813 – 1901) is best known for his operas, especially *Il Trovatore* (The Troubadour), first performed in 1853. The *Anvil Chorus*, from Act 2 of *Il Trovatore*, features Spanish gypsies who sing and strike anvils as they work in the early morning.

ART

Art in the style of Luminism began in the 1850s and was characterized by the use of light effects best seen in sea and landscapes. This American style is found in works by Frederic Church (*Twilight in the Wilderness*) and Martin Heade (*Sunlight and Shadow: The Newbury Marshes*).

WORLD

In 1853, when *Il Trovatore* premiered, the Ottoman Empire declared war on Russia, the Gadsden Purcha[se] (currently southern Arizona and New Mexico) was made and potato chips made their first tasty appearance.

6.7 ANVIL CHORUS

Pesante *(heavily)*

Giuseppe Verdi — TRA… 3

6.7 ANVIL CHORUS – Timpani

Pesante *(heavily)*

Giuseppe Verdi — TRA… 3

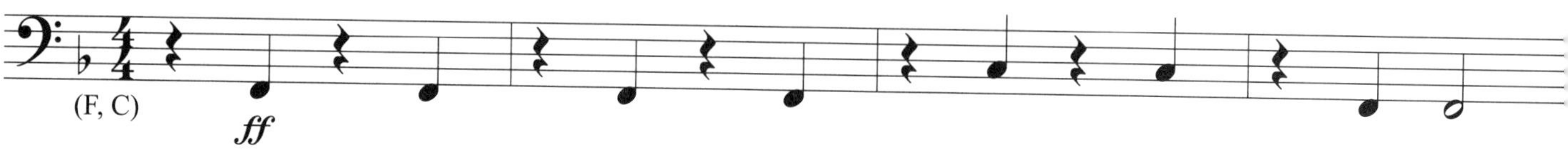

THEORY

MORE DYNAMICS

cresc. Sometimes this abbreviation is used in place of a crescendo sign. It means the same thing as the sign; gradually play louder.

decresc. Sometimes this abbreviation is used in place of a decrescendo sign. It means the same thing as the sign; gradually play softer.

6.8 YANKEE DOODLE CAME AND WENT

Moderato

American Folk Melody — TRA… 3

THEORY

MAJOR SCALE, ARPEGGIO, AND CHORD

A **major scale** has eight notes going up or down in consecutive order, all in the key signature of the scale name.

An **arpeggio** is the first, third, and fifth notes of a scale played in *succession.* It may also include the 8th scale note.

A **major chord** is the first, third, and fifth notes of a major scale played *simultaneously.*
Like the arpeggio, it may also include the 8th scale note.

Major scales, arpeggios, and chords are further explained in the keyboard percussion side of your book on page 43.

9 CONCERT B♭ MAJOR SCALE

TRACK 3 43

9 CONCERT B♭ MAJOR SCALE – Timpani

TRACK 3 43

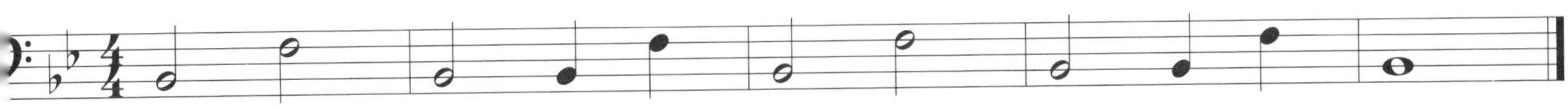

(B♭, F)

10 CONCERT B♭ MAJOR ARPEGGIO AND CHORD

TRACK 3 44

10 CONCERT B♭ MAJOR ARPEGGIO AND CHORD – Timpani

TRACK 3 44

(B♭, F)

10a LET'S ROLL – Snare Drum Solo

David Collier

TRACK 3 70

6.11 KUM BAH YAH

African Folk Song

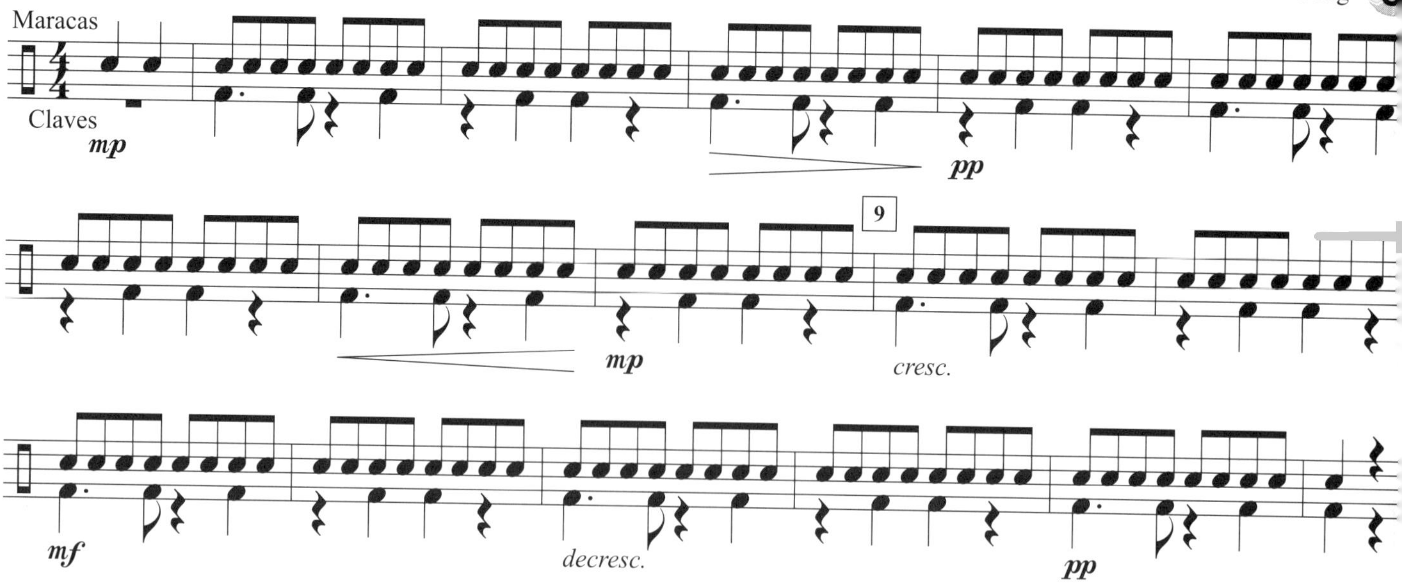

6.11 KUM BAH YAH – Timpani

African Folk Song

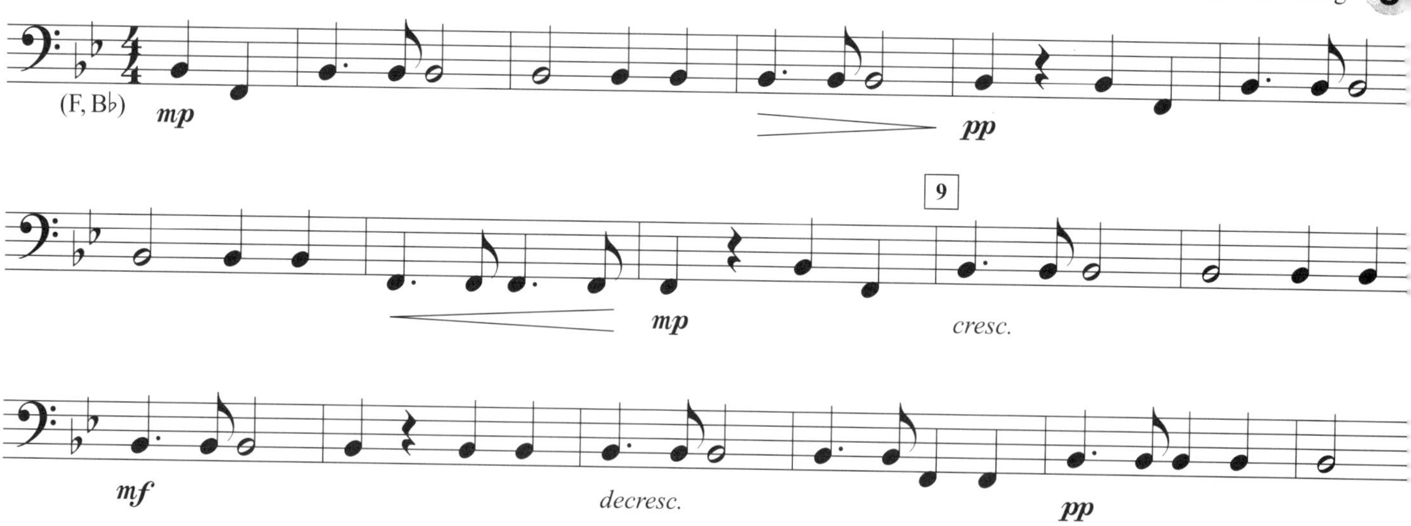

THEORY

INTERVALS

An **interval** is the distance between two pitches. You can figure out the interval by counting each line and space between the notes. Starting with "1" on the bottom note, count upward until you reach the top note. The number of the top note identifies the interval. Intervals are further explained in the keyboard percussion side of your book on page 44.

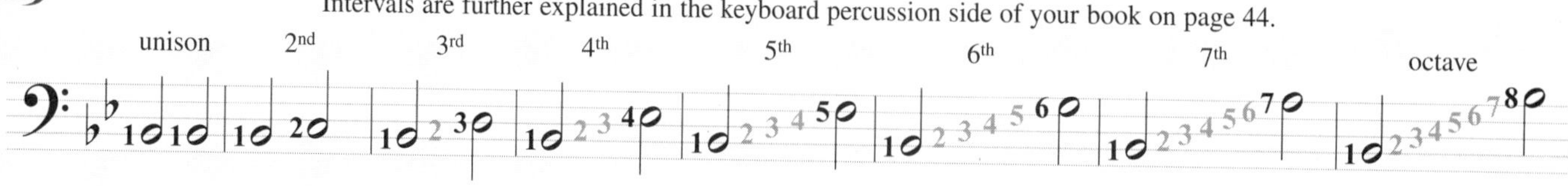

6.12 RANGE ROVER

ON THE PODIUM

.13 HATIKVAH

Israeli National Anthem

TRACK 3 48

6.14 HEY!

To play forte, strike the tambourine with your knuckles in the center of the head. Remember to start and end the shake rolls with a strike.

TRACK 3 48

N THE ODIUM

RHYTHM

MORE ABOUT SYNCOPATION

You already know the quarter-half-quarter syncopation. The most common syncopated rhythm is eighth-quarter-eighth. Here the syncopation occurs on the accented upbeat quarter note.

6.15 BEAT STREET

CLAP

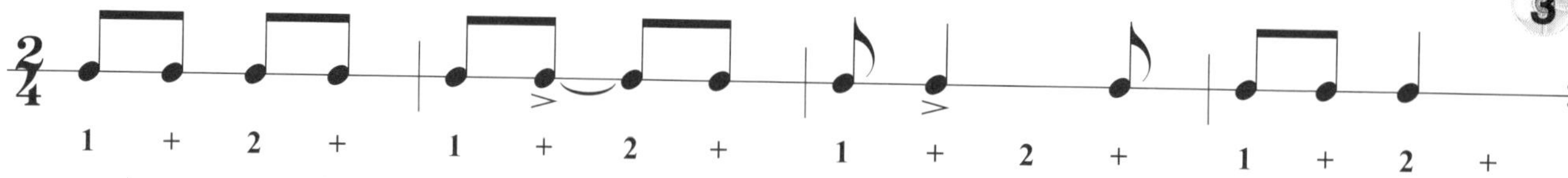

6.16 SYNCOPHOBIA

6.17 THE CAISSONS GO ROLLING ALONG

March tempo

Edmund L. Gruber

6.18 LI'L LIZA JANE

Moderato

American Folk Song

19 MAYIM, MAYIM – Duet

An ostinato is a musical pattern that is repeated over and over again. It is typically based on a short melodic or rhythmic idea and is generally performed by the same instrument part.

Israeli Folk Song — TRACK 3 53

.20 COVENTRY CAROL

English Carol — TRACK 3 54

.20 COVENTRY CAROL – Timpani

English Carol — TRACK 3 54

6.21 DIES IRAE

att. Thomas of Celano

Pesante

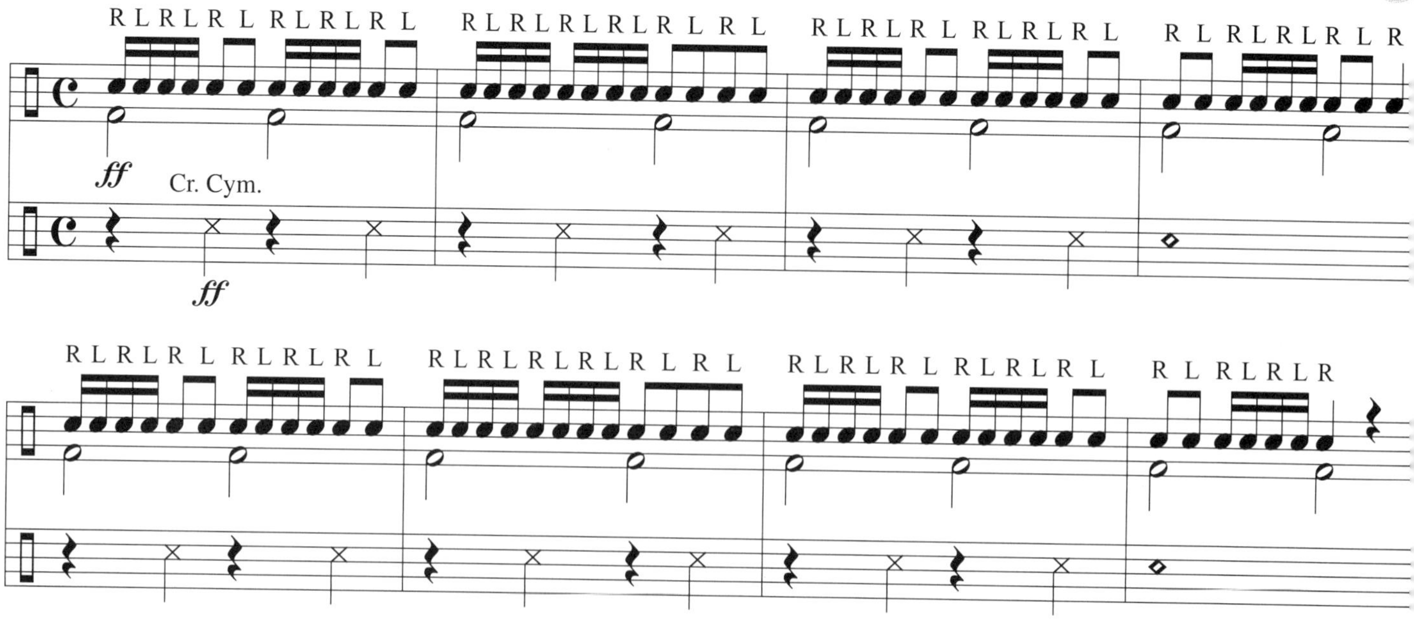

6.22 LEAGUE OF SUPERHEROES

Allegro

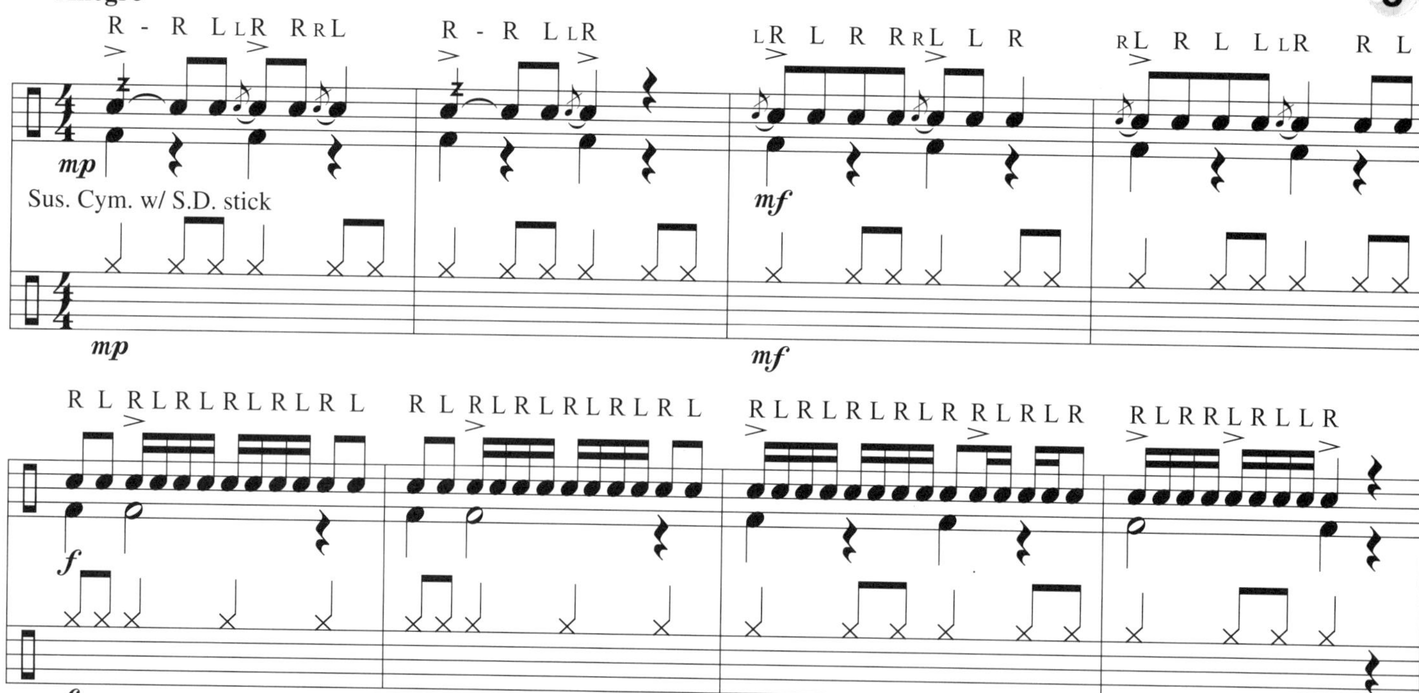

THEORY

CHROMATIC SCALE

A **half step** is the smallest interval between two pitches. Two consecutive half steps make a **whole step.** The **chromatic scale** has thirteen notes going up and down in consecutive half steps. The chromatic scale is further explained in the keyboard percussion side of your book on page 46.

6.23 CHROMATIC SCALE

STORY

MUSIC

Georges Bizet (1838 – 1875) was a child prodigy from Paris who composed his first symphony in 1855 when he was just 16! In his short 36-year life, he wrote many different types of music but is best known for his operas. His most famous opera is *Carmen*.

ART

The Impressionistic style was all the rage in the art world. Edgar Degas had painted *In Concert Cafe, The Song of the Dog*. American realist painter Thomas Eakins completed the *Gross Clinic*, a very real rendition of a surgeon overseeing an operation to remove part of a diseased thighbone.

WORLD

Events in 1875 included the first organized indoor ice hockey game in Montreal, the running of the first Kentucky Derby, and the patent of the electric dental drill.

.24 HABAÑERA (FROM CARMEN) – Duet *Where is the ostinato? Is there more than one?*

Georges Bizet TRACK 3 58

5.24 HABAÑERA (FROM CARMEN) – Timpani

Georges Bizet TRACK 3 58

OPUS 6 ENCORE!

INTERPRETATION STATION

Listen to CD 3 Track 59. For each musical example, decide if the melody is based on a **Scale** or an **Arpeggio.** Circle the letter that corresponds with your answer.

1. S A
2. S A
3. S A
4. S A

SIMON "SEZ"

Listen to CD 3 Track 60. You will hear a well-known piece. Listen first, sing it, then find the pitches on your keyboard instrument. You can then play along with the accompaniment track that follows. Can you match the notes and style of the initial recording?

COMPOSER'S CORNER

Performers sometimes compose music on the spot while they are playing! This is called **improvisation.** There is an ostinato below. Have the section play it (or use CD 3 Track 61 as a background track) while you improvise. Experiment with a variety of instruments and rhythms. You can also turn to page 47 in the keyboard percussion side of your book for a set of guide notes to use. Have fun!
Note: The CD recording repeats 4 times.

"WHATEVER!"

PENCIL POWER

In each box below, use *one note* with a z to show an alternate way of notating each type of roll.

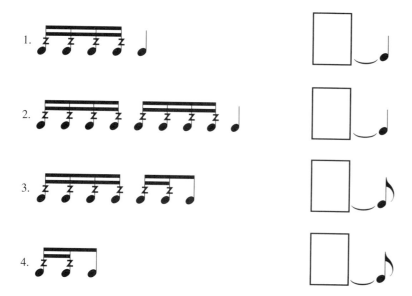

1. 

2. 

3. 

4. 

CURTAIN UP!

25 O CANADA

Canadian National Anthem
Calixa Lavallée, Sir Adolphe-Basile Routhier, and Justice R.S. Weir

TRACK 3 62

CURTAIN UP! FULL BAND

6.26 CHORALE IN B♭ MAJOR
(ALLE MENSCHEN MÜSSEN STERBEN)

Andante J. S. Bach

6.27 RABBLE ROUSER (Snare Drum, Bass Drum)

Allegro Robert Sheldon

.27 RABBLE ROUSER (Tambourine, Triangle, Crash Cymbals)

Robert Sheldon

TRACK 3 64

6.28 PROCESSION OF THE CHAMPIONS (Snare Drum, Bass Drum)

Brian Balmages

28 PROCESSION OF THE CHAMPIONS (Crash Cymbals, Suspended Cymbal, Triangle)

TRACK 3 65

Brian Balmages

6.28 PROCESSION OF THE CHAMPIONS (Timpani)

Brian Balmages

TRACK 3

29a MACHINES — Percussion Ensemble (Snare Drum, Bass Drum, Mounted Cowbell)

TRACK 3 71

Brian Balmages

6.29a MACHINES — Percussion Ensemble (Tambourine, Brake Drum, Sleigh Bells, Claves)

Brian Balmages

29a MACHINES — Percussion Ensemble (Triangle, Suspended Cymbal, Wood Block on table)

TRACK 3 71

Brian Balmages

SCALES AND TECHNIQUE

Percussionists have five options on these pages, each which focuses on different skills and accessory percussion. Your director will tell you which option you should play while the rest of the band plays their scales.

OPTION 1

OPTION 2

TION 3

PTION 4

PTION 5

RHYTHM REVIEW FOR PERCUSSION – OPUS 1-6

An additional rhythm review can be found in the keyboard percussion side of your book on page 52.

1A 

1B 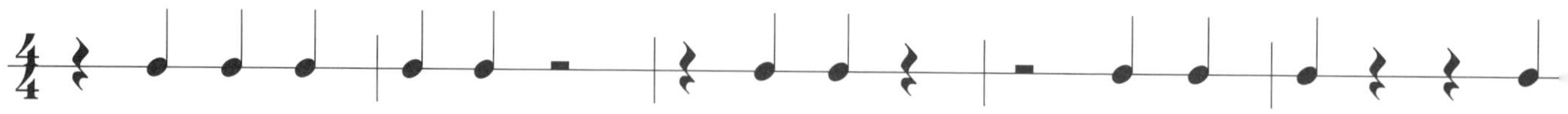

2A 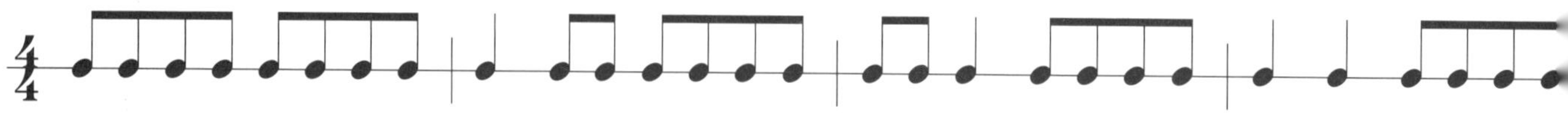

2B 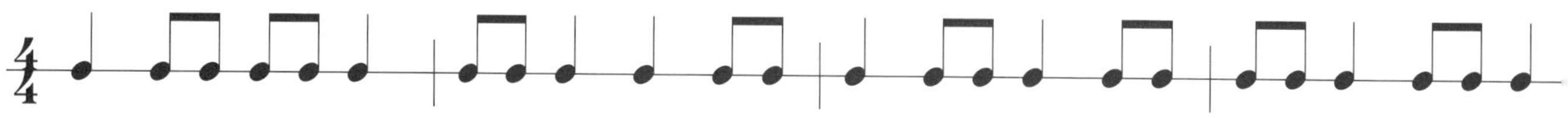

3A 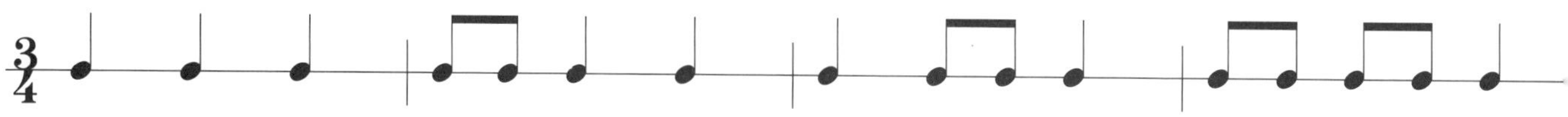

3B 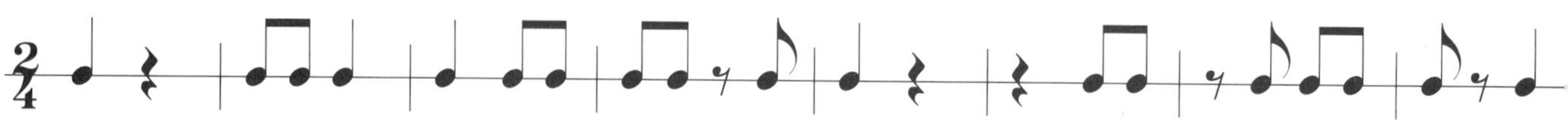

3C 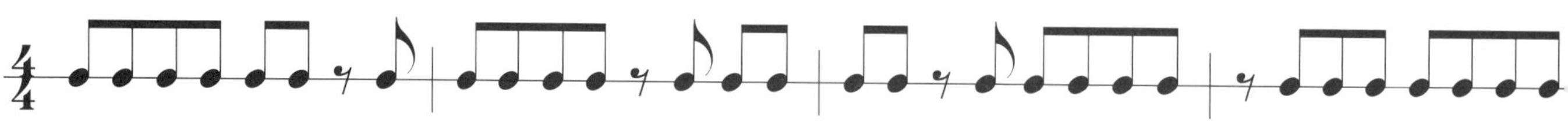

3D 

3E 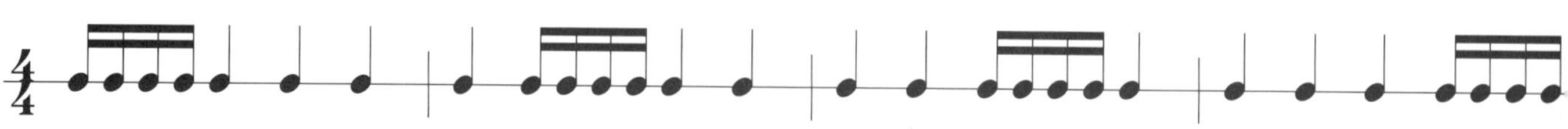

3F 

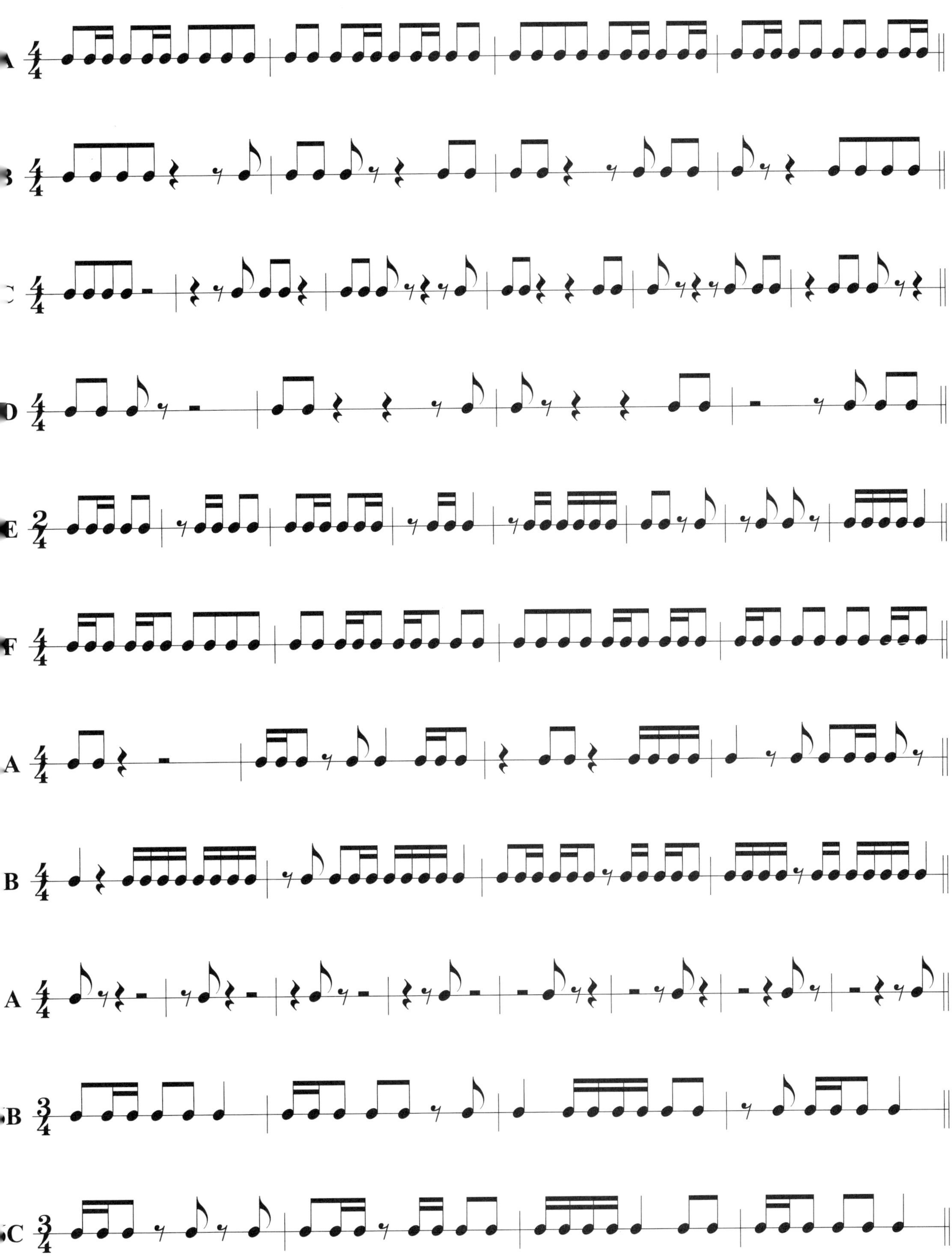
A
B
C
D
E
F
A
B
A
B
C

P.A.S. 40 INTERNATIONAL SNARE DRUM RUDIMENTS

I. ROLL RUDIMENTS

A. Single Stroke Roll Rudiments

1. SINGLE STROKE ROLL

R L R L R L R L

2. SINGLE STROKE FOUR

R L R L R L R L
L R L R L R L R

3. SINGLE STROKE SEVEN

R L R L R L R
L R L R L R L

B. Multiple Bounce Roll Rudiments

4. MULTIPLE BOUNCE ROLL

5. TRIPLE STROKE ROLL

R R R L L L R R R L L L

C. Double Stroke Open Roll Rudiments

6. DOUBLE STROKE OPEN ROLL

R R L L R R L L

7. FIVE STROKE ROLL

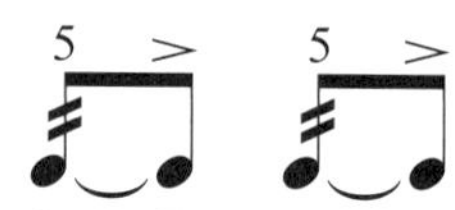

R R L L

8. SIX STROKE ROLL

R L R L
L R L R

9. SEVEN STROKE ROLL

R L R L
L R L R

10. NINE STROKE ROLL

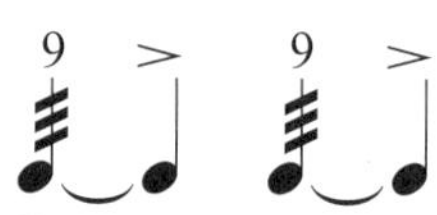

R R L L

11. TEN STROKE ROLL

R R L R R L
L L R L L R

12. ELEVEN STROKE ROLL

R R L R R L
L L R L L R

13. THIRTEEN STROKE ROLL

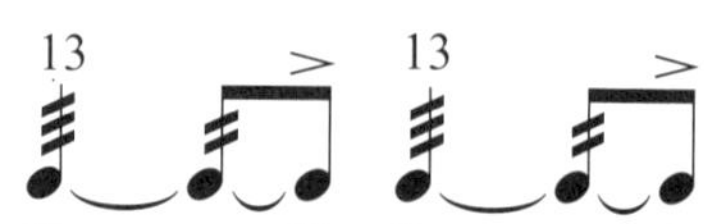

R R L L

14. FIFTEEN STROKE ROLL

R L R L
L R L R

15. SEVENTEEN STROKE ROLL

R R L L

Reprinted by permission of the Percussive Arts Society, Inc.
32 E. Washington, Suite 1400, Indianapolis, IN 46204-3516;
Email: percarts@pas.org; Web: www.pas.org.

I. DIDDLE RUDIMENTS

16. SINGLE PARADIDDLE

17. DOUBLE PARADIDDLE

18. TRIPLE PARADIDDLE

19. SINGLE PARADIDDLE-DIDDLE

II. FLAM RUDIMENTS

20. FLAM

21. FLAM ACCENT

22. FLAM TAP

23. FLAMACUE

24. FLAM PARADIDDLE

25. SINGLE FLAMMED MILL

26. FLAM PARADIDDLE-DIDDLE

27. PATAFLAFLA

28. SWISS ARMY TRIPLET

29. INVERTED FLAM TAP

30. FLAM DRAG

IV. DRAG RUDIMENTS

31. DRAG

32. SINGLE DRAG TAP

33. DOUBLE DRAG TAP

34. LESSON 25

35. SINGLE DRAGADIDDLE

36. DRAG PARADIDDLE #1

37. DRAG PARADIDDLE #2

38. SINGLE RATAMACUE

39. DOUBLE RATAMACUE

40. TRIPLE RATAMACUE

INDEX

RMS

COMPOSERS

WORLD MUSIC

HOLIDAY MUSIC

PERCUSSION INDEX

TERMS

SOLOS

Keyboard Percussion

Snare Drum

Timpani

ENSEMBLES

WARM-UPS and ADDITONA STUDIES

PERCUSSION BOOK 1
(INCLUDES KEYBOARD PERCUSSION)

MEASURES of SUCCESS®

A Comprehensive Musicianship Band Method

Includes Free Downloadable Recordings!

smartmusic.

DEBORAH A. SHELDON
BRIAN BALMAGES
TIMOTHY LOEST
ROBERT SHELDON

PERCUSSION WRITTEN AND EDITED BY DAVID COLLIER

THE F·J·H MUSIC COMPANY INC.
Frank J. Hackinson

PRACTICE LOG

Week	Date	Assignment	Mon	Tue	Wed	Thur	Fri	Sat	Sun	Total	Pa Init
1											
2											
3											
4											
5											
6											
7											
8											
9											
10											
11											
12											
13											
14											
15											
16											
17											
18											
19											
20											
21											
22											
23											
24											
25											
26											
27											
28											
29											
30											
31											
32											
33											
34											
35											
36											

MEASURES *of* SUCCESS®

A Comprehensive Musicianship Band Method

DEBORAH A. SHELDON • BRIAN BALMAGES • TIMOTHY LOEST • ROBERT SHELDON
PERCUSSION WRITTEN AND EDITED BY DAVID COLLIER

Welcome to *Measures of Success* and the amazing world of instrumental music! You are about to begin an exciting musical journey full of rewards and challenges. As you practice, you will find yourself sharing the gift of music with family, friends, and audiences. So get ready—your path to success begins now!

HISTORY OF PERCUSSION

Percussion instruments predate any other instruments. They have been found in nearly every society on Earth with examples dating back thousands of years. Historically, percussion instruments have played an important role in ceremonies, communication, military exercises, and musical expression. Percussion instruments are any instruments that produce a sound when they are struck, shaken or scraped. They are categorized by the way they produce their sounds. Instruments that vibrate when struck, like cymbals and triangles, are known as idiophones. Instruments that have a drumhead which vibrates, like snare drum and bass drum, are known as membranophones. Early drums were constructed from tree logs covered with animal skins. In the 13th century, small bowl-shaped drums of Arabic origin (called nakers) came to Europe. The timpani, derived from nakers, were added to the European orchestra in 1675, followed by cymbals in 1680, and bass drum in 1779. The snare drum was added much later.

The orchestra bells originated in Germany and were called "glockenspiel" (many composers continue to call them that to this very day). They originally were a set of bells of varying sizes. In the late 16th century, a musical keyboard design was introduced to make them easier to play. Handel is credited as the first major composer to use an early version of orchestra bells in a composition.

The percussion family is very large and includes timpani, drums of all kinds, keyboard percussion, cymbals and gongs, accessory instruments, world percussion, effects instruments, and the modern drumset. Today percussion plays a key role in wind bands, marching bands, orchestras, movie soundtracks, and jazz, rock and world music ensembles.

ABOUT THIS BOOK

Your book is divided into two main sections. The first section includes snare drum, bass drum, accessory percussion and timpani. These pages are often divided into A and B pages because there are multiple instruments you will learn. The second section contains all of the keyboard percussion exercises. Be sure to work from both sides of the book so that you become a *complete percussionist!*

Production: Frank J. Hackinson
Production Coordinators: Ken Mattis, Brian Balmages, and Philip Groeber
Cover Design and Interior Line Drawings: Danielle Taylor and Adrianne Hirosky / Interior Layout and Design: Andi Whitmer
Engraving: Tempo Music Press, Inc. / Printer: Tempo Music Press, Inc.

ISBN-13: 978-1-56939-819-7

THE F·J·H MUSIC COMPANY INC.
Frank J. Hackinson

BELLS ASSEMBLY

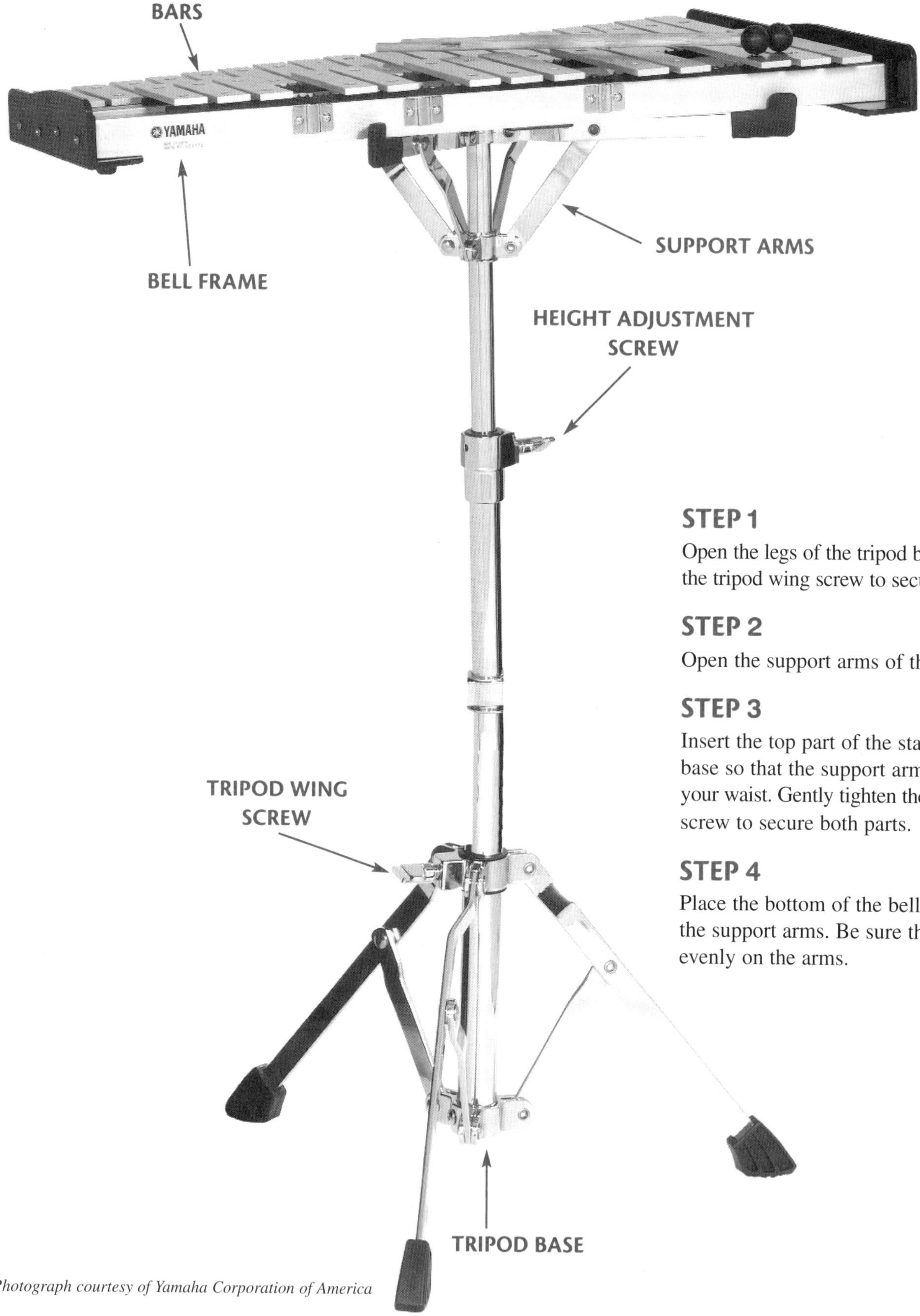

Photograph courtesy of Yamaha Corporation of America

STEP 1

Open the legs of the tripod base. Gently tight the tripod wing screw to secure the legs.

STEP 2

Open the support arms of the top.

STEP 3

Insert the top part of the stand into the tripo base so that the support arms are just below your waist. Gently tighten the height adjustme screw to secure both parts.

STEP 4

Place the bottom of the bell frame on top of the support arms. Be sure that it is balanced evenly on the arms.

PARTS OF THE MALLET

CHECK IT OUT!

)STURE CHECKLIST

and straight, tall and relaxed
eight of bells is just below your waist
and in the middle of the range you are playing
lbows comfortably away from your sides
rms are relaxed in front of body with a very
ight downward angle

ATCHED GRIP CHECKLIST

he grip is the same in both hands
rip point is 1/3 the way up from the end of the mallet
etween thumb and first finger
humb stays inline with the stick
emaining fingers gently wrap around the mallet handle
alms are facing down

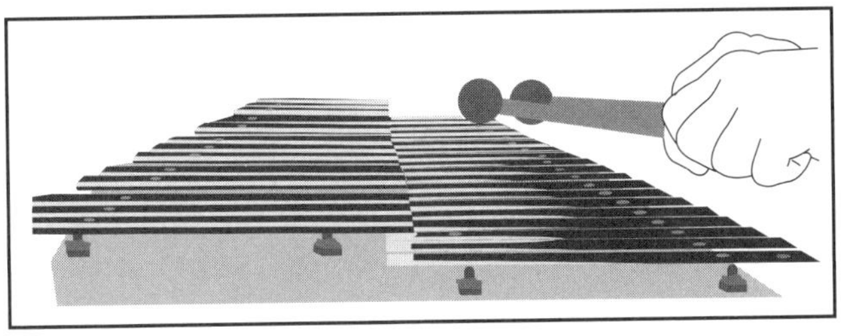

'ICK POSITION CHECKLIST
'HE REST POSITION)

Mallet heads rest 2 inches above the center of the bars
Mallets are held at an angle similar to a pizza slice
Right mallet is closest to body

TYPES OF STROKES

rimary Stroke — This is the basic stroke on keyboard percussion instruments. It is a tossing motion to the instrument ith a relaxed rebound or follow-through back to the up position. Since there is very little rebound on keyboard percussion astruments, the player has to use the wrist to return the mallet to the up position. When done smoothly, it is also known s a legato stroke.

STROKE PRODUCTION

tep 1: Place the mallets in the rest position.
tep 2: In one motion, use your wrist to raise the head of the right mallet from the rest position to a height of 10–12 inches (the up position) and toss it toward the center of the bar. Keep all fingers in contact with the mallet.
tep 3: Raise the mallet back to the up position.
tep 4: Repeat the process with the left mallet.
tep 5: When alternating hands, the mallet that is not moving waits in the rest position.

'or Practice: Hold a tennis ball in one hand. Toss it to the floor and catch it as it bounces back. Switch hands. This is the type of motion you will use when you make a primary stroke.

KEYBOARD PERCUSSION CARE

DAILY

- Check that the stand is assembled correctly and the wing screws are tightened before placing the bells on the stand
- Wipe away fingerprints with a soft cloth from all metal surfaces including the stand
- Always store your bells in its case when not in use

NEVER

- Never place any objects on the bars or frame
- Never keep any objects that can damage the bells inside its case

PRELUDE: SOUNDS BEFORE SYMBOLS

THEORY

PITCH, BEAT, AND RHYTHM

Pitch is the highness or lowness of a note or tone. The **beat** is the pulse of the music.
Rhythm is a pattern of short or long sounds (or silences) that fit with a steady beat.

ARTICULATION

Articulation is the result of a stroke and how you strike a bar.

Using just one bar on your keyboard instrument, play some of the familiar songs below. Since you are only using one bar, the *pitch* will stay the same, while the *rhythm* will identify the song. Be sure to strike in the center of the bar!

Bingo	**Jingle Bells**	**London Bridge**
Mary Had a Little Lamb	**Old MacDonald**	**Twinkle, Twinkle Little Star**

MAKING MUSIC

With your director's help, assemble your instrument. You are now ready for your first three notes!

NEW NOTE! **D**

NEW NOTE! **C**

NEW NOTE! **B♭**

Play each note four times and then rest for four beats.
Remember to focus on posture, hand position, and striking location.

AND WE'RE OFF!

(hold) (rest)

D → | – – – – | D D D D | – – – – | (repeat this with your other two new notes)

1 2 3 4 1 2 3 4 1 2 3 4 1 2 3 4

AU CLAIRE DE LA LUNE

B♭ B♭ B♭ C | D – C – | B♭ D C C | B♭ → – – |

1 2 3 4 1 2 3 4 1 2 3 4 1 2 3 4

HOT CROSS BUNS

D → C → | B♭ → – – | D → C → | B♭ → – – | B♭ B♭ B♭ B♭ | C C C C | D → C → | B♭ → – – |

1 2 3 4 1 2 3 4 1 2 3 4 1 2 3 4 1 2 3 4 1 2 3 4 1 2 3 4 1 2 3 4

MARY HAD A LITTLE LAMB

D C B♭ C | D D D – | C C C – | D D D – | D C B♭ C | D D D – | C C D C | B♭ → – – |

1 2 3 4 1 2 3 4 1 2 3 4 1 2 3 4 1 2 3 4 1 2 3 4 1 2 3 4 1 2 3 4

COMPOSER'S CORNER

It is your turn to compose your *own* piece of music! Use the three notes you know to complete this piece.
Give it a title and perform it for a friend or family member!

Title:____________________ **Composer (your name):**____________________

B♭ __ __ __ | __ – __ – | __ __ __ – | __ __ B♭ – |

OPUS 1

ORY

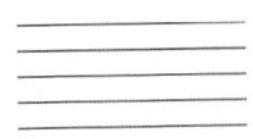

MUSIC STAFF

The **music staff** is where notes and rests are written. It has 5 lines and 4 spaces.

LONG TONE

A **long tone** is a held note. The fermata (𝄐) indicates to hold the note until your teacher tells you to rest.

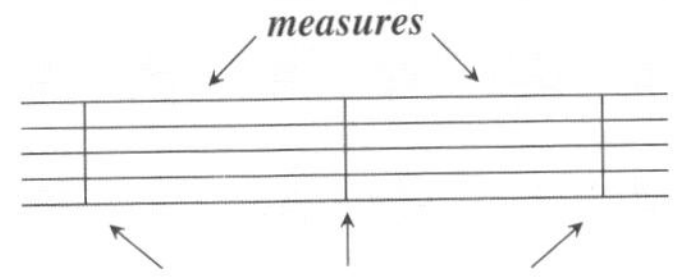

BAR LINES

Bar lines divide the music staff into measures.

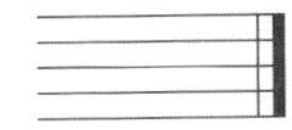

FINAL BAR LINE

A **final bar** line indicates the end of a piece.

FIRST NOTE *Percussionists use* **R** *and* **L** *to refer to right and left hands. Throughout this book, you will see these* ***stickings*** *as a guide.*

TRACK 1 2

W TE!

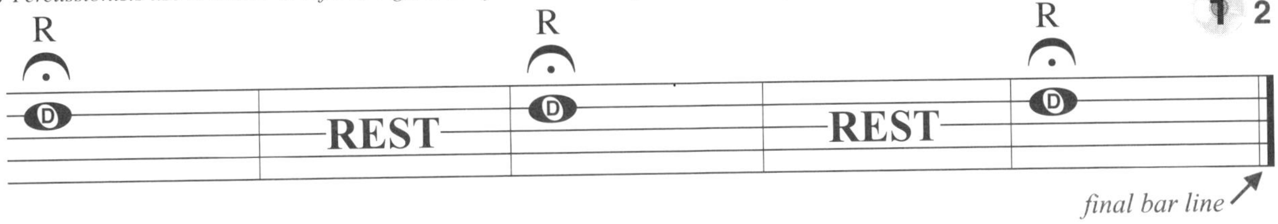

YTHM

BEAT

The **beat** is the pulse of the music. Tap your foot to keep a steady beat!

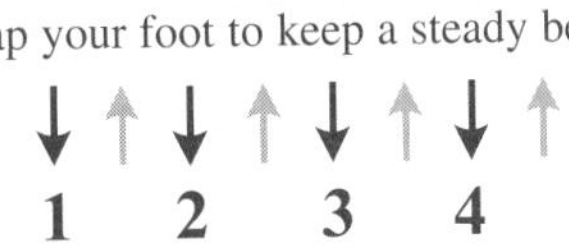

NOTES AND RESTS

Notes represent sound. **Rests** represent silence.

Quarter Note = 1 beat of sound

Quarter Rest = 1 beat of silence

2 FOUR IN A ROW *This piece has four beats in each measure. Remember to tap your foot.*

TRACK 1 3

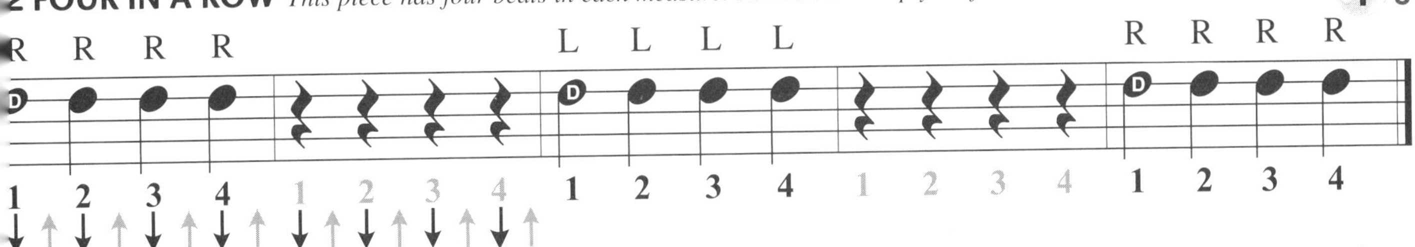

3 SECOND NOTE

TRACK 1 4

EW OTE!

.4 FOUR MORE *How many measures do you see?*

TRACK 1 5

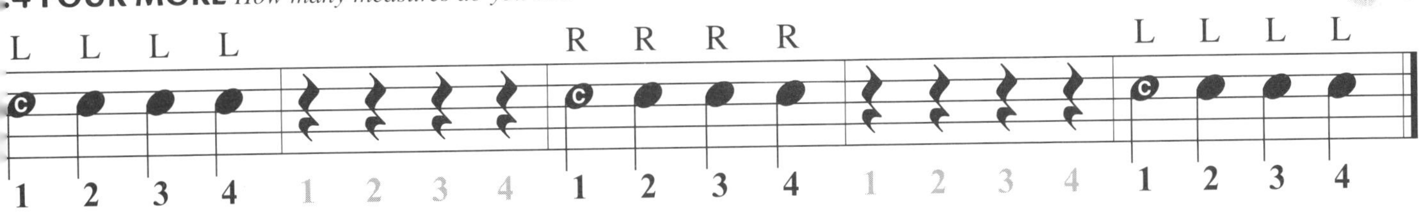

.5 UP AND DOWN *Any time you see a Bonus Box, write in the note name.*

TRACK 1 6

ONUS BOX

.6 ALL MIXED UP

TRACK 1 7

ONUS BOX

THEORY

ACCIDENTALS

Accidentals are signs that alter a note's pitch. They are placed to the left of the note.

Flat (♭) A flat sign lowers the pitch by one half-step. This pitch remains lowered for the rest of the measure.

Sharp (♯) A sharp sign raises the pitch by one half-step. This pitch remains raised for the rest of the measure.

Natural (♮) A natural sign cancels a flat or sharp. It remains cancelled for the rest of the measure.

1.7 THIRD NOTE'S A CHARM

NEW NOTE! B♭

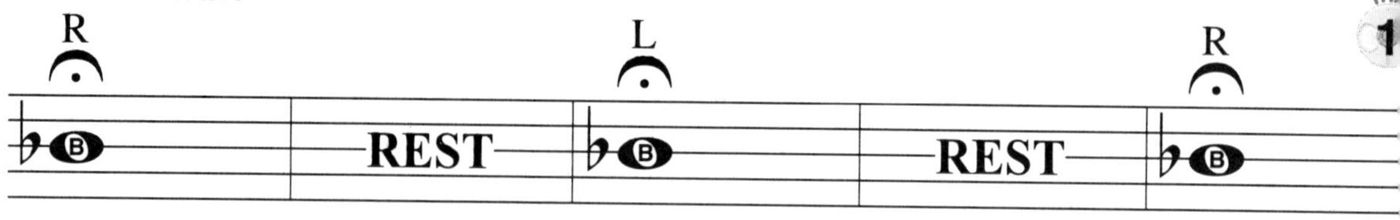

1.8 ALL TOGETHER

1.9 WHAT GOES UP...

BONUS BOX

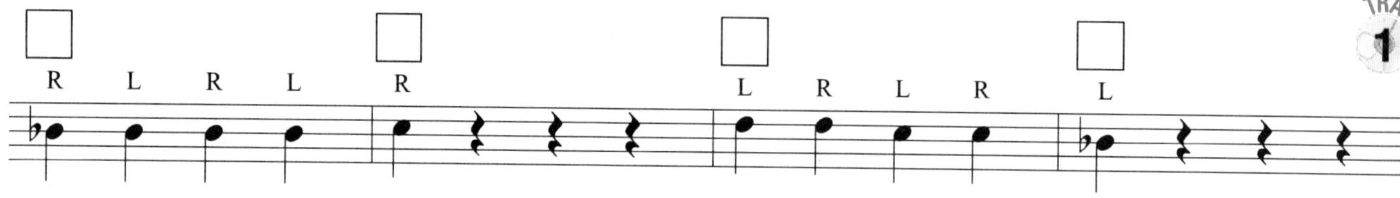

1.10 RHYTHM RENDEZVOUS

THEORY

CLEFS

Clefs are signs that help name notes.

The **treble clef**, also called the **G clef**, names G on the treble staff. The inside tail wraps around 2nd line G. The musical alphabet uses A B C D E F and G. Each line and space of the staff has a note name. To find a treble clef note, move up or down by lines and spaces in the musical alphabet sequence.

LEDGER LINES

Ledger lines extend the staff. Notes written above or below the staff appear with ledger lines.

NAME THAT NOTE... *Use your knowledge of the musical alphabet to fill in the Bonus Boxes!*

BONUS BOX

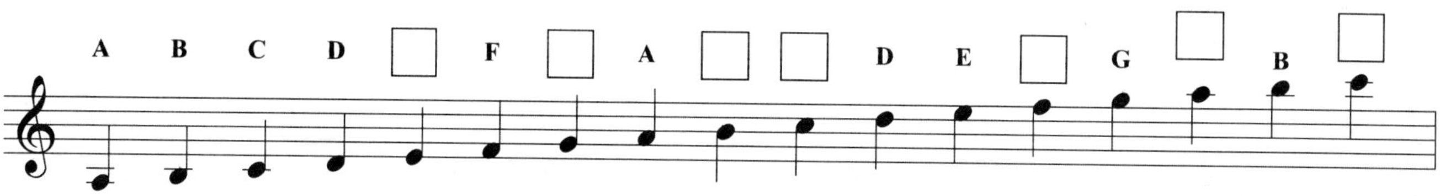

THM

HALF NOTES AND WHOLE NOTES

Half Note
2 beats of sound

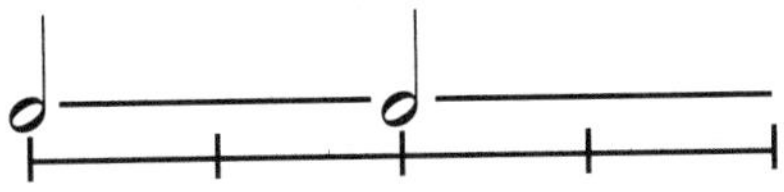

Whole Note
4 beats of sound

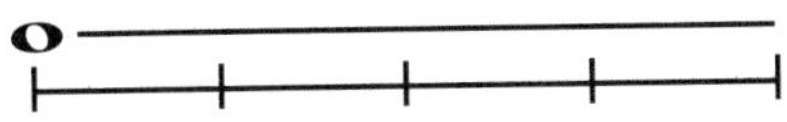

HALF RESTS AND WHOLE RESTS

Half Rest
2 beats of silence
(sits on a line)

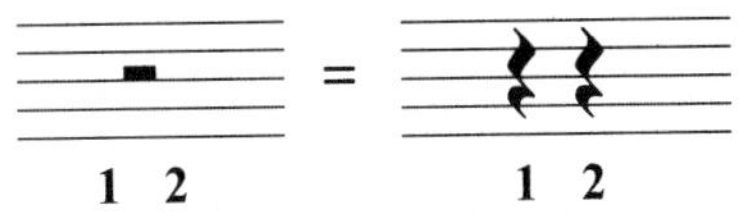

Whole Rest
4 beats of silence
(hangs from a line)

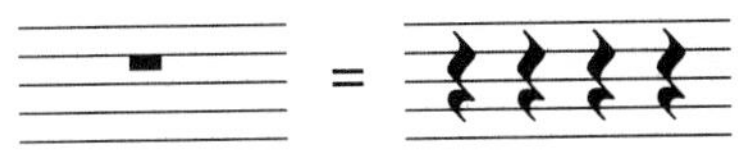

TIME SIGNATURE

The top number shows the number of beats in each measure.
The bottom number shows the type of note that receives one beat.
Hint: Replace the top number with a "1" and you will get a fraction that equals the type of note that gets one beat!

Number of beats in a measure
Type of note that gets one beat

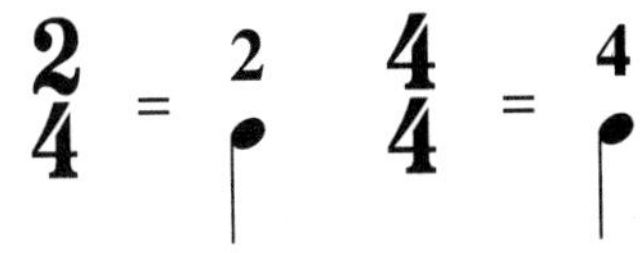

11 GOING PLACES *Circle the half rests.*

TRACK 1 12

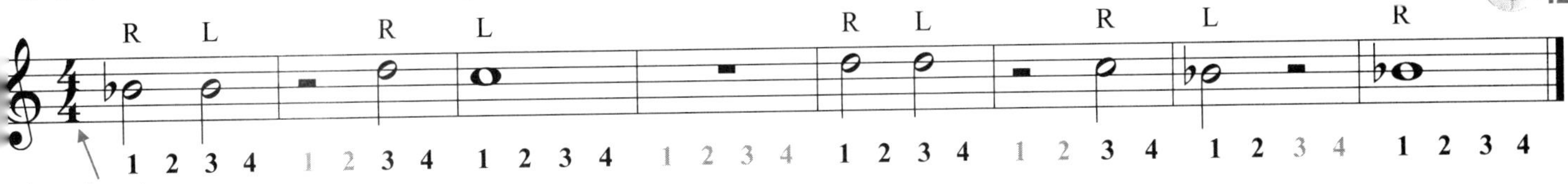

HEORY

FERMATA

When playing on your own, hold a note with a **fermata** longer than its assigned value.

.12 COUNTDOWN *Hold the note with a fermata longer than its assigned value.*

TRACK 1 13

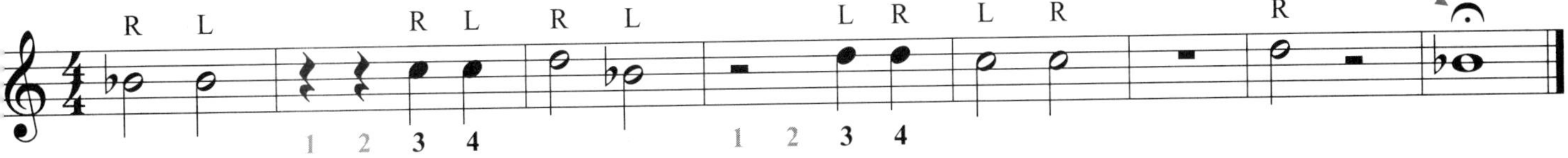

HEORY

REPEAT SIGN

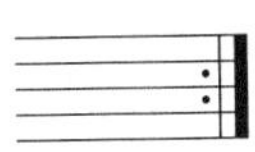

A **repeat sign** is a final bar line with two dots. Without stopping, go back to the beginning and play the music a second time.

1.13 TURN AROUND *Say the note names before you play.*

TRACK 1 14

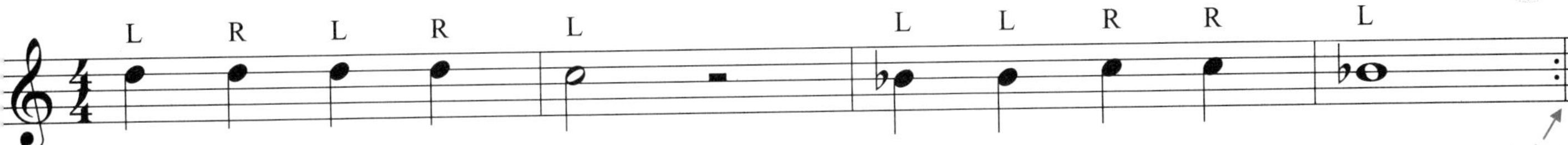

1.14 HOT CROSS BUNS

English Folk Song

TRACK 1 15

1.15 HERE WE GO! *Draw in the bar lines, then play!*

TRACK 1 16

BONUS BOX

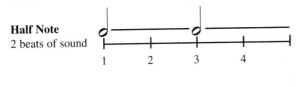

1.16 AU CLAIRE DE LA LUNE *Musicianship Challenge! – Without the CD, play 1st time quietly, 2nd time loudly.*

French Folk Song

1.17 MARY HAD A LITTLE LAMB

Traditional

1.18 MARY HAD A COOL LAMB

Traditional Melody

THEORY

STYLE AND FORM: DUET

A **duet** has two different parts performed simultaneously by two individuals or groups.

1.19 BEAT STREET — Duet *A Beat Street exercise indicates to clap the rhythm.*

CLAP

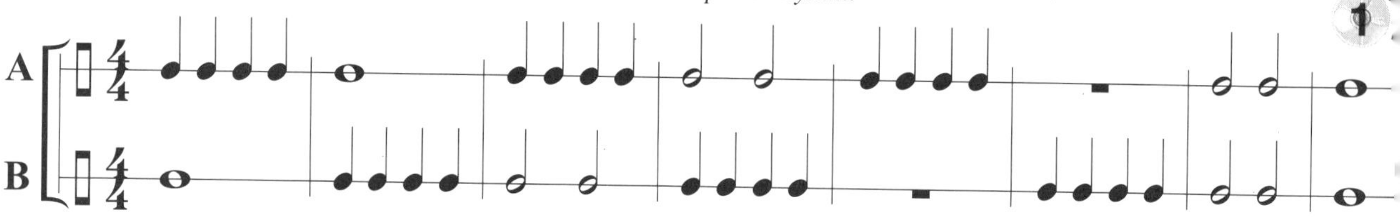

1.20 DUET LIKE THIS

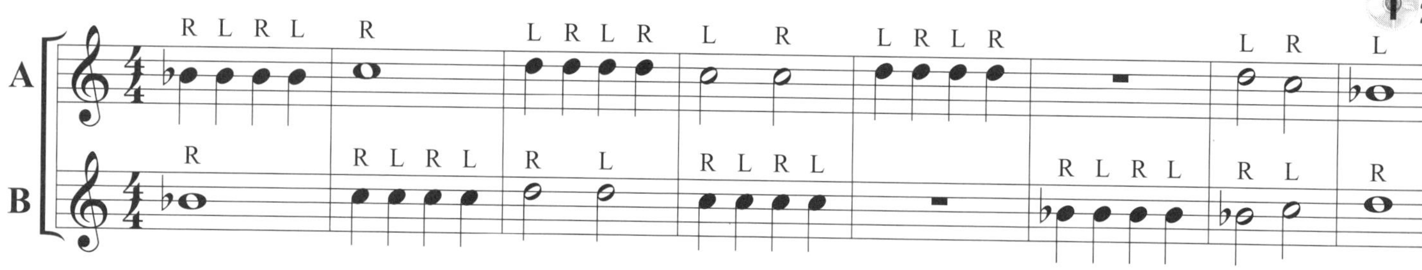

1.21 CLIMBING HIGHER

NEW NOTE! E♭

1.22 HOME BASE

1.23 EVEN HIGHER! *Trace the clef!*

NEW NOTE! F

ORY

PHRASING

A **phrase** in music is similar to a sentence in speech. It should continue uninterrupted until the music indicates a breath. Always listen for the phrasing in the winds.

24 DOWN BY THE STATION

American Folk Song — TRACK 1 25

TORY

MUSIC

Stephen Collins Foster (1826 – 1864) was an American songwriter born in Pennsylvania. He published his first piece when he was 18 years old. Some of his most famous songs are *Oh! Susanna, Camptown Races,* and *Some Folks Do.* His compositions capture the spirit of American folk music during the 1800s.

ART

During this time in history, artists of the Hudson River School were hard at work in the United States. Frederic Church painted *Morning, Looking East Over the Hudson Valley from the Catskill Mountains* about the same time that *Camptown Races* was written.

WORLD

The world was introduced to Ebenezer Scrooge (the famous character in Charles Dickens' *A Christmas Carol*), Abraham Lincoln delivered the Gettysburg Address, and the stapler was patented.

25 SOME FOLKS DO

Before you play, draw these symbols where they belong: Treble Clef, Time Signature, Final Bar Line.

Stephen C. Foster — TRACK 1 26

.26 SCALING THE WALL *Work with another student to learn this piece.*

TRACK 1 27

ONUS BOX

N THE ODIUM

CONDUCTING IN $\frac{4}{4}$ TIME

Your band director has been conducting a four-beat pattern. Now it is your turn to conduct! Place your right hand in a "handshake" position and follow the diagram to conduct in $\frac{4}{4}$ time.

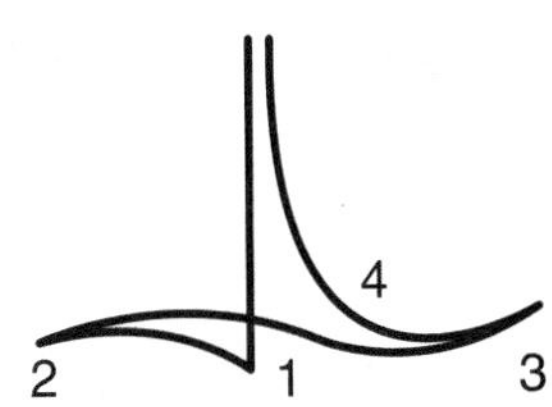

.27 GOOD KING WENCESLAS *Conduct a partner, your section, or the entire class!*

English Carol — TRACK 1 28

N THE ODIUM

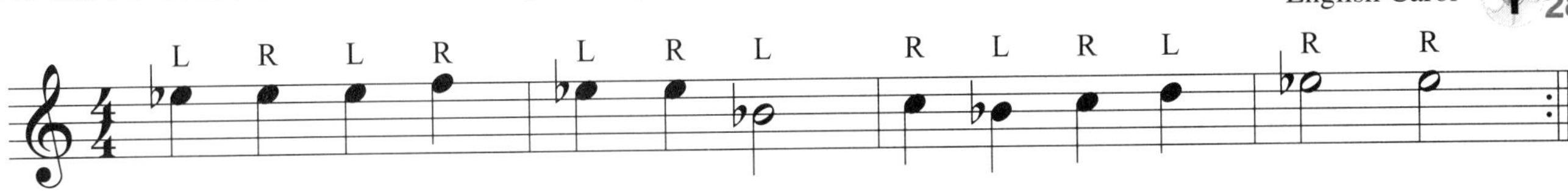

.28 STOMP ROCK

TRACK 1 29

OPUS 1 ENCORE!

INTERPRETATION STATION

Listen to CD 1 Track 30. Describe the music and how it makes you feel.

SIMON "SEZ"

Your director will give you a starting note. Listen to the rhythms your director plays and echo them back. Listen carefully!

COMPOSER'S CORNER

A composer is someone who creates original music. It is YOUR turn to be a composer!
Using the notes you already know, complete this composition. Guide rhythms have been provided for you in parentheses.

Title:______________________________ **Name:**__________________

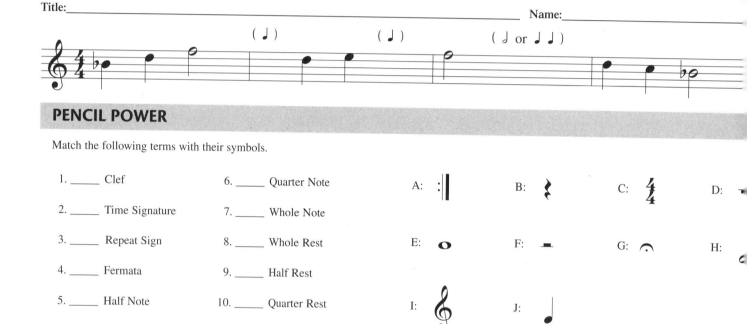

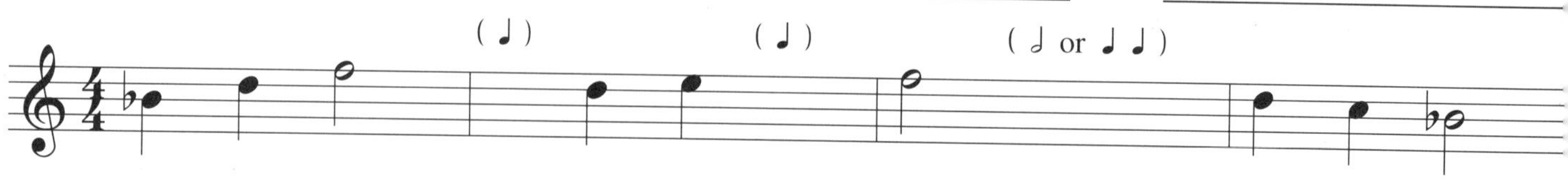

PENCIL POWER

Match the following terms with their symbols.

1. _____ Clef
2. _____ Time Signature
3. _____ Repeat Sign
4. _____ Fermata
5. _____ Half Note
6. _____ Quarter Note
7. _____ Whole Note
8. _____ Whole Rest
9. _____ Half Rest
10. _____ Quarter Rest

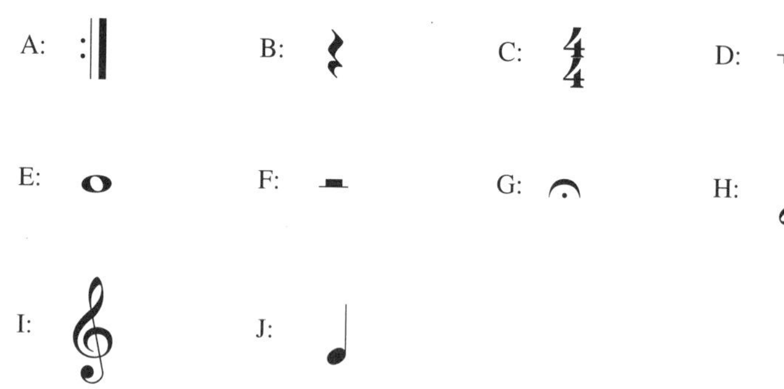

CURTAIN UP!

Time to perform! Practice these pieces and play them for friends or family members. Introduce each piece by its title.
Remember to bow when you are finished!

1.29 GO TELL AUNT RHODY *Teach your audience to conduct a four-beat pattern!*

American Folk Song

ON THE PODIUM

1.30 CUCKOO SAMBA

1.31 LIGHTLY ROW — Duet *Pair up with a friend to perform this piece for your audience. Switch parts on the repeat!*

Traditional

OPUS 2

HISTORY

MUSIC

Ludwig van Beethoven (1770 – 1827) lived most of his life in Vienna, Austria. His music became a bridge between Classical and Romantic music. When *Symphony No. 9* and its *Ode to Joy* were performed for the first time, Beethoven was completely deaf!

ART

Romanticism in art was an important movement in Europe and themes often included nationalism. Eugene Delacroix was one of the most important French artists. His *Liberty Leading the People* commemorates the French Revolution of 1830 and the overthrow of King Charles X.

WORLD

Around this time in history, Mexico became a republic, trains first carried passengers in England, the first photograph was taken, and ice cream was first sold in the United States!

2.1 ODE TO JOY

Musicianship Challenge! – Without the CD, play the 1st phrase gently, the 2nd phrase majestically.
Hint: This piece uses 4-measure phrases.

Ludwig van Beethoven — TRACK 1 34

2.2 OUTER LIMITS

TRACK 1 35

NEW NOTE! G

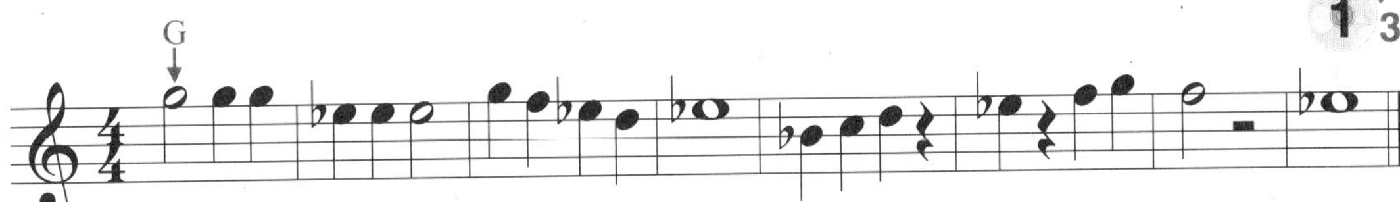

2.3 OLD MACDONALD

American Folk Song — TRACK 1 36

continue to the next line

2.4 SHARK!

Musicianship Challenge! – Without the CD, play this like you are being chased.

TRACK 1 37

NEW NOTE! A

Choose any note you have learned!

2.5 CRUSADER'S HYMN

Silesian Folk Song — TRACK 1 38

THEORY

KEY SIGNATURE

The **key signature** indicates which notes to play sharp or flat. It appears at the beginning of each staff.

- There can be up to 7 sharps in a key signature. **Sharps** (♯) follow this order: F, C, G, D, A, E, B
- There can be up to 7 flats in a key signature. **Flats** (♭) follow this order: B, E, A, D, G, C, F
- Your key signature in 2.6, *Keynote March,* indicates that all Bs and Es should be played as B-flats and E-flats.

This is the key of B♭ **Major.**

2.6 KEYNOTE MARCH

Musicianship Challenge! – Play this piece like you would hear it in a parade.

TRACK 1 39

HISTORY

MUSIC

Wolfgang Amadeus Mozart (1756 – 1791) was born in Salzburg, Austria. He was a child genius and composed his first minuet when he was just five years old! During his short life of 35 years, he wrote over 600 musical compositions. Many of his works continue to be performed today.

ART

As Mozart wrote in the Classical style, Neoclassicism in visual art was being explored by artists such as Jacques-Louis David, a French painter. This style can be seen in his painting, *The Death of Socrates,* which was completed in 1787.

WORLD

The thirteen American Colonie broke away from the British Empire in the American Revolutionary War, the *Declaration of Independence* was signed, and Johnny Appleseed was born.

2.7 STAR SEARCH *This piece is in the key of _______ Major.*

French Melody
adapted by Wolfgang A. Mozart

THEORY

DYNAMICS

Dynamics indicate how loudly or softly to play. Italian terms are often used in music to indicate volume.

p (*piano*) – play softly ***f*** (*forte*) – play loudly

DYNAMICS AND MALLET HEIGHTS

On keyboard percussion instruments, change dynamics by changing the height of your mallets.
f = 10" above the center of the bar. ***p*** = 2" above the center of the bar.

2.8 BEAT STREET *Clap the rhythm with dynamics!*

CLAP

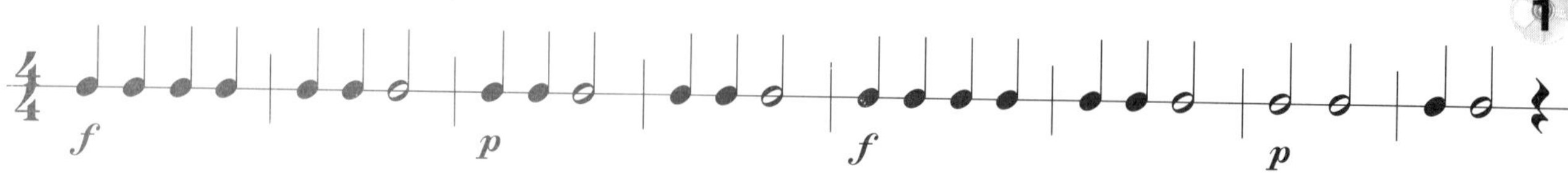

2.9 LONDON BRIDGE

English Folk Song

2.10 JINGLE BELLS – Duet *Remember to adjust your mallet height when playing dynamics.*

James Pierpont

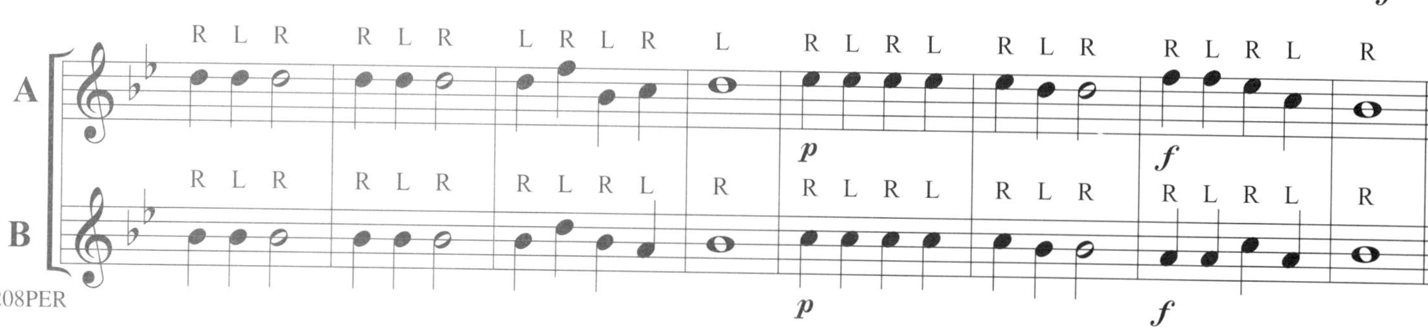

When dynamics indicate *loud*, a conductor's gestures are **bigger.**
When dynamics indicate *soft*, gestures are smaller.
Practice conducting a four-beat pattern with dynamics!

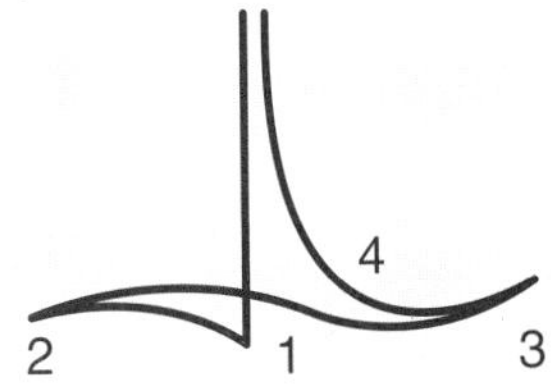

2.11 DREIDEL SONG

Traditional Hannukah Song — TRACK 1 44

DYNAMICS

Mezzo is an Italian term that means "medium" or "moderately." The letter *m* is an abbreviation used in dynamics.

mp (*mezzo piano*) – play moderately soft ***mf*** (*mezzo forte*) – play moderately loud

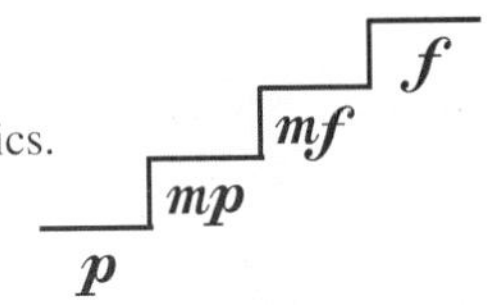

DYNAMICS AND MALLET HEIGHTS

mf = 6–8" above the center of the bar. ***mp*** = 4" above the center of the bar.

2.12 BEAT STREET *Clap the dynamics!*

TRACK 1 45

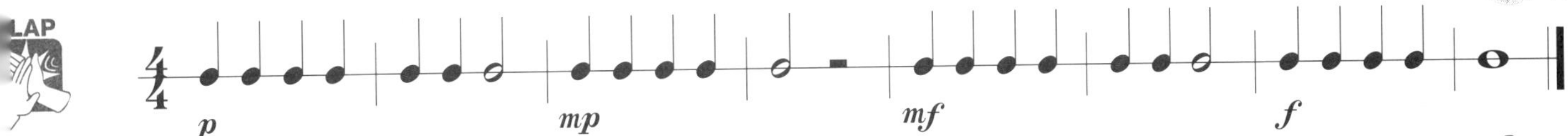

2.13 DYNAMIC DOODLE ALL DAY

American Folk Melody — TRACK 1 46

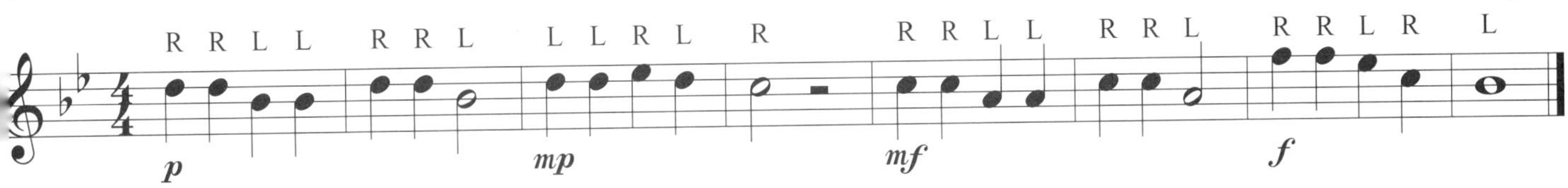

PICK-UP NOTES

Pick-up notes lead into the first full measure of a phrase.
When pick-up notes are used to begin a piece, their combined rhythmic value is often subtracted from the last measure.

2.14 A–TISKET, A–TASKET

American Folk Song — TRACK 1 47

2.15 OH! SUSANNA – Duet

Stephen C. Foster — TRACK 1 48

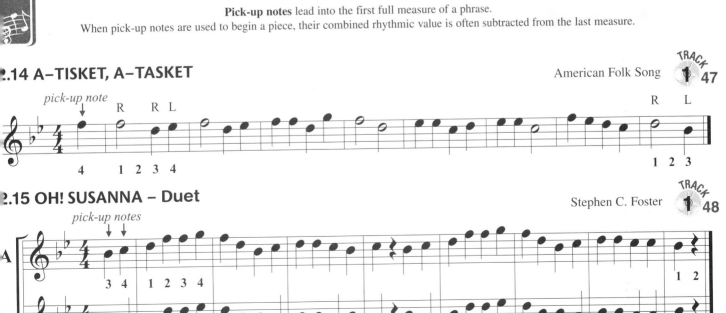

2.16 AFRICAN SAFARI

NEW NOTE!
G

THEORY

ARTICULATION: ACCENT

> An **accent** indicates to emphasize a note by playing louder. Be sure to use the correct mallet height!

2.17 LEAN ON IT

2.18 WALK TO MY LOU

American Folk Melody

RHYTHM

SYNCOPATION

Music has strong beats and weak beats. Most of the time, we stress strong beats (**1** 2 **3** 4).
Sometimes, we shift the stress onto weak beats (1 **2** 3 **4**).
This is known as **syncopation**. Longer, accented notes that occur on weak beats often identify syncopation.

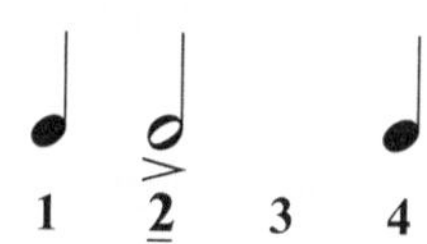

2.19 BEAT STREET

CLAP

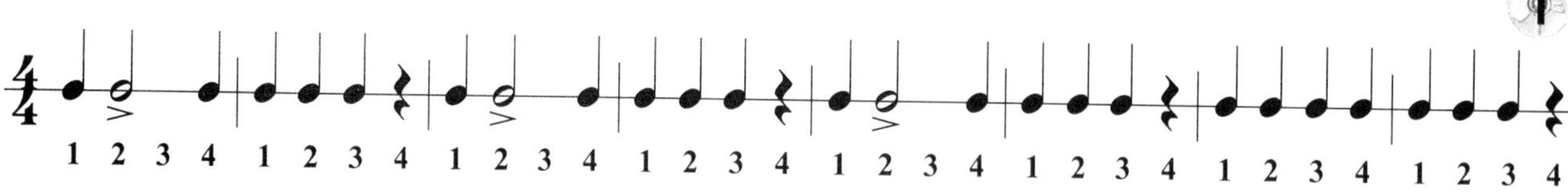

2.20 SHOO FLY

American Folk Song

2.21 CHANT

OPUS 2 ENCORE!

INTERPRETATION STATION

TRACK 1 55

Listen to CD 1 Track 55. You will hear two performances of the same piece. Which one is more musical and why?

SIMON "SEZ"

TRACK 1 56

Listen to CD 1 Track 56. You will hear a well-known song. Listen first, sing it, then find the pitches on your instrument. You can then play along with the accompaniment track that follows. Can you match the initial recording?

COMPOSER'S CORNER

Use the notes and rhythms you have learned to complete the composition. Be sure to give it a title!

tle:______________________________ Name:______________________

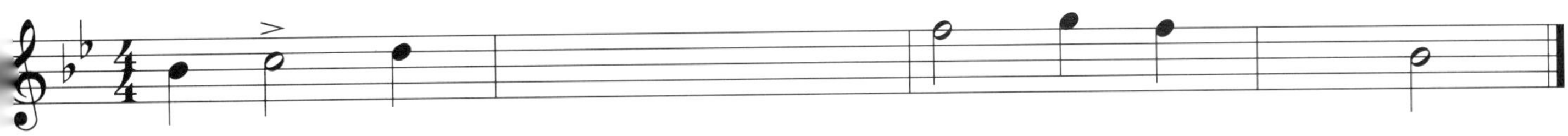

PENCIL POWER

The Secret Decoder: Name the notes and solve the puzzles!

Beethoven went __ __ __ __ towards the end of his life.

The __ __ __ __ __ in the __ __ __ __ __ photo h__ __ __ __ __ __ __ __ with time.

3. 

H__ h__ __ to pay an extra __ __ __ for the __ i __ __ __ __ __ __ __ __ __ __ __.

4. 

He __ __ __ __ __ __ __ when he mistakenly ate __ __ __ corned __ __ __ __ __ and __ __ __ __ __ __ __ __ __ __!

CURTAIN UP!

2.22 TOKECANG

Traditional Indonesian

TRACK 1 57

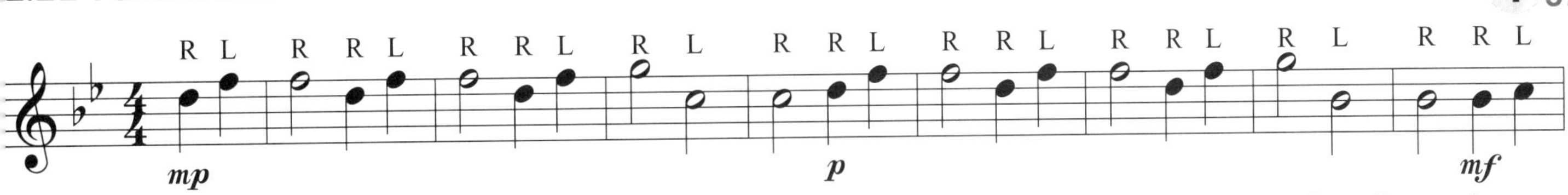

CURTAIN UP! FIRST CONCERT

2.23 CONCERT WARM-UP NO. 1

2.24 CONCERT WARM-UP NO. 2

2.25 THE SYNCOPATED ROW BOAT – Duet

Traditional Melody

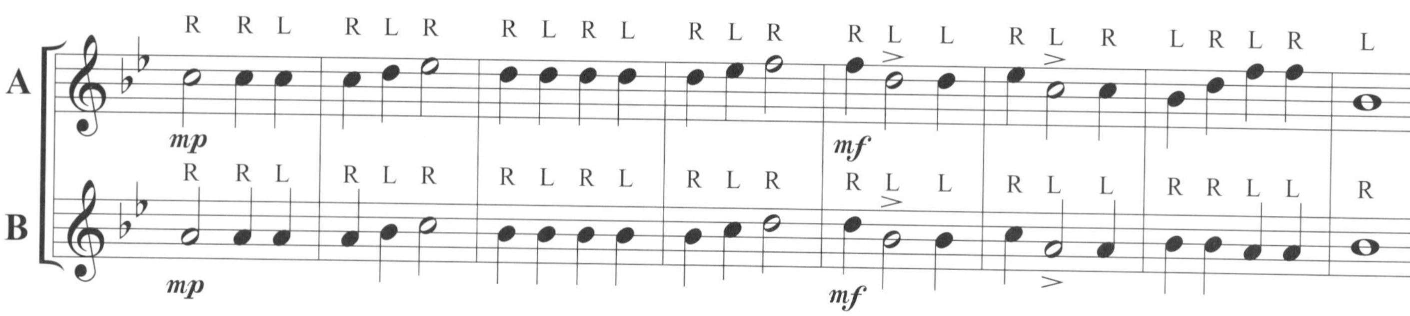

2.26 CROWN OF MAJESTY – Full Band

Robert Sheldon

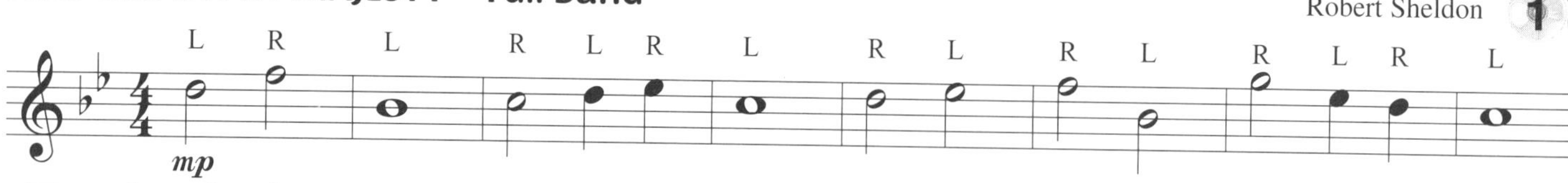

2.27 OBWISANA – Duet or Full Band with Percussion

Ghanian Folk Song

2.28 FANFARE FOR A WINTER CELEBRATION – Full Band

arr. Brian Balmages

TRACK 1 63

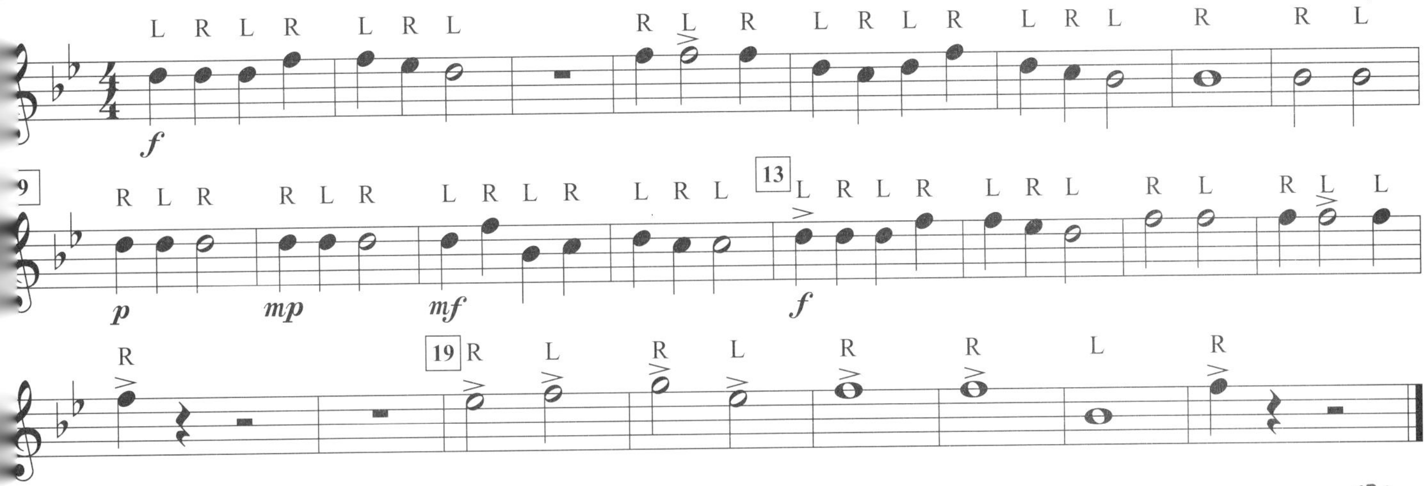

29 THE SECTION BATTLE RAG – Full Band

Brian Balmages

TRACK 1 64

2.30 ON CARIBBEAN SHORES (MARY ANN) – Full Band

Jamaican Folk Song
arr. Robert Sheldon

TRACK 1 65

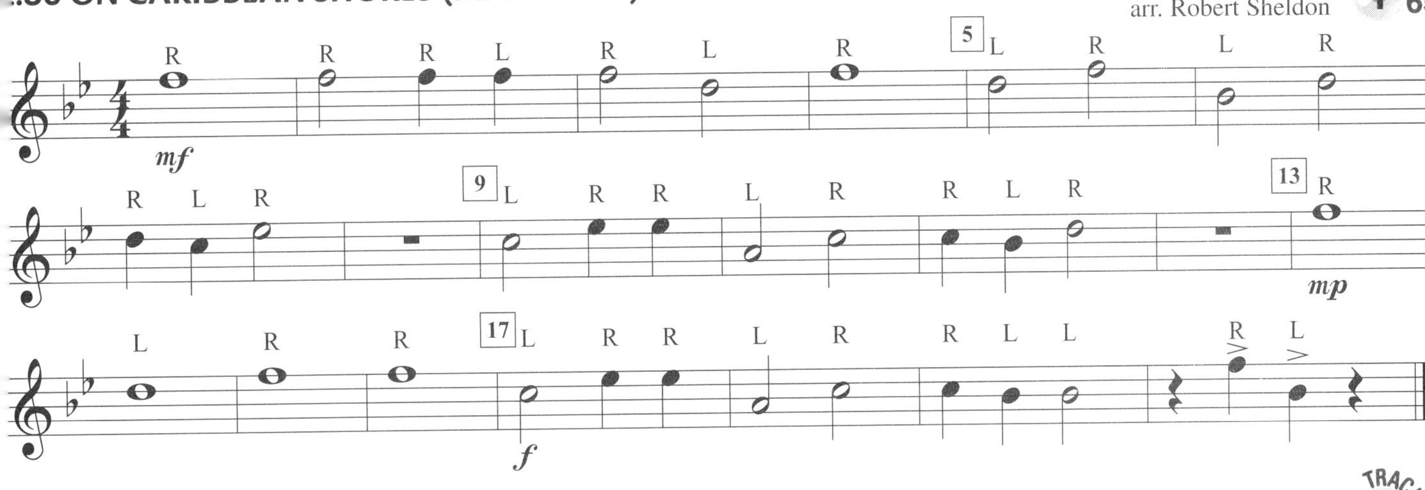

2.31 ROCK THE HOUSE – Full Band

Brian Balmages

TRACK 1 66

OPUS 3

RHYTHM

MORE TIME SIGNATURES

$\frac{3}{4}$ **3 beats** in each measure
Quarter note gets one beat

$\frac{2}{4}$ **2 beats** in each measure
Quarter note gets one beat

3.1 BEAT STREET

CLAP

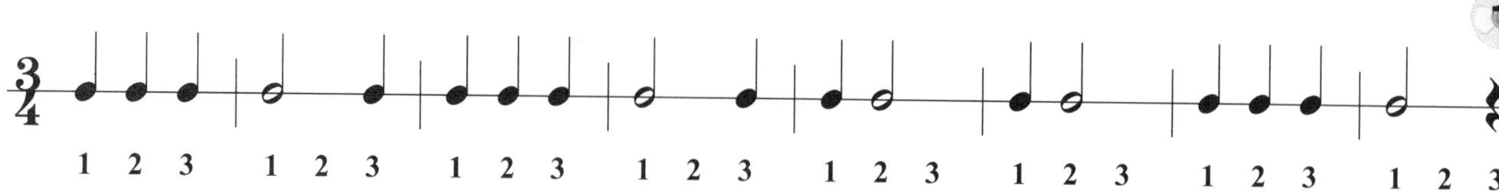

3.2 THREE'S A CROWD

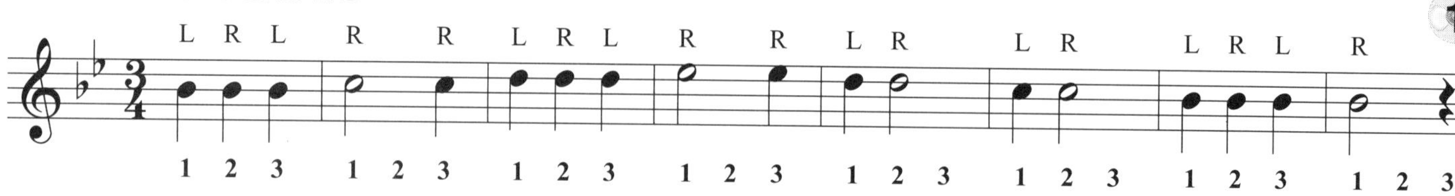

3.3 THREE POINTER

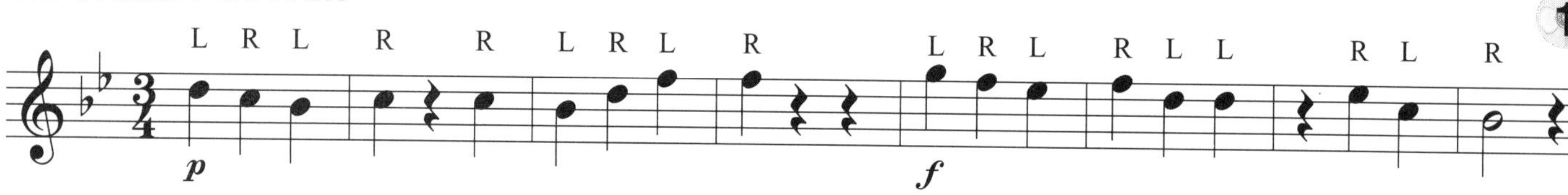

3.4 BEAT STREET

CLAP

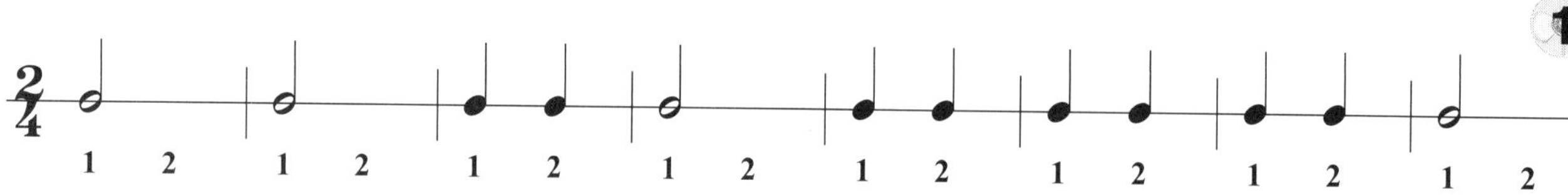

3.5 RAIN, RAIN, GO AWAY

Traditional

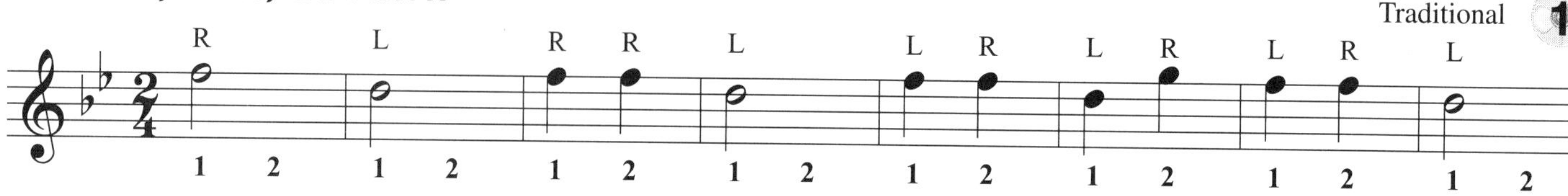

ON THE PODIUM

CONDUCTING IN $\frac{2}{4}$ TIME

It is your turn to conduct a two-beat pattern. With your right hand in a "handshake" position, follow the diagram to conduct in $\frac{2}{4}$ time.

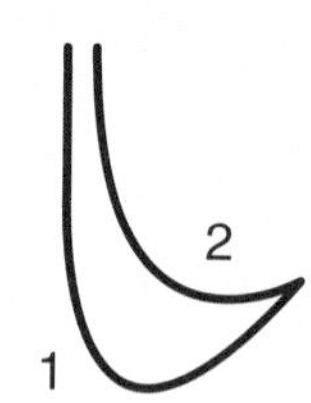

3.6 TWO FOR YOU

ON THE PODIUM

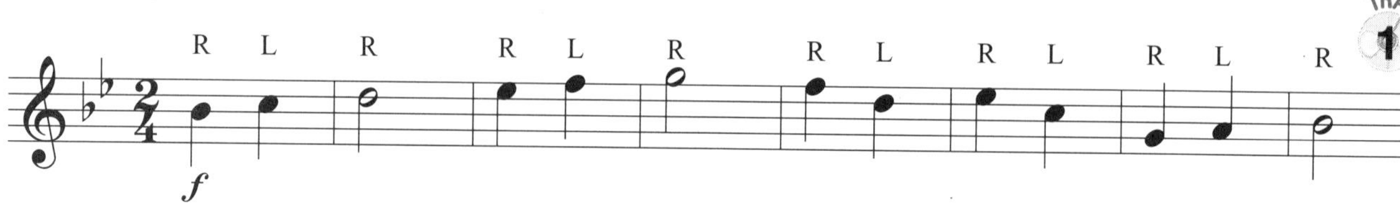

3.7 TERRIBLE TWOS

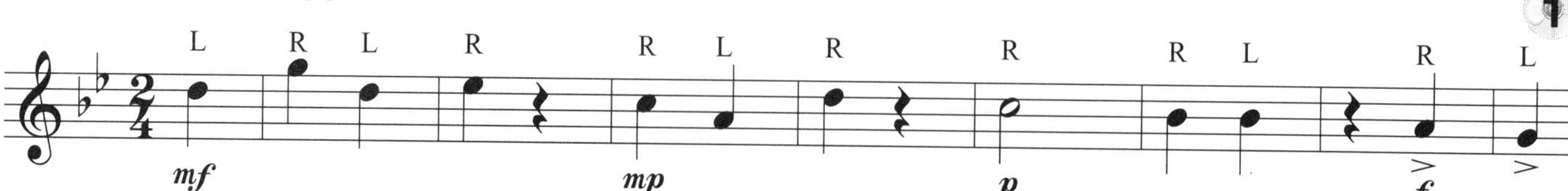

EORY

REVISITING ACCIDENTALS

Accidentals include **flat** (♭), **sharp** (♯), and **natural** (♮) signs found in front of notes, but not in the key signature.
A flat sign (♭) lowers the pitch one half-step. It remains in effect for the rest of the measure.

8 CANYONS

TRACK 1 74

EW TE!

EORY

NEW KEY SIGNATURE

This is the key of E♭ **Major.**

This key signature indicates that all Bs, Es, and As should be played as B-flats, E-flats, and A-flats.

9 ROYAL SCEPTER *Musicianship Challenge! – Play this piece in a noble style.*

TRACK 1 75

.10 THINGS ARE LOOKING UP

TRACK 1 76

EW TE!

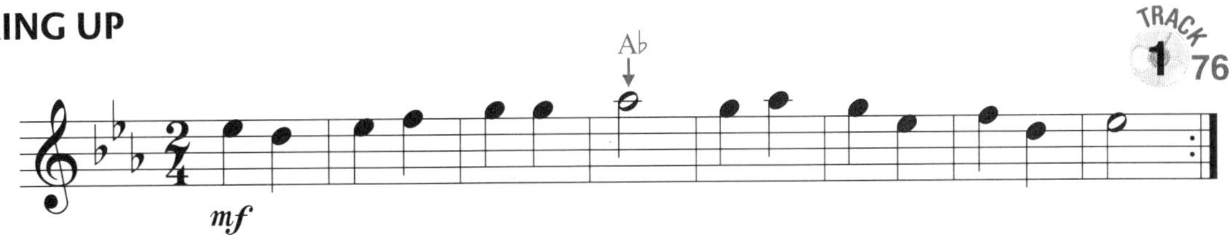

YTHM

THE RULE OF THE DOT

Adding a dot after a note increases the length of the note *by half its value.*
When adding a dot to a half note, it becomes a **dotted half note.**

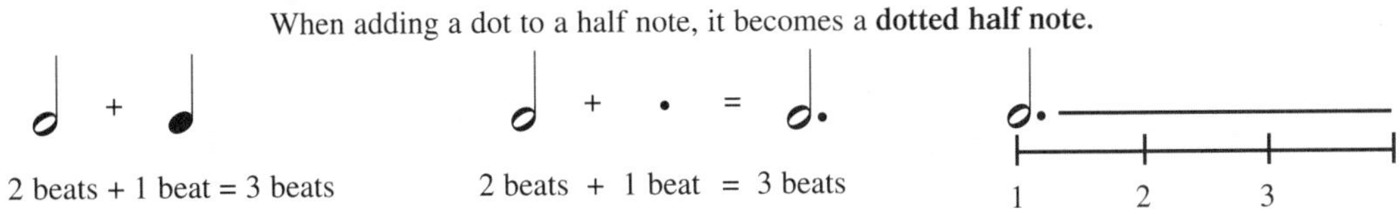

.11 BEAT STREET

Begin CD 2

TRACK 2 1

LAP

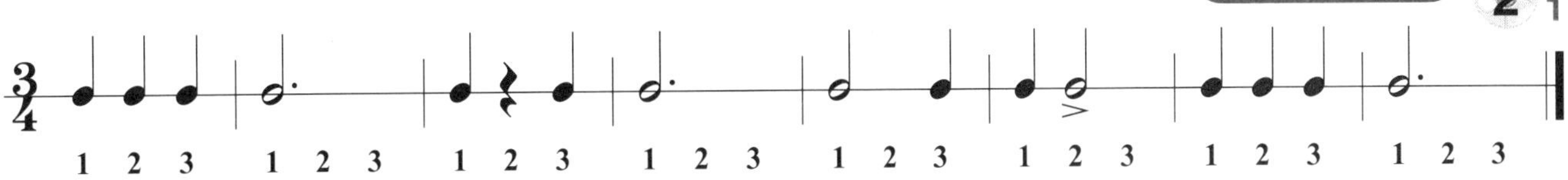

.12 TRIPLE CROWN

TRACK 2 2

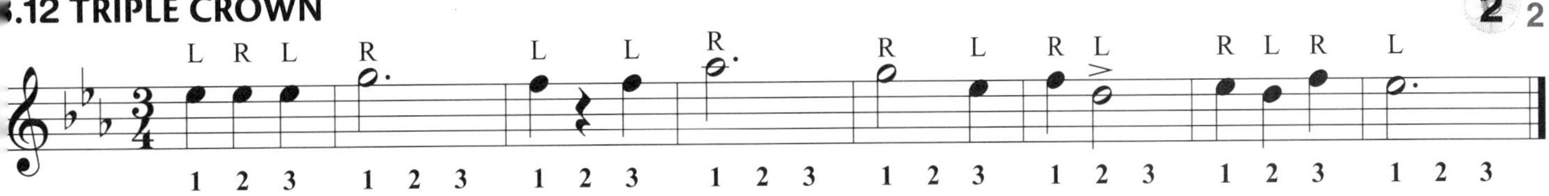

.13 MINUET

Daniel G. Türk

TRACK 2 3

3.14 JUNGLE RITUAL

TRACK 2

3.15 VOLGA BOATMEN *p–f* Play *piano* the 1st time and *forte* the 2nd time.

Russian Folk Song

TRACK 2

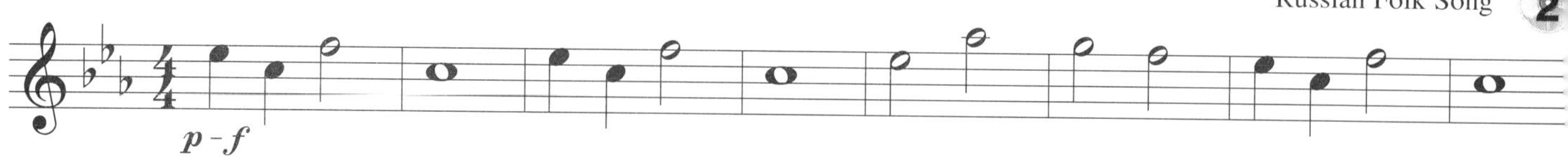

3.16 SHE WORE A YELLOW RIBBON

Traditional American

TRACK 2

3.17 CAMPTOWN RACES – Duet

Stephen C. Foster

TRACK 2

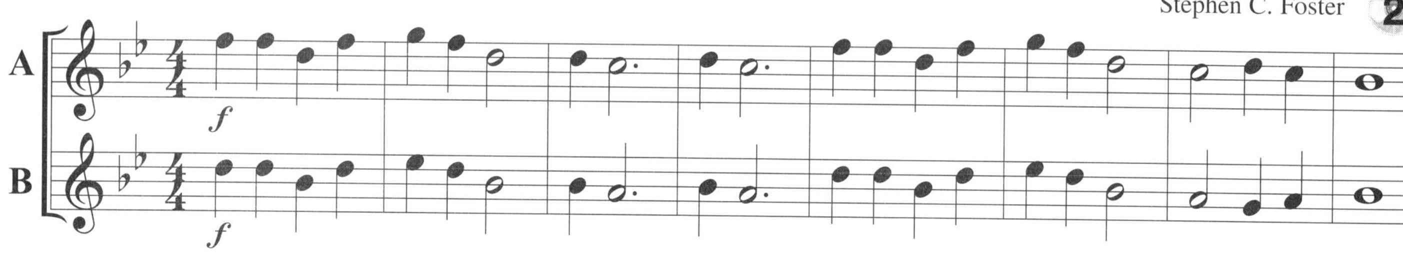

RHYTHM

EIGHTH NOTES

Eighth Note = half beat of sound

Flagged Eighth Notes

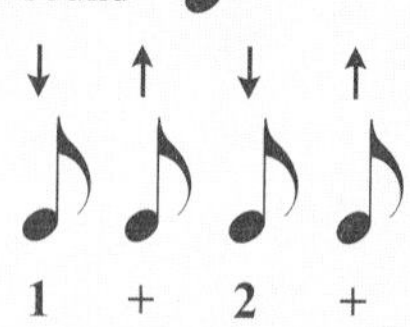

Beamed Eighth Notes

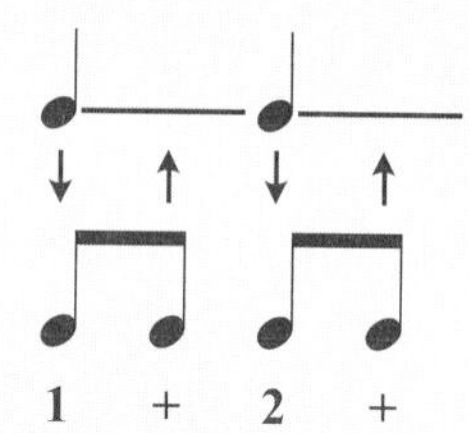

3.18 BEAT STREET *Tap your foot to keep a steady beat!*

TRACK 2

CLAP

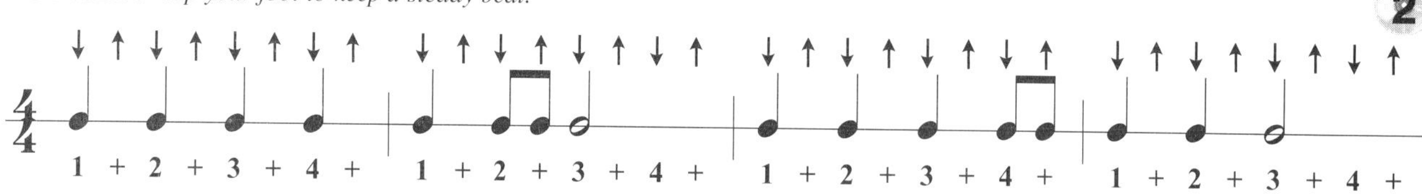

3.19 EIGHTH NOTE EXPRESS

TRACK 2

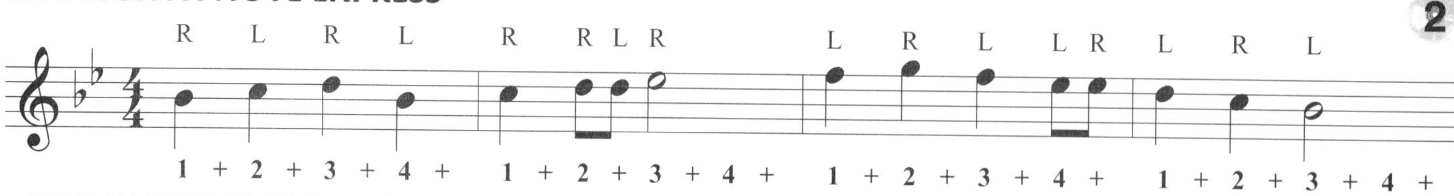

THEORY

COMMON TIME

C The **common time** symbol means the same thing as $\frac{4}{4}$ time.

3.20 GRANDMA GRUNTS

Traditional American

TRACK 2

21 SKIP TO MY LOU

American Folk Song — TRACK 2 11

WHOLE MEASURE REST

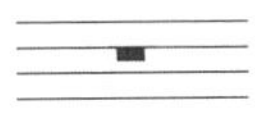

Rest for the entire measure. Check the time signature!

22 WALTZING LOU *How should you play these dynamics?*

American Folk Melody — TRACK 2 12

ENCLOSED REPEAT SIGNS

Repeat the music between the two signs.

23 TWO BY FOUR

TRACK 2 13

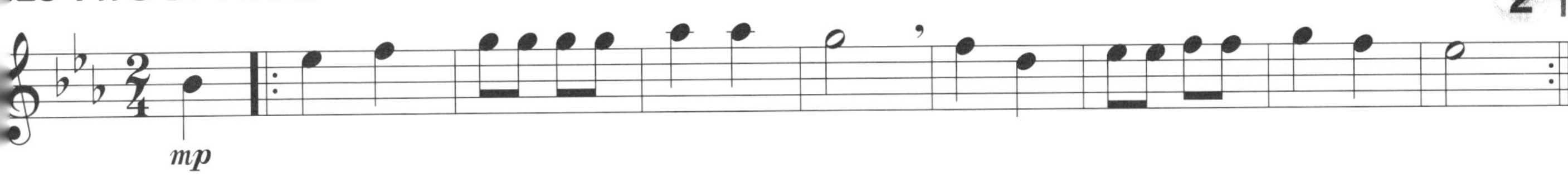

STYLE AND FORM: ROUND

In a **round**, each musician plays the same part, but enters at a different time.

24 FRÉRE JACQUES – Round *As each musician reaches ②, the next musician should begin playing at ①.*

French Folk Song — TRACK 2 14

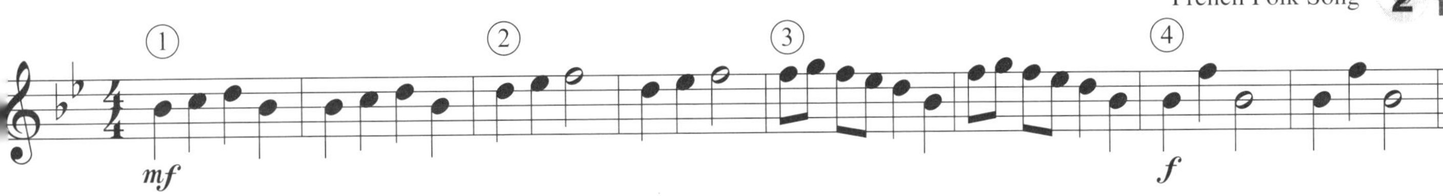

STYLE AND FORM: THEME AND VARIATIONS

Composers create a **variation** when they change a melody in some way. Changes can be made to the notes, rhythm, key, and even the time signature! While you will notice the differences in each variation, you will still be able to recognize the original theme.

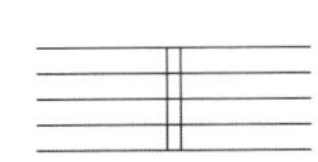

A **double bar line** indicates the end of one section and the beginning of another.

25 VARIATIONS ON A FRENCH MELODY

TRACK 2 15

THEORY

DYNAMICS

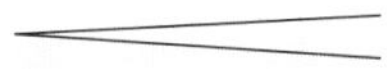

Crescendo means to gradually play louder.

Decrescendo means to gradually play softer.

3.26 IT'S SWELL *Clap first, then play! Use the provided stickings as a guide.*

TRACK 2

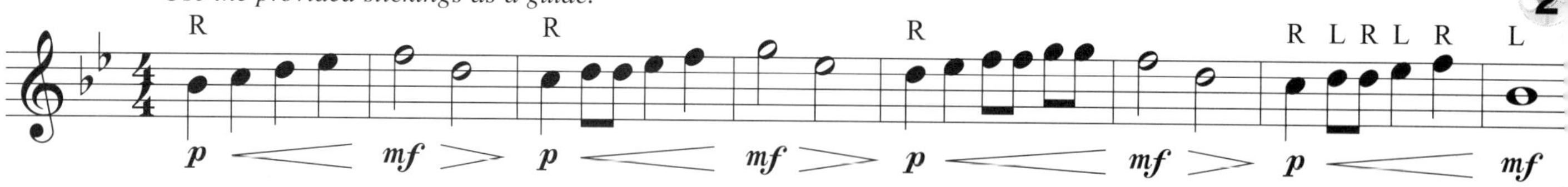

3.27 OUTTA MY WAY

TRACK 2

3.28 REGAL FANFARE

TRACK 2

NEW NOTE! F

HISTORY

MUSIC

German born **George Frideric Handel** (1685 – 1759) composed many types of music including oratorios, operas, and orchestral works. *Music for the Royal Fireworks* was written when George II of Great Britain hired him to write music to accompany fireworks in London. The event commemorated the signing of the Treaty of Aix-la-Chapelle in 1749.

ART

During colonial times, American painting and drawing focused on portraiture. Joseph Badger painted portraits of prominent figures and children in colonial Boston. His style can be seen in the portrait of *Jeremiah Belknap*, painted in 1758.

WORLD

Sir Isaac Newton stated the three universal laws of motion. In the same publication he used the Latin word *gravitas* that would become known as gravity. Also, America founded its first hospital in Pennsylvania.

3.29 MUSIC FOR THE ROYAL FIREWORKS

TRACK 2

George F. Handel

RHYTHM

BEAM GROUPS

3.30 SCALE THE WALL

TRACK 2

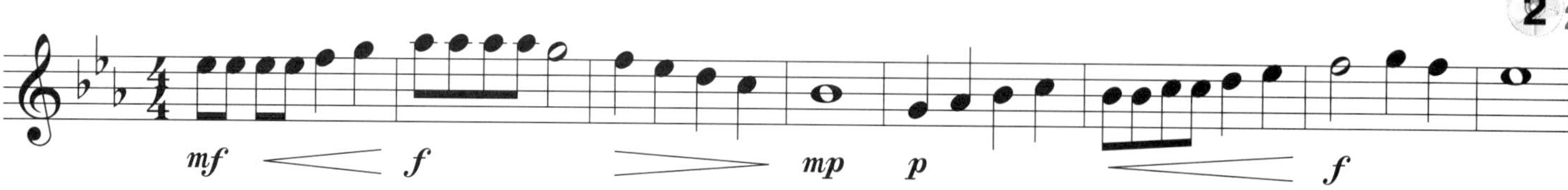

1 NEW FRONTIERS

TRACK 2 21

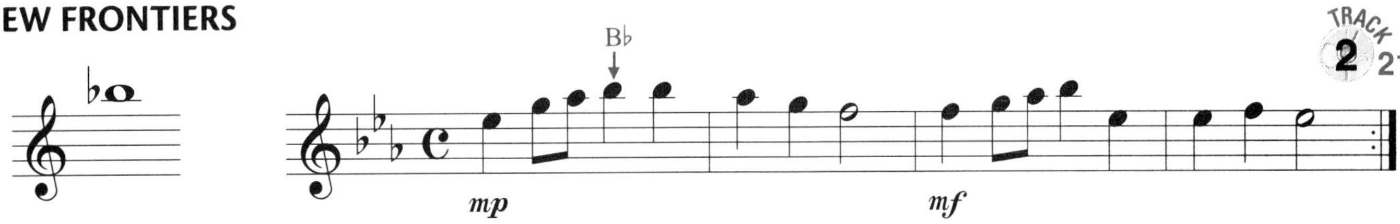

2 THE SAINTS GO MARCHING IN *Pick-up notes lead into measure 1.*

Traditional Spiritual

TRACK 2 22

THE
IUM

CONDUCTING IN $\frac{3}{4}$ TIME

It is your turn to conduct a three-beat pattern. With your right hand in a "handshake" position, follow the diagram to conduct in $\frac{3}{4}$ time.

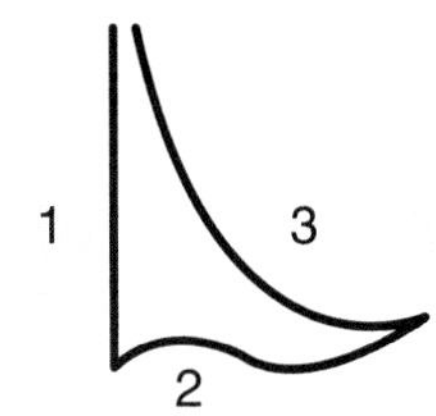

33 ROLLING ALONG

THE
IUM

TRACK 2 23

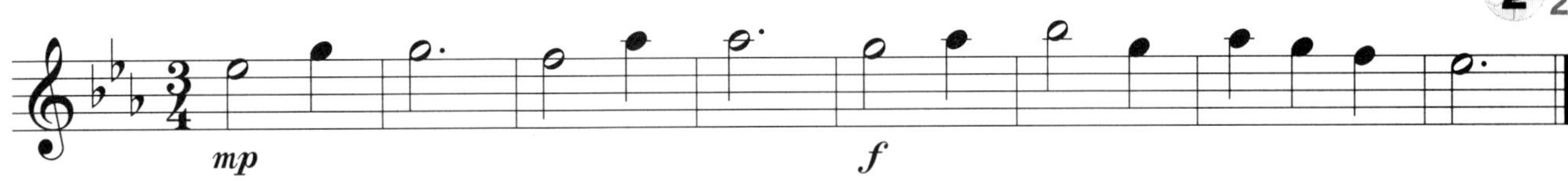

EORY

FIRST AND SECOND ENDINGS

At the **first ending**, play through it to the repeat sign. Go back to the beginning or the previous repeat sign and play again. Skip the first ending – play the **second ending** instead.

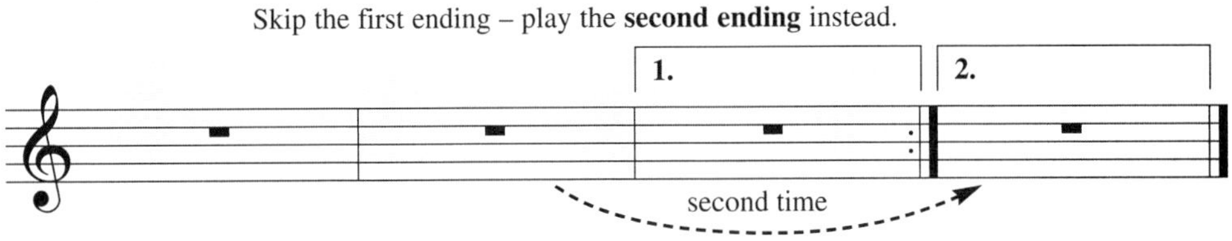

34 LONG, LONG AGO

Traditional

TRACK 2 24

35 JOLLY OLD SAINT NICHOLAS – Duet

American Carol

TRACK 2 25

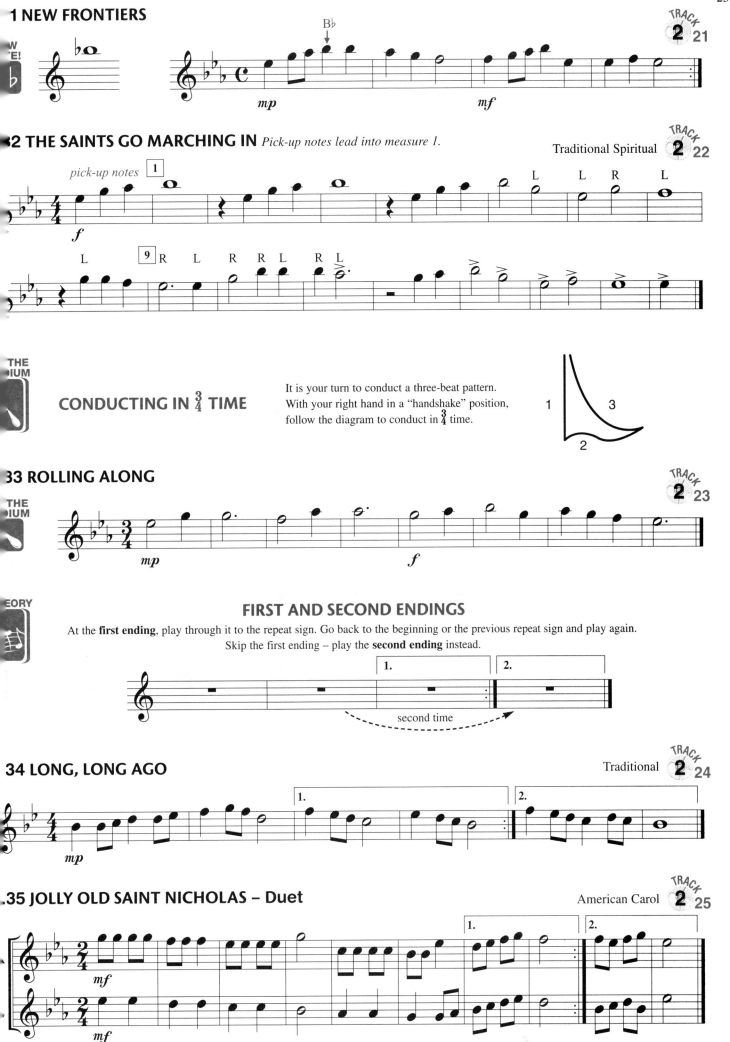

OPUS 3 ENCORE!

INTERPRETATION STATION

Listen to CD 2 Track 26. You will hear four musical examples, all composed using a different time signature. As you listen, pay close attention to how rhythmic ideas are grouped. Circle the correct time signature for each example.

1. $\frac{3}{4}$ $\frac{4}{4}$ 2. $\frac{2}{4}$ $\frac{3}{4}$ 3. $\frac{3}{4}$ $\frac{4}{4}$ 4. $\frac{2}{4}$ $\frac{3}{4}$

SIMON "SEZ"

Listen to CD 2 Track 27. You are going to hear a piece called *One Note Wonder.* It gets its title because it uses only one pitch! You will hear dynamics that make it very interesting. Play along with the accompaniment track that follows, imitating the dynamics and rhythm of the initial recording to make it musical.

COMPOSER'S CORNER

It is your turn to be a composer again! Use notes and rhythms you have learned to complete each measure (remember to look at the time signature). Then give your piece a title and perform it for a friend or family member!

Title:____________________________ **Name:**________________

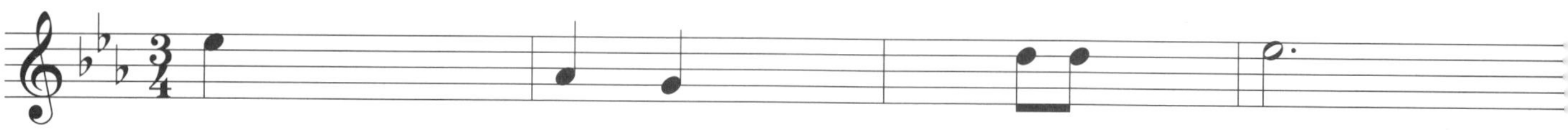

PENCIL POWER

Each measure below is rhythmically incomplete! For each example, add *one note* to complete the measure and make it correct.

1. 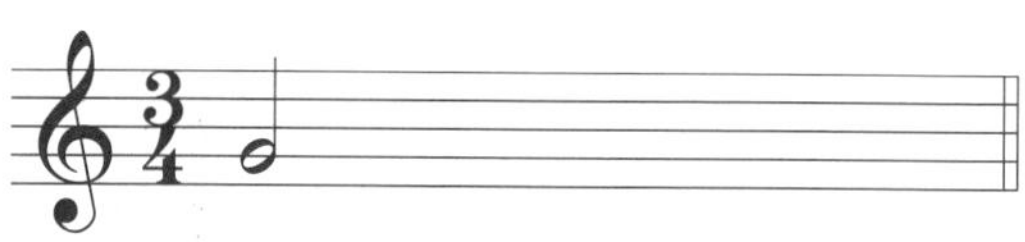

2. 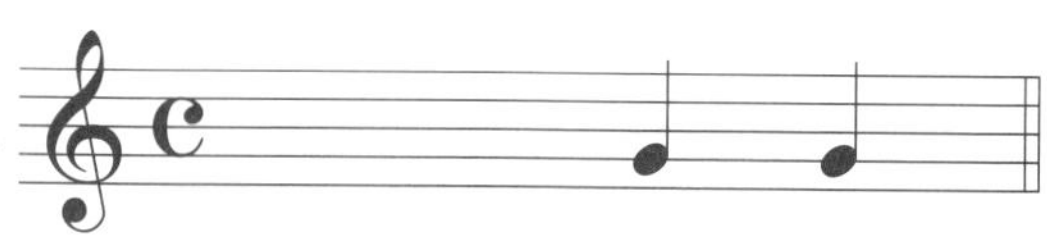

3. 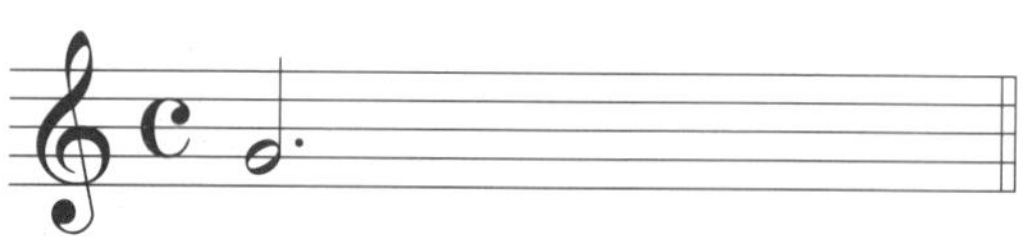

4. 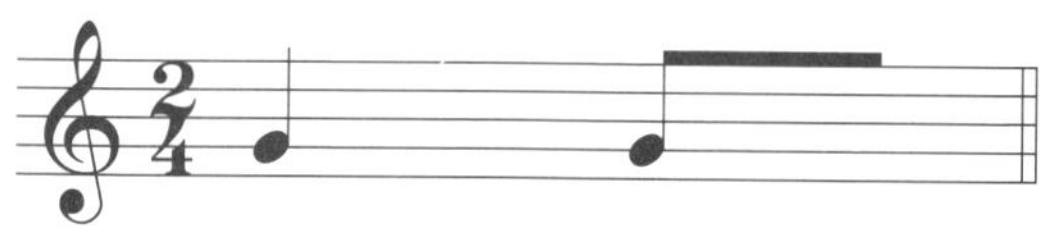

CURTAIN UP!

3.36 ZUM GALI GALI – Round

Traditional Hebrew Song

3.37 DRY BONES

Spiritual

CURTAIN UP! FULL BAND

ORY

MULTIPLE MEASURE REST

In some pieces, there will be instances when you rest for a few measures at a time. When this happens, you will see the **multiple measure rest** symbol. The number above the symbol tells you how many measures of rest to count.

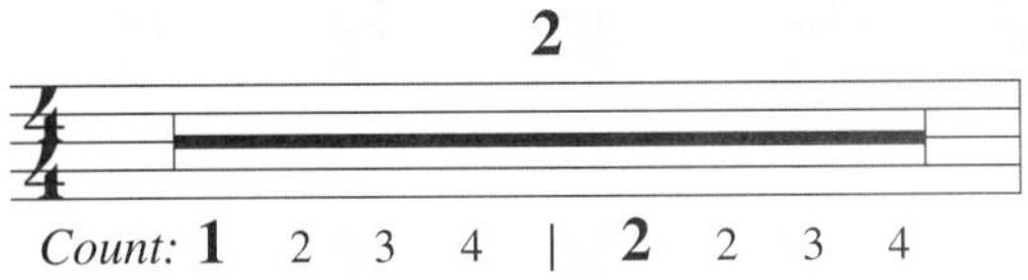

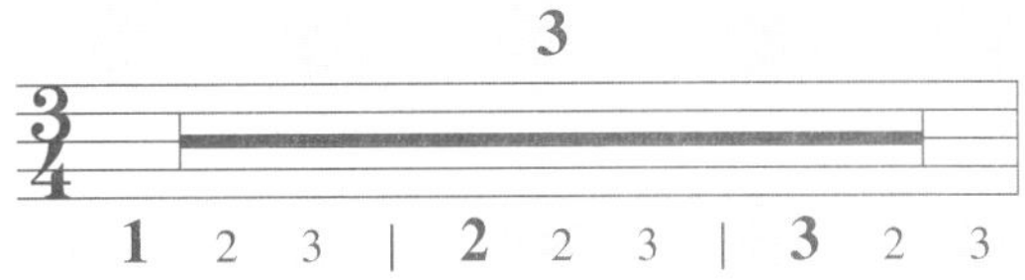

This symbol tells you to rest for two measures in $\frac{4}{4}$ time.

This symbol tells you to rest for three measures in $\frac{3}{4}$ time.

38 WILLIAM TELL OVERTURE

Gioachino Rossini
arr. Brian Balmages

TRACK 2 30

39 ABOVE THE CLOUDS

Robert Sheldon

TRACK 2 31

OPUS 4

4.1 CIRCUS ACT

NEW NOTE! E

4.2 DAYBREAK

ON THE PODIUM

THEORY

NEW KEY SIGNATURE

This is the key of **F Major.**

This key signature indicates that all Bs should be played as B-flats.

4.3 CHIAPANECAS

Mexican Folk Song

BONUS BOX

4.4 SLURRED NOT SHAKEN

NEW NOTE! A

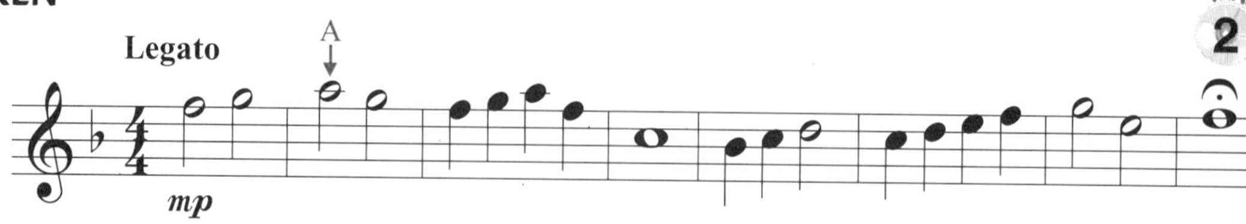

4.5 SLIP 'N' SLIDE

ORY

TEMPO

Tempo is the speed of the beat. Music can move at different rates of speed.

Largo – a slow tempo **Moderato** – a medium tempo **Allegro** – a fast tempo

5 MUSETTE

J.S. Bach TRACK 2 37

Moderato

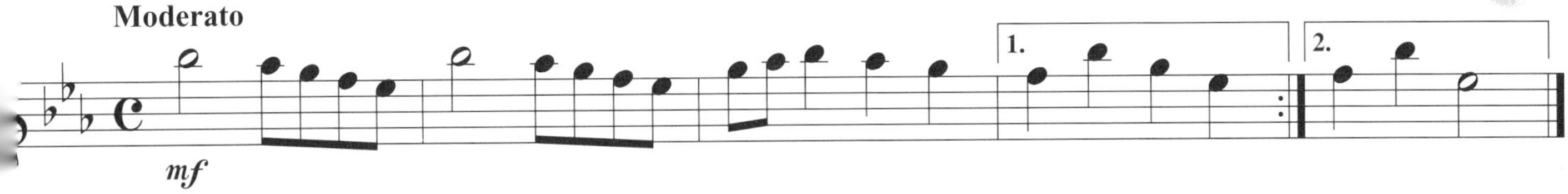

mf

7 CIELITO LINDO

Mexican Folk Song TRACK 2 38

THE
UM

Allegro

f

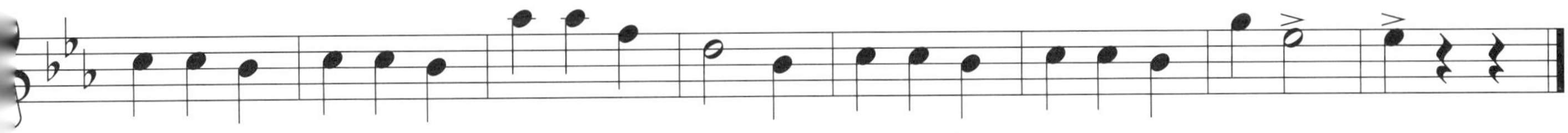

TORY

MUSIC

Gustav Mahler (1860 – 1911) was a noted composer and conductor of the late Romantic era. He spent time in New York conducting the Metropolitan Opera and the New York Philharmonic Orchestra. He is mainly known for his large symphonies (his *Symphony No. 8* uses over a thousand performers!).

ART

The world saw the emergence of Cubism, a style in which objects were broken up, then reassembled in abstract forms. Pablo Picasso became one of the most famous Cubists in history. His *Ma Jolie* (1911) is an early example of the style.

WORLD

Mark Twain published *The Adventures of Tom Sawyer*, Sir Arthur Conan Doyle introduced the world to Sherlock Holmes, and the coin-operated telephone was invented.

8 THEME FROM SYMPHONY NO. 1 – Round

Gustav Mahler TRACK 2 39

Largo

mp

mf *p*

YTHM

TIE

A **tie** is a curved line that connects notes of the *same* pitch. These notes are "tied" together and played to sound like one longer note.

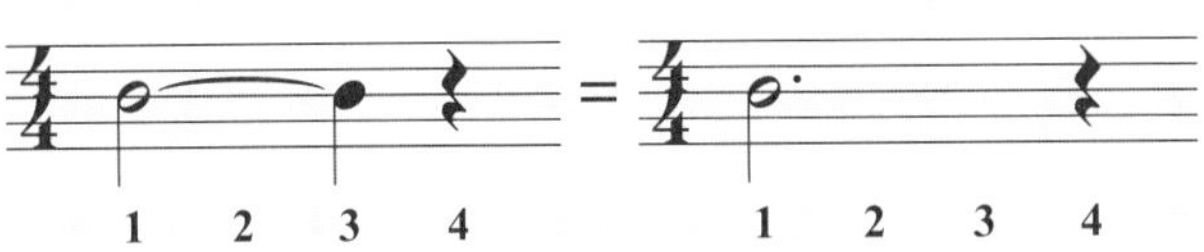

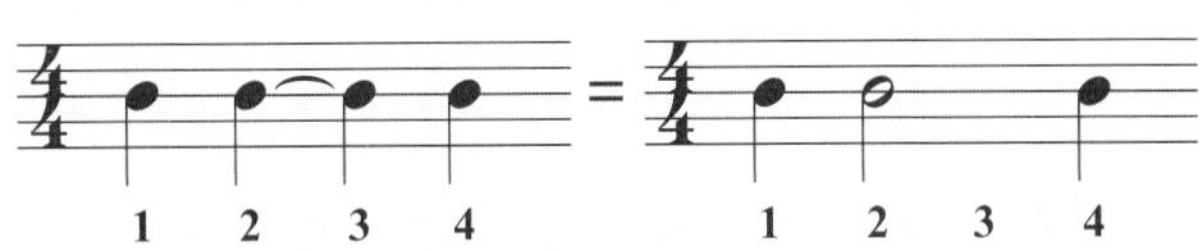

9 MAKING CONNECTIONS

TRACK 2 40

mp *f* *mp*

10 ALL TIED UP

TRACK 2 41

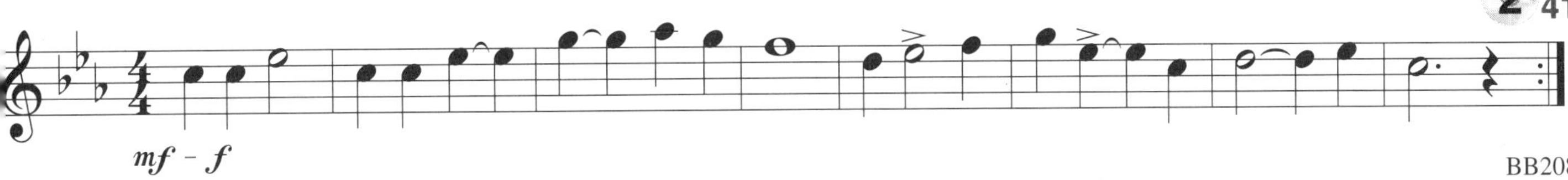

mf – *f*

HISTORY

MUSIC

Pyotr Ilyich Tchaikovsky (1840 – 1893) was a Russian composer who studied music at a very young age. His most famous works include the ballet *The Nutcracker* and the exciting *1812 Overture*. He composed *Capriccio Italien* after a visit to Italy during Carnivale season.

ART

In 1880, the Arts and Crafts Movement was going strong in England. This style is reflected in art, architecture, and interior design. Works by British architect Herbert Tudor Buckland and American architect Frank Lloyd Wright are typical of the Arts and Crafts style.

WORLD

Wabash, Indiana became the first town to be complet illuminated using electric light and the Statue of Liberty was presented to th United States by the peopl of France.

4.11 CAPRICCIO ITALIEN

Allegro

Pyotr I. Tchaikovsky

4.12 BARCAROLLE

NEW NOTE!

D♭

Moderato

Jacques Offenbach

THEORY

NEW KEY SIGNATURE

This is the key of A♭ **Major.**

This key signature indicates that all Bs, Es, As, and Ds should be played as B-flats, E-flats, A-flats, and D-flats.

4.13 THE BLUE BELLS OF SCOTLAND

Maestoso *(majestically)*

Scottish Folk Song

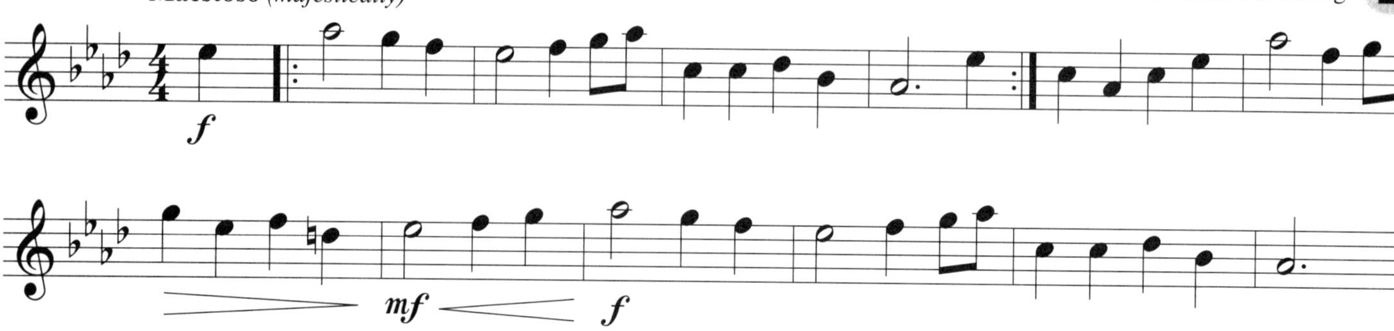

HISTORY

MUSIC

John Philip Sousa (1854 – 1932) was a violinist, composer, and conductor born in Washington, D.C. He conducted the United States Marine Band from 1880 until 1892. His marches, such as *The Stars and Stripes Forever, Semper Fidelis*, and the *Liberty Bell*, are well known and important to American culture.

ART

In the early 20th century, artist Salvador Dali of Spain was mostly known as a surrealist and emphasized visions of the subconscious. *The Persistence of Memory* (1931), a scene with melting clocks, is one of his best known works.

WORLD

Elsewhere in 1917, the Russian revolution began, World War I was still raging, and the first commercial recordings of jazz music were available to the public.

4.14 HIGH SCHOOL CADETS

March tempo

John Philip Sousa

5 IT'S ONLY NATURAL

US K

TRACK 2 46

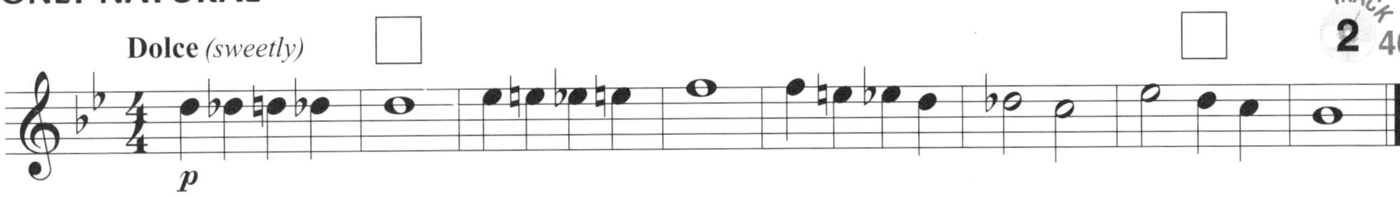

6 ACCIDENTAL BLUES – Duet

TRACK 2 47

THM 3 4

RETURN OF THE DOT RULE

Adding a dot after a note increases the length of the note by half its value. Here, the dot is used with a quarter note to create a **dotted quarter note.**

17 BEAT STREET *Tap your foot to keep a steady beat.*

TRACK 2 48

AP

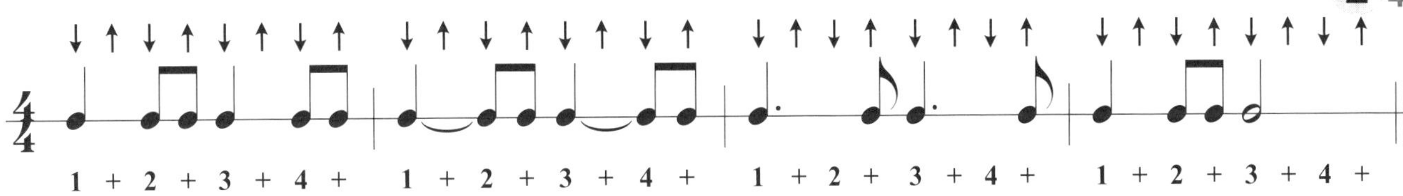

.18 DOTS A LOT

TRACK 2 49

EORY

RITARDANDO

Ritardando – abbreviated "*rit.*" – means to make the tempo gradually slower.

.19 ALL THROUGH THE NIGHT

Welsh Folk Song

TRACK 2 50

ONUS OX

4.20 AMERICA

Maestoso — Traditional

THEORY

D.C. AL FINE

D.C. is an abbreviation for *da capo*, an Italian term that refers to the beginning.
At the **D.C. al Fine**, return to the beginning and play again until the **Fine**.

4.21 ALOUETTE

French-Canadian Folk Song

Moderato

4.22 BANANA BOAT SONG *Calypso is a blend of African and Caribbean music.*

Calypso — Caribbean Folk Song

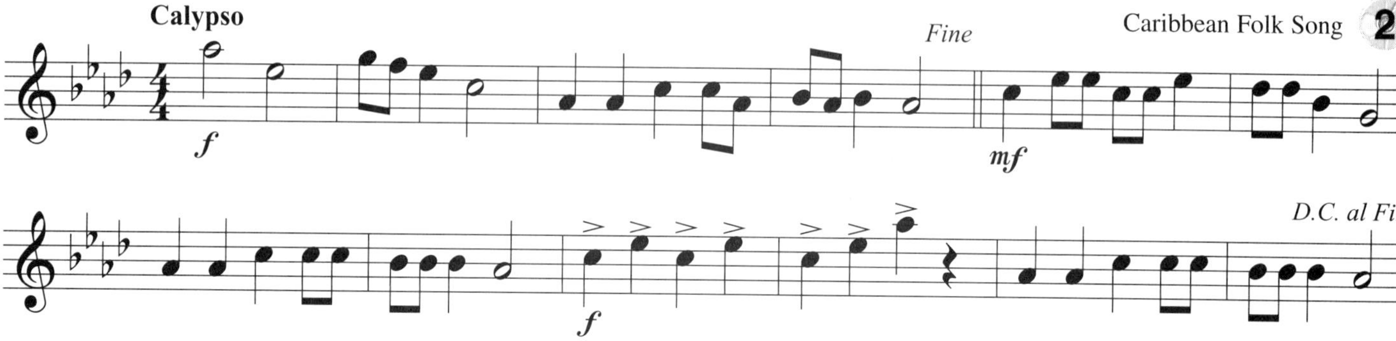

HISTORY

MUSIC

Antonín Dvořák (1841 – 1904) was from a small town near Prague, in the Czech Republic. He eventually moved to the United States and became the director of the New York Conservatory of Music. In 1888, the Conservatory welcomed African-Americans while other schools were still practicing segregation. His *Symphony No. 9 ("From the New World")* was composed during his brief time in America. It is influenced by Native American music and African-American spirituals.

ART

French artist Georges Seurat painted *A Sunday Afternoon on the Island of La Grande Jatte*. This large painting, depicting a scene of recreation in Paris, was created using a technique called pointillism. Composed entirely of painted dots, it took him nearly two years to finish.

WORLD

Congress abolished slavery in the U.S. Territories, Albert Einstein was born, the World's Columbian Exposition was held in Chicago, and New York became the first state to require license plates on cars

4.23 THEME FROM THE NEW WORLD SYMPHONY

Largo — Antonín Dvořák

THM

MORE ABOUT THE DOT

While a dotted quarter note is usually followed by an eighth note, the eighth note sometimes appears *before* the dotted quarter note.

.4 BEAT STREET

TRACK 2 55

AP

1 + 2 + 3 + 4 + 1 + 2 + 3 + 4 + 1 + 2 + 3 + 4 + 1 + 2 + 3 + 4 +

25 CARIBBEAN CARNIVAL

TRACK 2 56

Calypso

1 + 2 + 3 + 4 + 1 + 2 + 3 + 4 + 1 + 2 + 3 + 4 + 1 + 2 + 3 + 4 +

26 GOOD NIGHT LADIES

Traditional TRACK 2 57

THE
IUM

Brightly

27 GOING TO KENTUCKY

American Folk Song TRACK 2 58

Allegro

EW
TE!
E♭

.28 FILL 'ER UP *A deep breath and full airstream will help you play with a beautiful sound.*

TRACK 2 59

EW
TE!
E

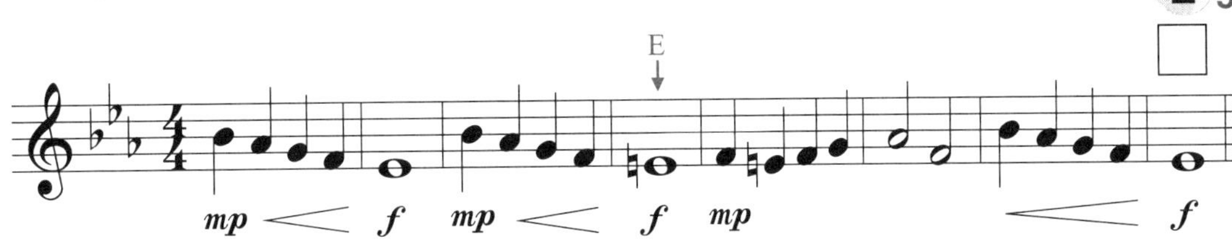

.29 MARCHE MILITAIRE

Franz Schubert TRACK 2 60

Marziale *(in a march style)*

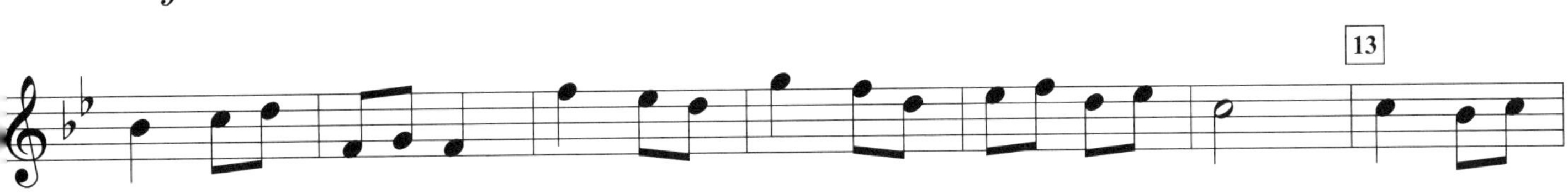

OPUS 4 ENCORE!

INTERPRETATION STATION

Listen to CD 2 Track 61. For each example, decide if the tempo is ***L**argo*, ***M**oderato*, or ***A**llegro*.
Circle the correct answer.

1. L M A 2. L M A 3. L M A 4. L M A

SIMON "SEZ"

Listen to CD 2 Track 62. You are going to hear 4 examples.
Match the performance to its correctly notated example. The first one has been done for you!

No. 1 = B No. 2 = ____ No. 3 = ____ No. 4 = ____

A.

B.
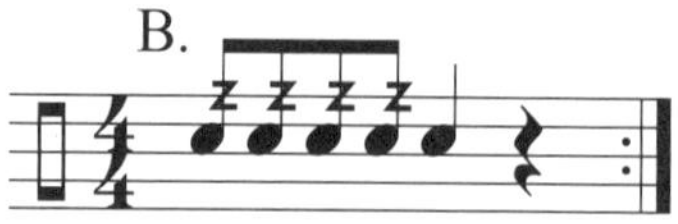

C.

D.

COMPOSER'S CORNER

Sometimes a composer takes an existing melody and presents it in a new way. This is called **arranging**. Change the rhythms of the music in *Alouette in Four* so it is playable in $\frac{2}{4}$ time. *Hint: Cut the rhythmic value of each note in half!* The arrangement has been started for you.

ALOUETTE IN FOUR

ALOUETTE IN TWO

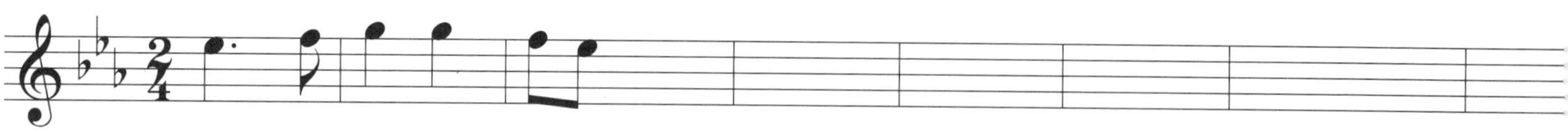

PENCIL POWER – MATCH THE COMPOSER

Match the composer with the correct fact by writing in the appropriate letter.

____ Wolfgang Amadeus Mozart

____ Antonín Dvořák

____ Gustav Mahler

____ John Philip Sousa

____ Ludwig van Beethoven

____ Pyotr Ilyich Tchaikovsky

A. Russian composer who wrote the famous ballet, *The Nutcracker*

B. U.S. Marine Band conductor and composer known for his marches

C. His *Symphony No. 9* reveals the influence of African-American spirituals

D. Child genius who composed over 600 works in a short life of 35 years

E. Continued to compose music after becoming completely deaf

F. Composer of the late Romantic era known for his large symphonies

CURTAIN UP!

4.30 HAVA NASHIRA – Round

Israeli Folk Song

31 LITTLE SWALLOW

Chinese Folk Song
arr. Robert Sheldon
TRACK 2 64

32 FURY

Brian Balmages
TRACK 2 65

4.33 HAIL THE CONQUERING HERO

Instrumental Solo

George F. Handel
arr. Brian Balmages

Piano Accompaniment

OPUS 5

Begin CD 3

. CATAPULT!

TRACK 3 1

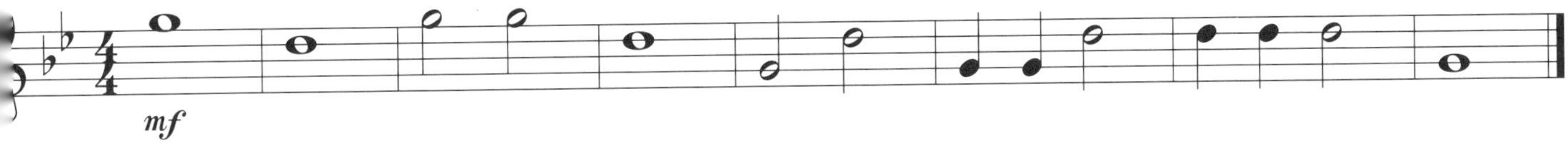

2 UP AND OVER

TRACK 3 2

3 SMOOTH HORIZONS

TRACK 3 3

4 UP, UP AND AWAY!

TRACK 3 4

.5 CLIMB ON

TRACK 3 5

.6 OVER EASY

TRACK 3 6

.7 ZERO GRAVITY

TRACK 3 7

.8 BREAKING THROUGH

TRACK 3 8

.9 THE MOON TURNS DARK

French Folk Melody

TRACK 3 9

Misterioso *(mysteriously)*

5.10 IN ORBIT

TRACK 3

5.11 CLEAR SKIES

TRACK 3

5.12 SPIRIT!

TRACK 3

Marziale

5.13 BREAK IT DOWN

TRACK 3

NEW NOTE! C

5.14 SHALOM, CHAVERIM

TRACK 3

Allegro

Hebrew Folk Song

5.15 THE UNDISCOVERED PLANET

TRACK 3

Aggressively

THEORY

TEMPO

Andante is a tempo between *Largo* and *Moderato.*

slow ⟵⟶ fast

Largo – Andante – Moderato – Allegro

5.16 SAKURA, SAKURA

TRACK 3

Andante

Japanese Folk Song

TORY

MUSIC

German composer **Johannes Brahms** (1833 – 1897) was also an accomplished pianist and gave the first performance of many of his own works. *Lullaby (Wiegenlied)* was composed in 1868 to celebrate the birth of his friend's son.

ART

In the mid 1800s, Realists were concerned with objectivity. American artist James Whistler titled many of his works "harmonies" or "arrangements." An example is his *Arrangement in Grey and Black No. 1: Portrait of the Artist's Mother.*

WORLD

In 1868, floats appeared in New Orleans' Mardi Gras parade for the first time and the first Memorial Day was celebrated in the United States.

17 LULLABY – Duet

Johannes Brahms TRACK 3 17

Cantabile *(in a singing style)*

YTHM

EIGHTH RESTS

The **eighth rest** receives one-half beat in $\frac{4}{4}$ time.

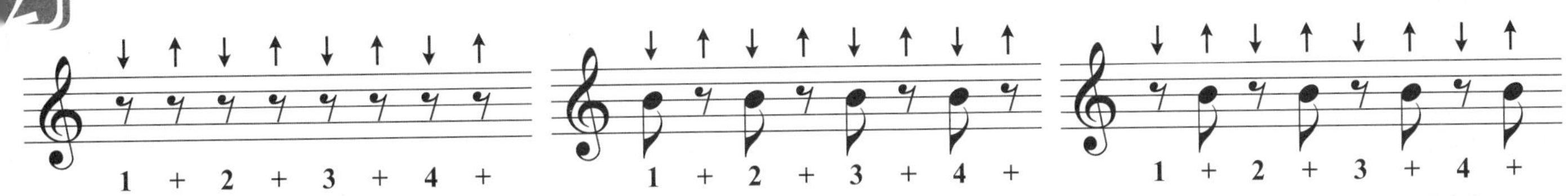

Eighth rests can replace upbeat eighth notes. Eighth rests can replace downbeat eighth notes.

.18 BEAT STREET

TRACK 3 18

LAP

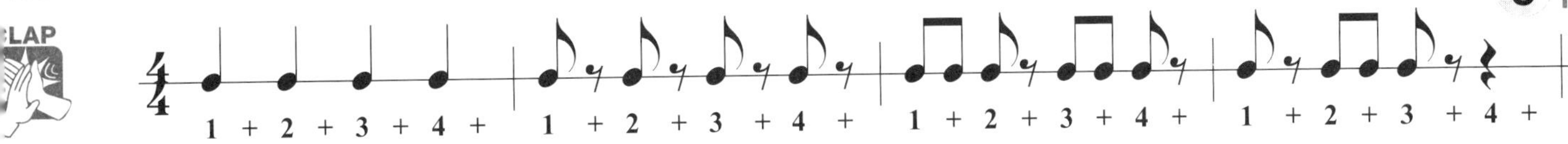

.19 SCALING WITH EIGHTH RESTS

TRACK 3 19

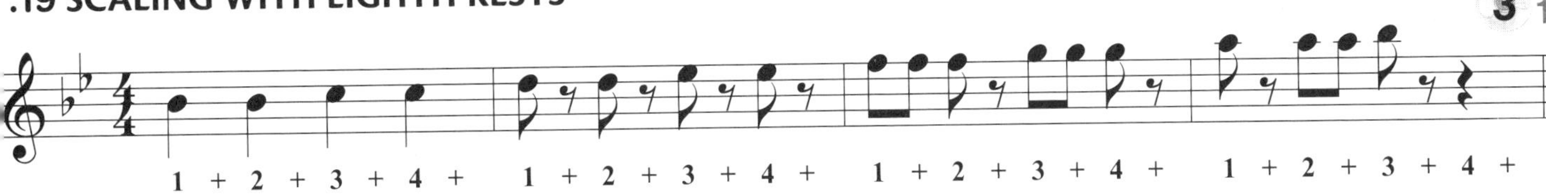

ISTORY

MUSIC

German composer **Johann Sebastian Bach** (1685 – 1750) began learning music as a young boy, studying violin and organ. He is thought to be one of the greatest composers who ever lived. His work is the model of the Baroque style.

ART

Peter Paul Rubens painted a series of works in the Baroque Style for Marie de Medici at the Luxembourg Palace in Paris, France. These works are now on display at the Louvre, one of the most famous art museums in the world.

WORLD

The tuning fork was invented by Englishman John Shore, the first folding umbrella was manufactured in France, and infamous pirate Edward Teach (Blackbeard) terrorized people along the Atlantic coast.

5.20 MINUET NO. 1

J. S. Bach TRACK 3 20

Moderato

5.21 BEAT STREET

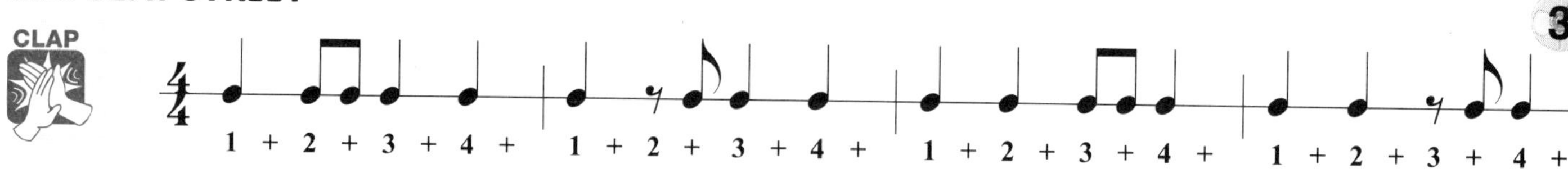

5.22 STEPPIN' OFF THE EIGHTH

5.23 TIPTOE TANGO *Tango is a type of music and dance that originated in Buenos Aires, Argentina.*

5.24 ROCK ON, ROCK OFF – Duet

ORY

ARTICULATION: TENUTO AND STACCATO

Tenuto
Play with full value.

Staccato
Play light and separated.

25 LONG AND SHORT OF IT

Listen carefully to the winds. As you become more advanced, you will learn more about these articulations.

TRACK 3 25

TORY

MUSIC

Austrian composer **Franz Joseph Haydn** (1732 – 1809) is often referred to as the father of the symphony (He wrote 108 of them!). *Symphony No. 94* is often called the *Surprise Symphony*. Haydn surprised listeners with an unexpected loud chord that came after some very quiet music.

ART

Americans saw paintings by countryman John Trumbull (his historical painting *Declaration of Independence* is on the back of the $2 bill). In England, young artist Joseph Turner was setting the tone for Impressionism.

WORLD

The United States Bill of Rights was ratified, the world's first Sunday newspaper (*The Observer)* was published in England, and Benjamin Franklin invented bifocals!

26 SURPRISE SYMPHONY

Franz J. Haydn — TRACK 3 26

Andante

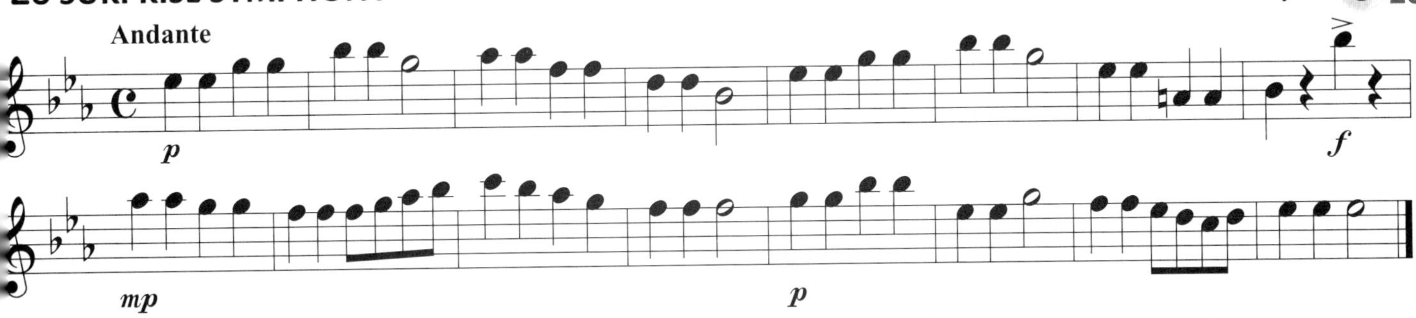

STORY

MUSIC

Paul Abraham Dukas (1865 – 1935) was a French composer who wrote in the Romantic style. His most famous work, *The Sorcerer's Apprentice,* is based on a poem by Johann Wolfgang von Goethe. The poem describes an apprentice who loses control of an enchanted broomstick.

ART

Edvard Munch, from Norway, painted in the Expressionist style which uses symbolism to portray many different themes. One of his best-known works is *The Scream* (1893).

WORLD

The 19th Amendment gave women the right to vote, author Madeleine L'Engle was born, and the first underground metro railway opened in Boston.

.27 THE SORCERER'S APPRENTICE

Paul A. Dukas — TRACK 3 27

Misterioso

.28 GO DOWN MOSES

Spiritual — TRACK 3 28

NEW NOTE! G♭

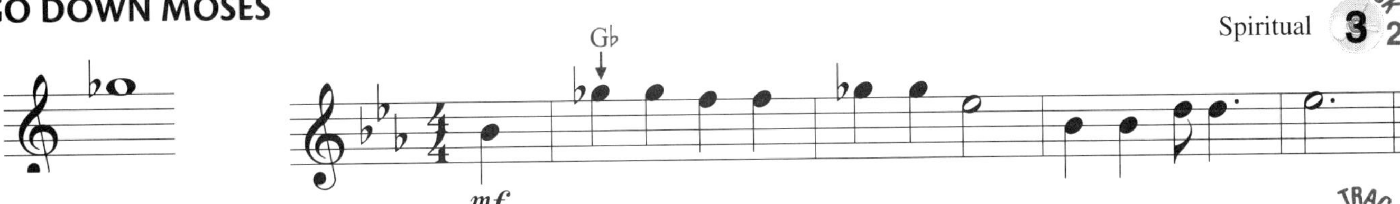

.29 JITTERS, CRITTERS

TRACK 3 29

Misterioso

OPUS 5 ENCORE!

INTERPRETATION STATION

Listen to CD 3 Track 30. For each example, decide if the articulation is ***L**egato* or ***S**taccato.*
Circle the letter that corresponds with your answer.

1. L S 2. L S 3. L S 4. L S

SIMON "SEZ"

Listen to CD 3 Track 31. You will hear a well-known song. Listen first, sing it, then find the pitches on your instrument. You can then play along with the accompaniment track that follows. Can you match the notes and style of the initial recording?

COMPOSER'S CORNER

Writing a theme is just one part of a composer's process. Composers also use dynamics to make their music more expressive.
Add your own dynamics and then play the piece expressively. Choose from the following:

p ***mp*** ***mf*** ***f*** < >

PENCIL POWER – MATCH THE STYLE TERMS

Match the style term with the correct definition by writing in the appropriate letter.

_____ Legato	A. In a singing style
_____ Maestoso	B. In a march style
_____ Dolce	C. Smooth and flowing
_____ Marziale	D. Sweetly
_____ Cantabile	E. Blend of African and Caribbean music
_____ Calypso	F. Majestically

CURTAIN UP!

5.30 LOCH LOMOND

Scottish Folk Song

Cantabile

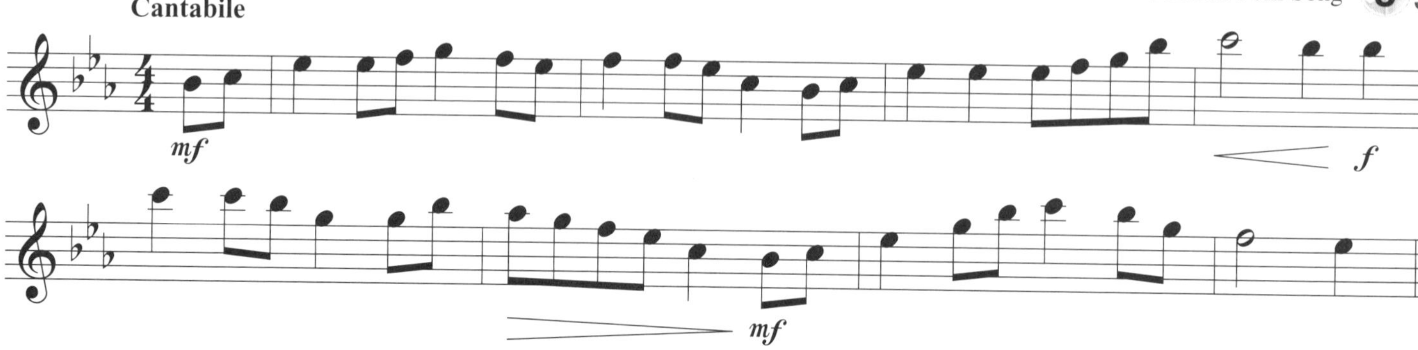

CURTAIN UP! FULL BAND

31 LA MORISQUE (RENAISSANCE DANCE)

Tielman Susato
arr. Brian Balmages

TRACK 3 33

.32 COSSACK'S MARCHING SONG

Russian Folk Song
arr. Robert Sheldon

TRACK 3 34

OPUS 6

THEORY

ENHARMONICS

Two notes that have the same pitch but different names are called **enharmonics**. An example would be G♭ and F♯. They have different names but share the same bar on a keyboard instrument!

6.1 ENHARMONIC ZONE

TRACK 3

NEW NOTE! F♯/G♭

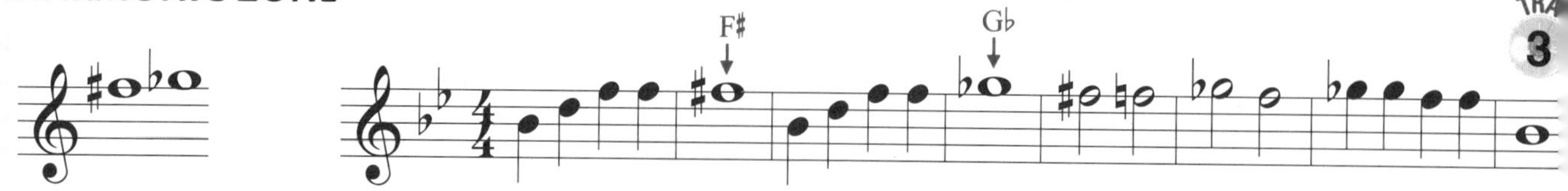

6.2 THE SPHINX

TRACK 3

6.3 THE SPY

TRACK 3

NEW NOTE! C♯/D♭

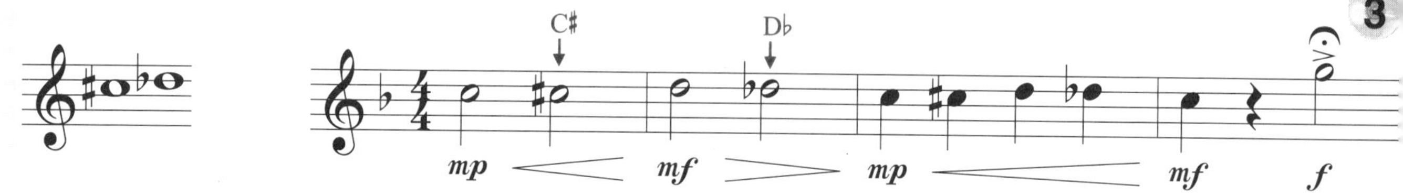

6.4 FINAL FRONTIER

TRACK 3

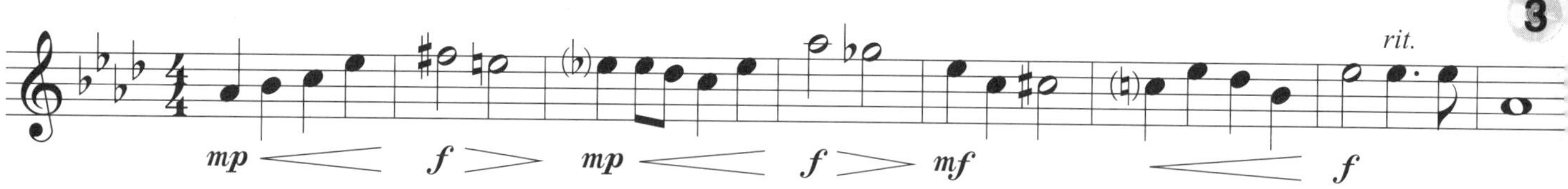

6.5 MARCH SLAV

TRACK 3

Maestoso

Pyotr I. Tchaikovsky

THEORY

DYNAMICS

pp (*pianissimo*) – play very soft

ff (*fortissimo*) – play very loud

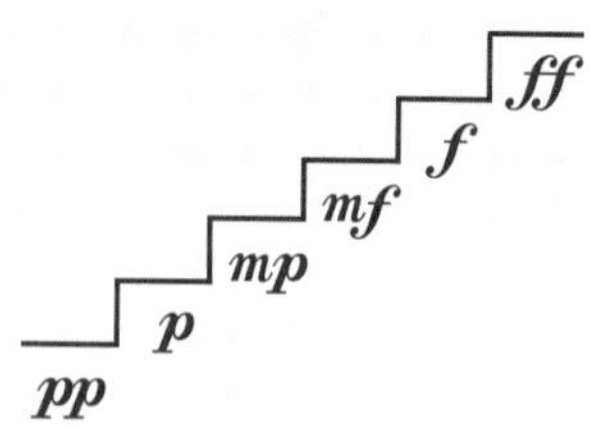

DYNAMICS AND MALLET HEIGHTS

ff = 12" above the bar. *pp* = 1" above the bar.
Remember to always play in the center of the bar!

6.6 ARIRANG

ON THE PODIUM

TRACK 34

Andante

Korean Folk Song

TORY

MUSIC

Italian born **Giuseppe Verdi** (1813 – 1901) is best known for his operas, especially *Il Trovatore* (The Troubadour), first performed in 1853. The *Anvil Chorus*, from Act 2 of *Il Trovatore*, features Spanish gypsies who sing and strike anvils as they work in the early morning.

ART

Art in the style of Luminism began in the 1850s and was characterized by the use of light effects best seen in sea and landscapes. This American style is found in works by Frederic Church (*Twilight in the Wilderness*) and Martin Heade (*Sunlight and Shadow: The Newbury Marshes*).

WORLD

In 1853, when *Il Trovatore* premiered, the Ottoman Empire declared war on Russia, the Gadsden Purchase (currently southern Arizona and New Mexico) was made, and potato chips made their first tasty appearance.

7 ANVIL CHORUS

TRACK 3 41

Giuseppe Verdi

Pesante *(heavily)*

EORY

MORE DYNAMICS

cresc. Sometimes this abbreviation is used in place of a crescendo sign. It means the same thing as the sign; gradually play louder.

decresc. Sometimes this abbreviation is used in place of a decrescendo sign. It means the same thing as the sign; gradually play softer.

.8 YANKEE DOODLE CAME AND WENT

TRACK 3 42

American Folk Melody

Moderato

HEORY

MAJOR SCALE, ARPEGGIO, AND CHORD

A **major scale** has eight notes going up or down in consecutive order, all in the key signature of the scale name. In your key of B♭ Major, all eight notes are in the key signature of B♭ Major, which has 2 flats. The top and bottom notes are both B♭. The distance between these notes is called an **octave**.

An **arpeggio** is the first, third, and fifth notes of a scale played in *succession*. It may also include the 8th scale note.

A **major chord** is the first, third, and fifth notes of a major scale played *simultaneously*. Like the arpeggio, it may also include the 8th scale note.

.9 CONCERT B♭ MAJOR SCALE

TRACK 3 43

6.10 CONCERT B♭ MAJOR ARPEGGIO AND CHORD

TRACK 3 44

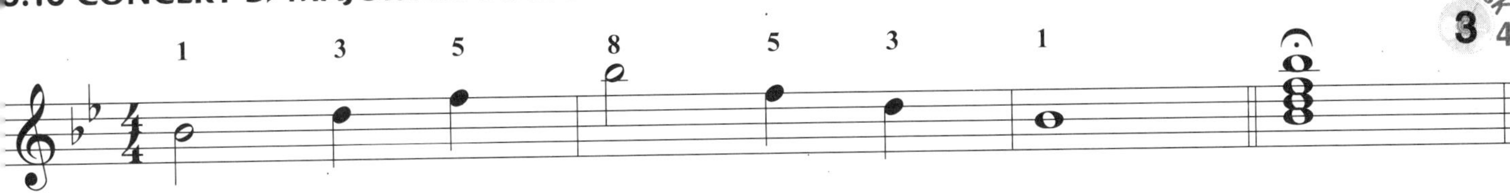

6.11 KUM BAH YAH *Circle the arpeggios.*

TRACK 3

African Folk Song

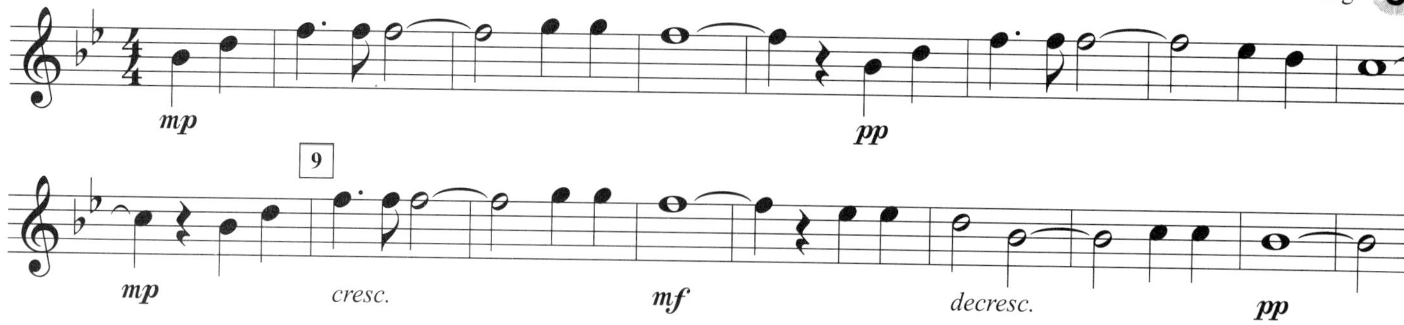

THEORY

INTERVALS

An **interval** is the distance between two pitches. You can figure out the interval by counting each line and space between the notes. Starting with "1" on the bottom note, count upward until you reach the top note. The number of the top note identifies the interval.

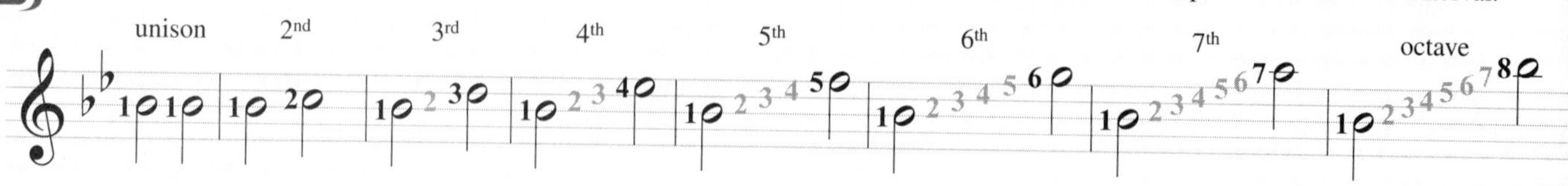

6.12 RANGE ROVER *Identify each interval, counting from the bottom note.*

TRACK 3

ON THE PODIUM

6.13 HATIKVAH

TRACK 3

Israeli National Anthem

6.14 HEY!

TRACK 3 4

ON THE PODIUM

MORE ABOUT SYNCOPATION

You already know the quarter-half-quarter syncopation. The most common syncopated rhythm is eighth-quarter-eighth. Here the syncopation occurs on the accented upbeat quarter note.

15 BEAT STREET

TRACK 3 49

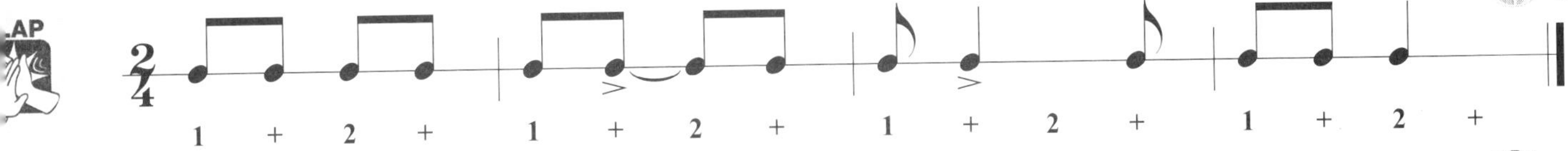

16 SYNCOPHOBIA

TRACK 3 50

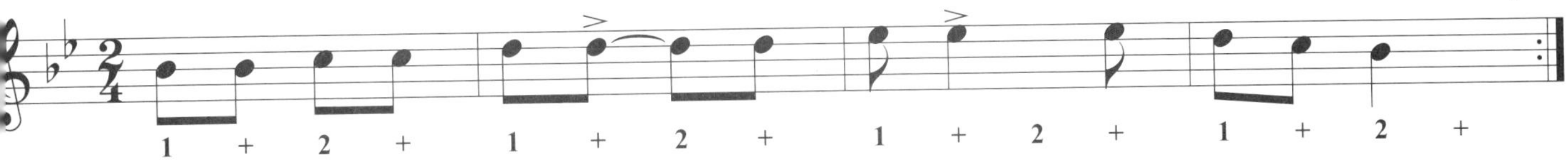

17 THE CAISSONS GO ROLLING ALONG

Edmund L. Gruber

TRACK 3 51

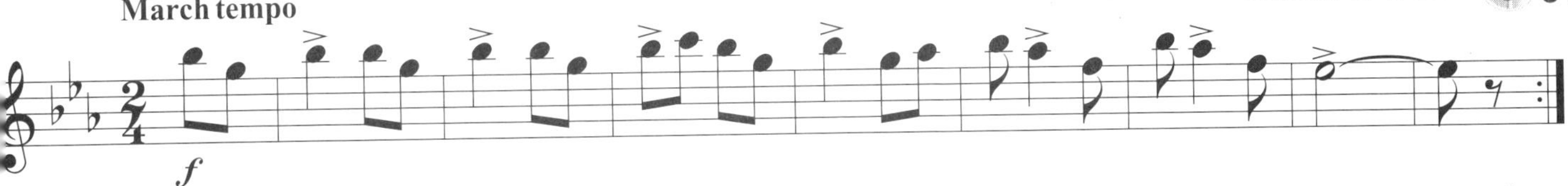

18 LI'L LIZA JANE

American Folk Song

TRACK 3 52

19 MAYIM, MAYIM – Duet

An ostinato is a musical pattern that is repeated over and over again. It is typically based on a short melodic or rhythmic idea and is generally performed by the same instrument part.

Israeli Folk Song

TRACK 3 53

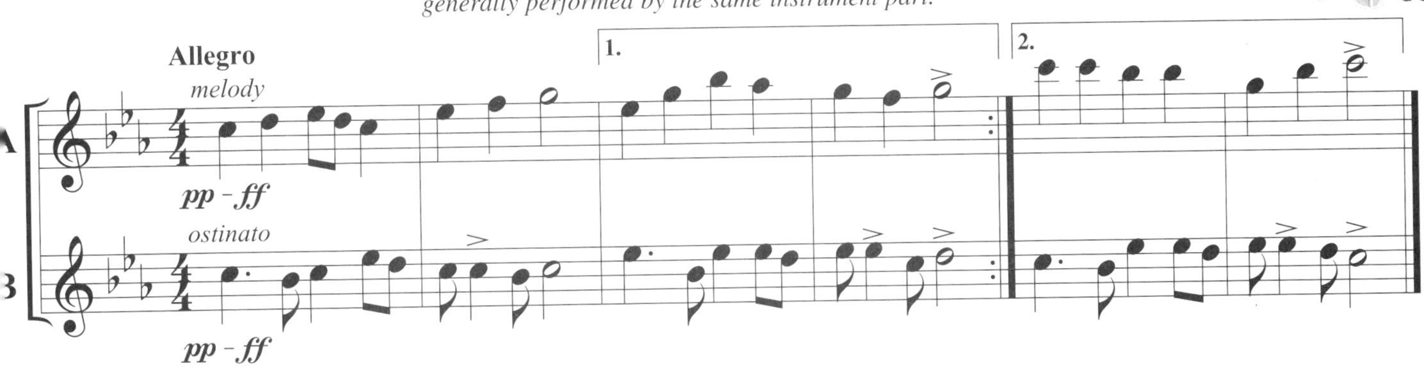

20 COVENTRY CAROL

English Carol

TRACK 3 54

NEW NOTE! B

6.21 DIES IRAE

Pesante — att. Thomas of Celano

6.22 LEAGUE OF SUPERHEROES

Allegro

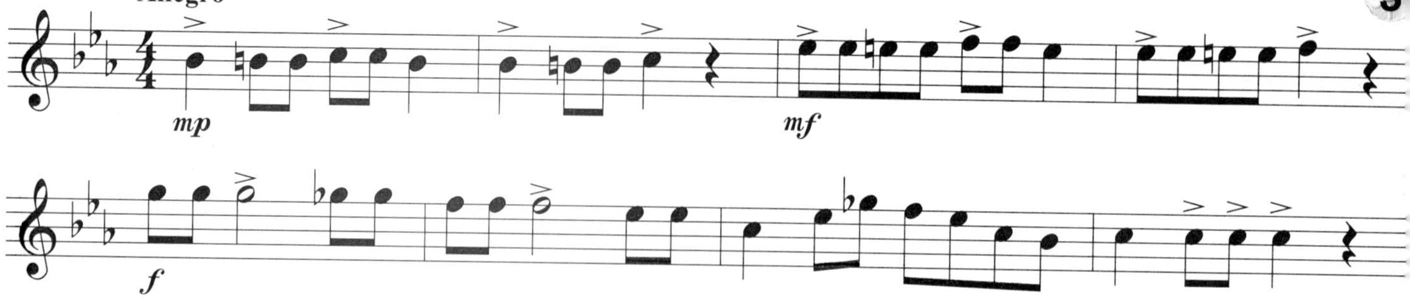

CHROMATIC SCALE

A **half step** is the smallest interval between two pitches. Two consecutive half steps make a **whole step.** The **chromatic scale** has thirteen notes going up and down in consecutive half steps.

6.23 CHROMATIC SCALE

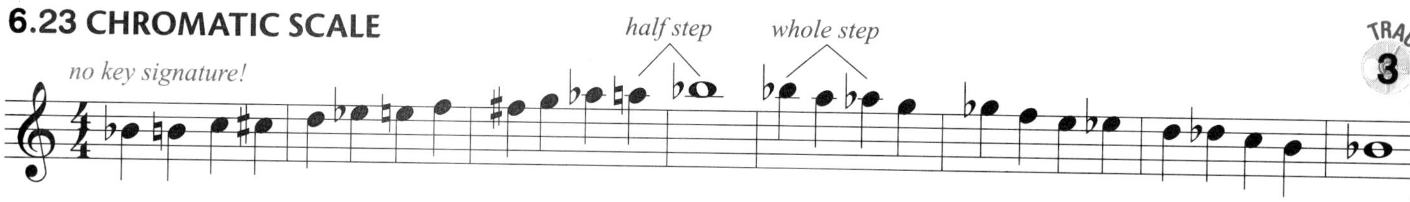

MUSIC

Georges Bizet (1838 – 1875) was a child prodigy from Paris who composed his first symphony in 1855 when he was just 16! In his short 36-year life, he wrote many different types of music but is best known for his operas. His most famous opera is *Carmen*.

ART

The Impressionistic style was all the rage in the art world. Edgar Degas had painted *In Concert Cafe*, *The Song of the Dog*. American realist painter Thomas Eakins completed the *Gross Clinic*, a very real rendition of a surgeon overseeing an operation to remove part of a diseased thighbone.

WORLD

Events in 1875 included the first organized indoor ice hockey game in Montreal, the running of the first Kentucky Derby, and the patent of the electric dental drill.

6.24 HABAÑERA (FROM CARMEN) – Duet *Where is the ostinato?*

Moderato — Georges Bizet

OPUS 6 ENCORE!

NTERPRETATION STATION

TRACK 3 59

isten to CD 3 Track 59. For each musical example, decide if the melody is based on a <u>S</u>cale or an <u>A</u>rpeggio.
ircle the letter that corresponds with your answer.

1. S A 2. S A 3. S A 4. S A

IMON "SEZ"

TRACK 3 60

istén to CD 3 Track 60. You will hear a well-known piece. Listen first, sing it, then find the pitches on your instrument.
ou can then play along with the accompaniment track that follows. Can you match the notes and style of the initial recording?

COMPOSER'S CORNER

erformers sometimes compose music on the spot while they are playing! This is called **improvisation.** There is an ostinato below.
lave a partner play it (or use CD 3 Track 61 as a background track) while you improvise. Use the guide notes to help you out. Have fun!
ote: The CD recording repeats 4 times.

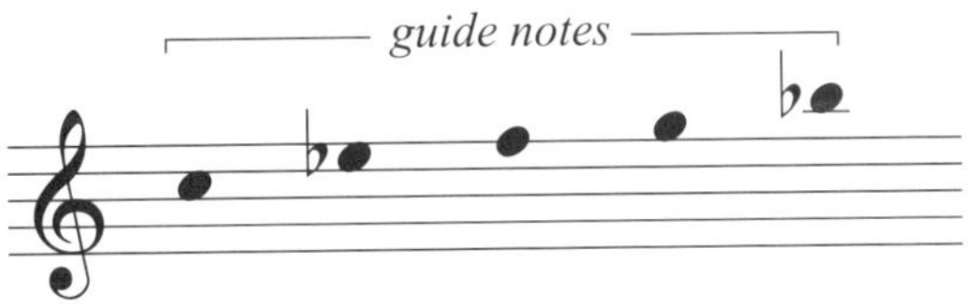

VHATEVER!"

TRACK 3 61

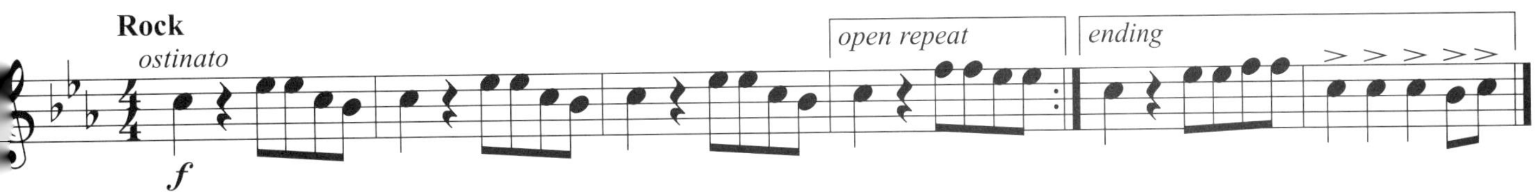

PENCIL POWER

)n the staff below, notate the enharmonic for each note. See if you can figure out the bonus notes!

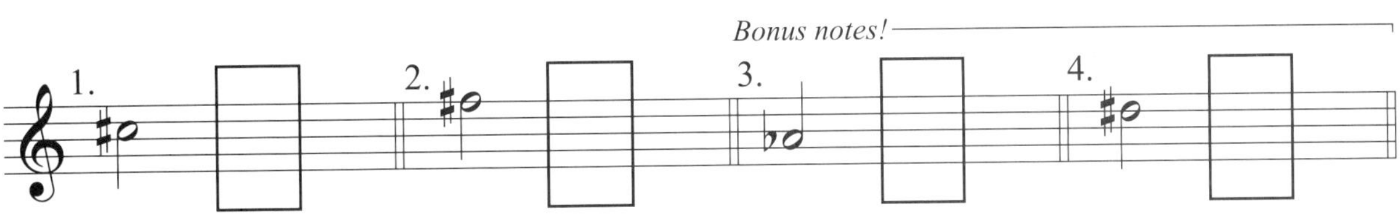

CURTAIN UP!

.25 O CANADA

TRACK 3 62

Canadian National Anthem
Calixa Lavallée, Sir Adolphe-Basile Routhier, and Justice R.S. Weir

6.26 CHORALE IN B♭ MAJOR
(ALLE MENSCHEN MÜSSEN STERBEN)

J. S. Bach

6.27 RABBLE ROUSER

Robert Sheldon

28 PROCESSION OF THE CHAMPIONS

Brian Balmages

TRACK 3 65

6.29 ROYAL MARCH OF THE LION

Instrumental Solo

Camille Saint-Saëns
arr. Brian Balmages

Piano Accompaniment

Note: Sections are repeated in the accompaniment for spacing reasons and do not always follow the solo part.

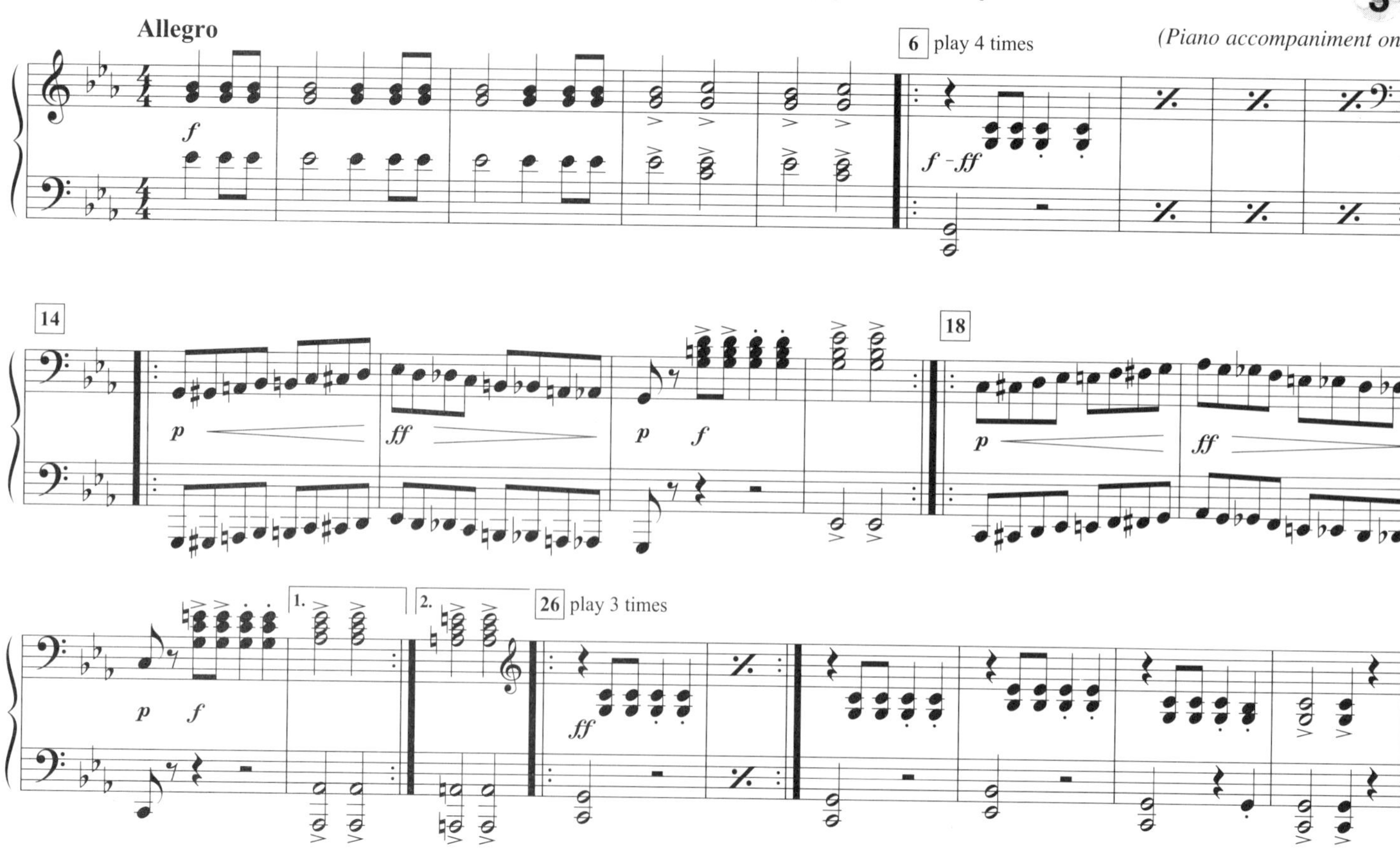

SCALES AND TECHNIQUE

CONCERT B♭ MAJOR

CALE

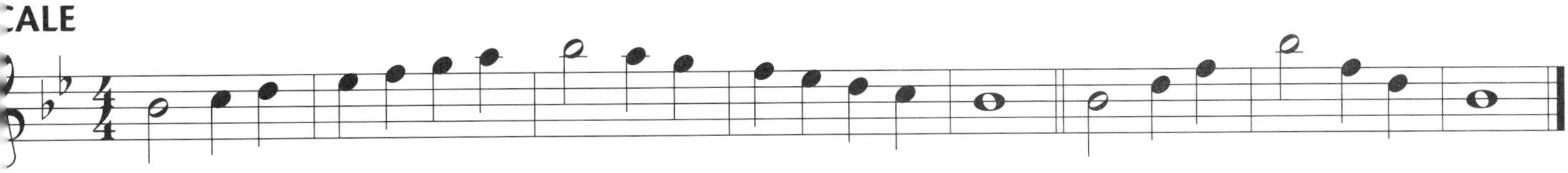

CALE IN THIRDS

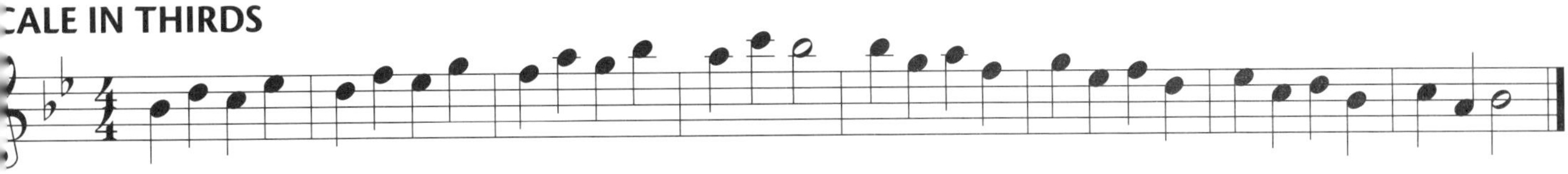

CONCERT E♭ MAJOR

CALE

CALE IN THIRDS

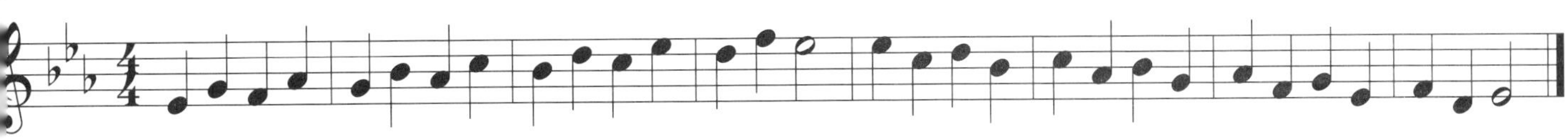

CONCERT A♭ MAJOR

CALE

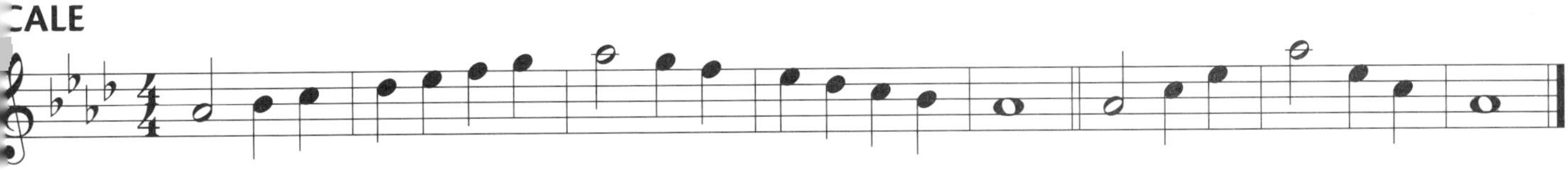

CALE IN THIRDS

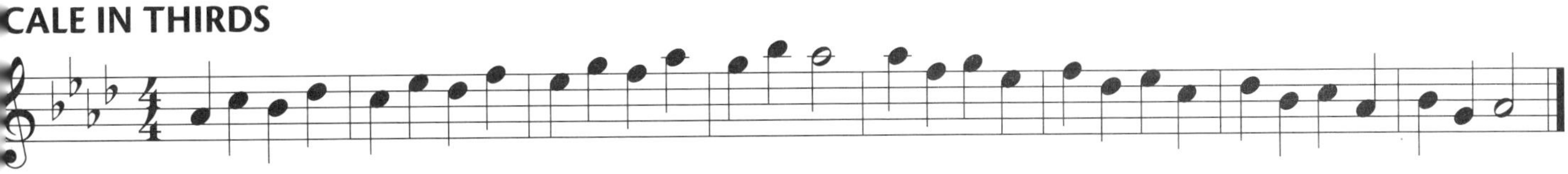

CONCERT F MAJOR

CALE

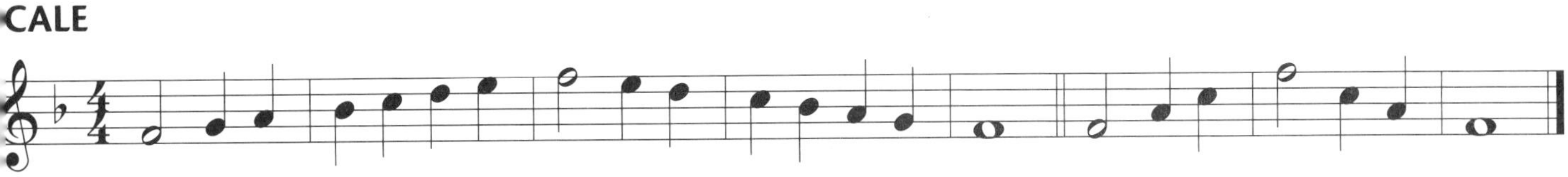

CALE IN THIRDS

CHROMATIC SCALE

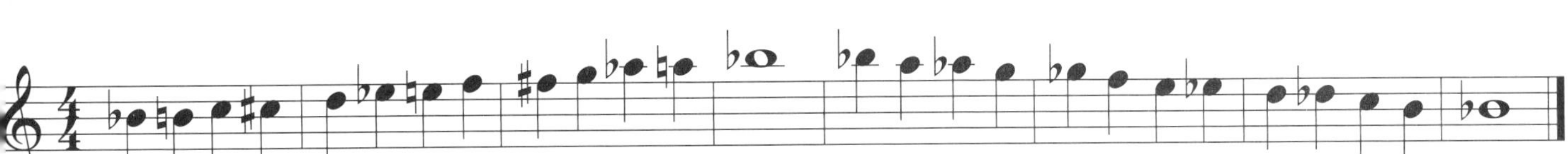

RHYTHM REVIEW – OPUS 1-6

An additional rhythm review can be found in the first section of your book on page 52.

1A

1B
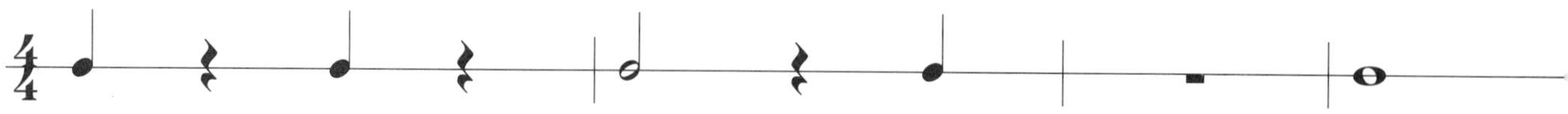

2A
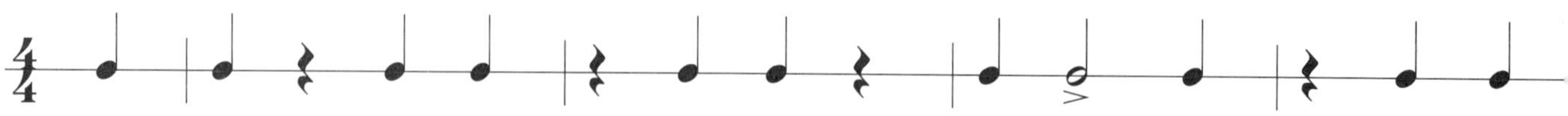

2B

3A

3B

3C
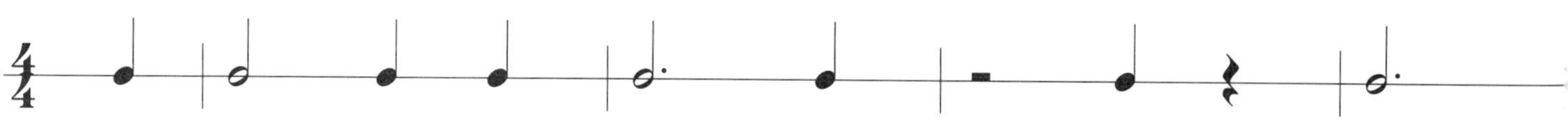

3D
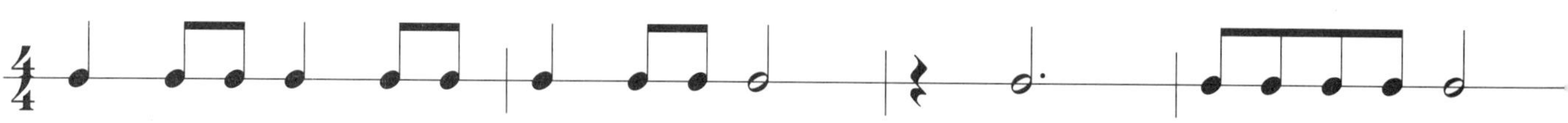

3E

4A
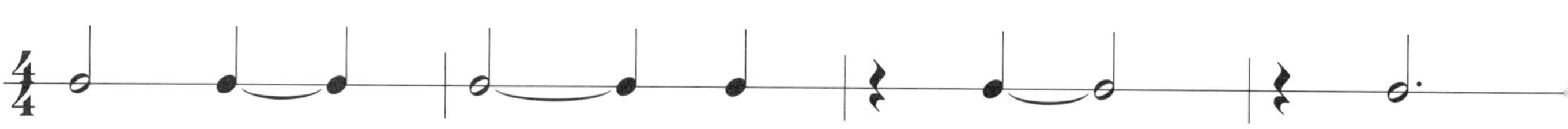

KEYBOARD PERCUSSION LAYOUT

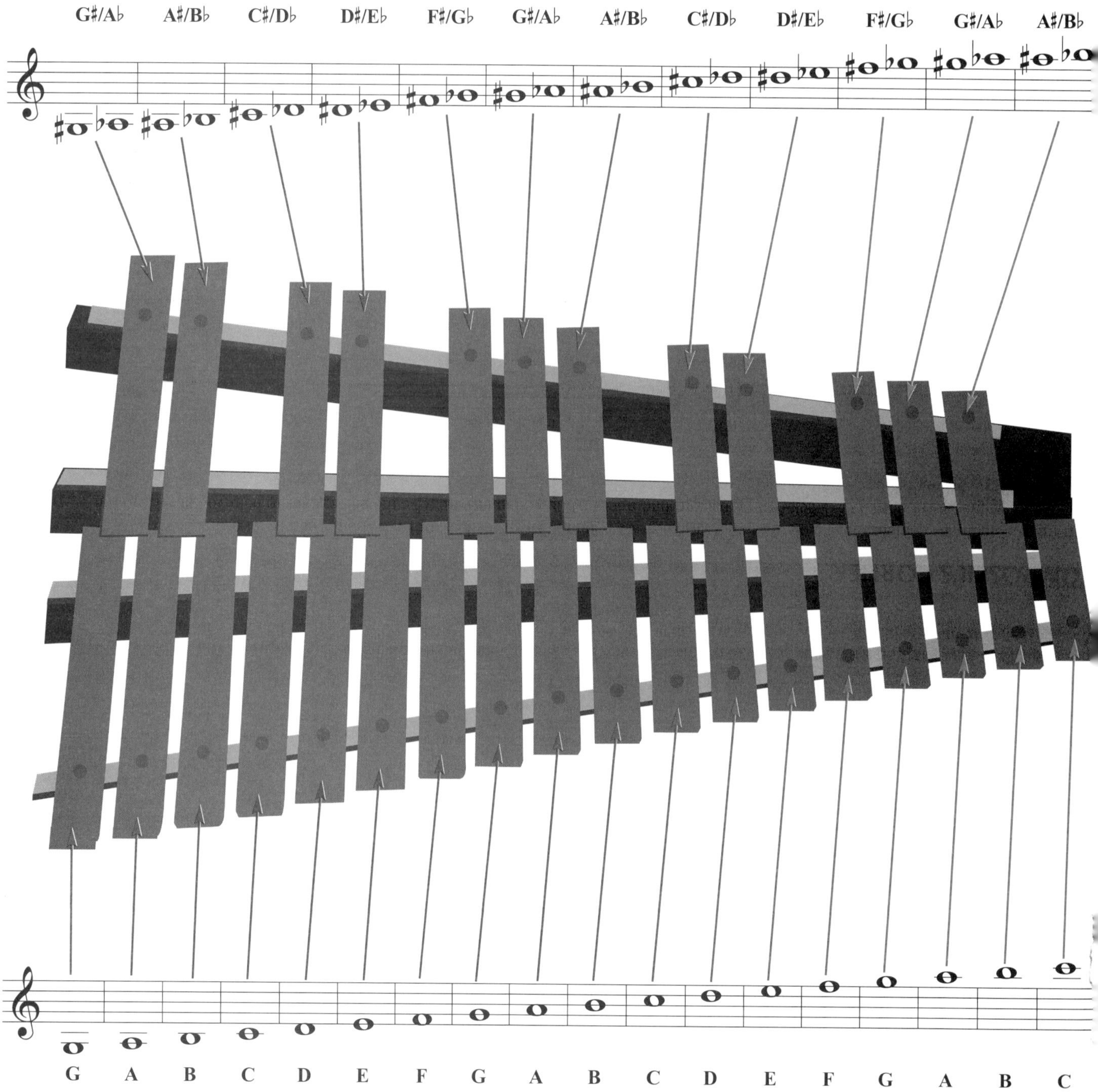

KEYBOARD PERCUSSION

:LLS

- ars – metal alloy or steel
- allets – hard rubber, ard plastic or brass
- ounds 2 octaves higher an written

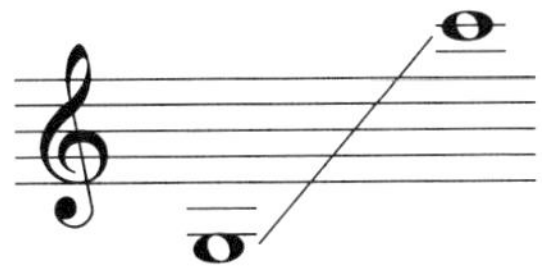

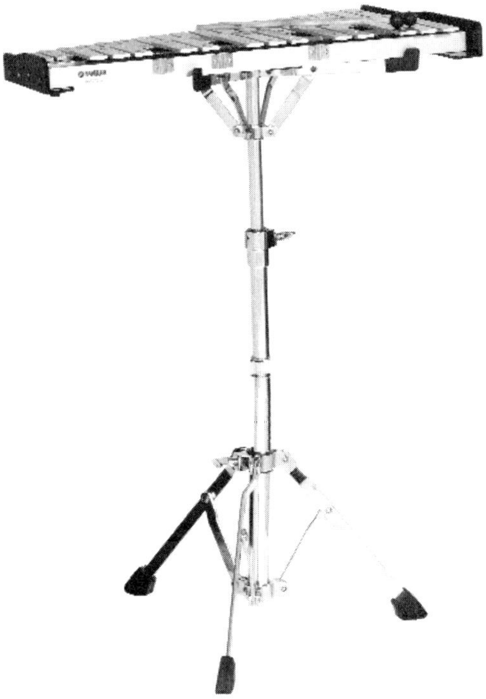

HIMES

- 3ars – metal tubes
- Mallets – plastic, rawhide or wooden
- Sounding pitch is the same s written pitch

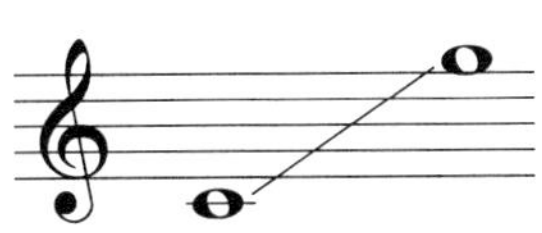

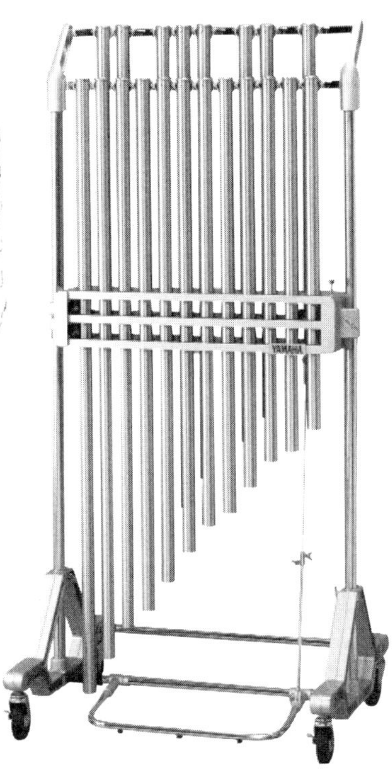

otographs courtesy of Yamaha Corporation of America

XYLOPHONE

- Bars – wooden or synthetic, with a resonating tube below each bar
- Mallets – hard rubber
- Sounds 1 octave higher than written

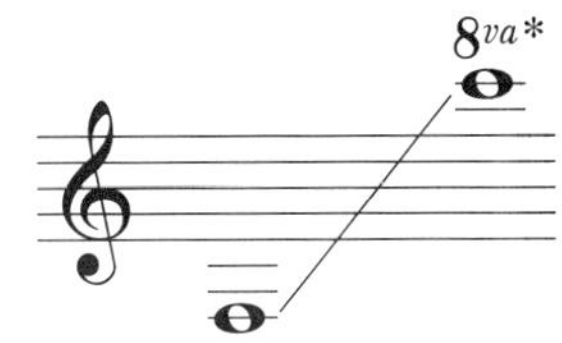

*8va = one octave higher

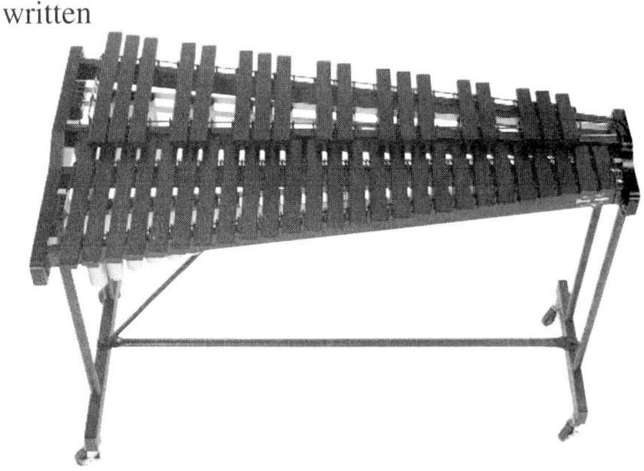

MARIMBA

- Bars – wooden, wider than xylophone bars, with a resonating tube below each bar
- Mallets – soft to medium yarn covered
- Sounding pitch is the same as written pitch
- Reads bass and treble clefs

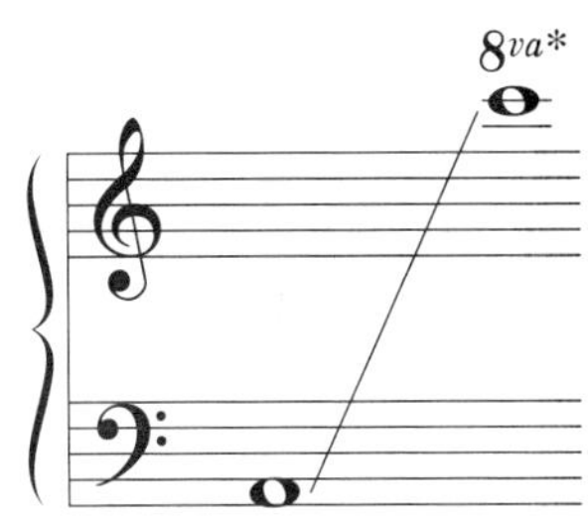

*8va = one octave higher

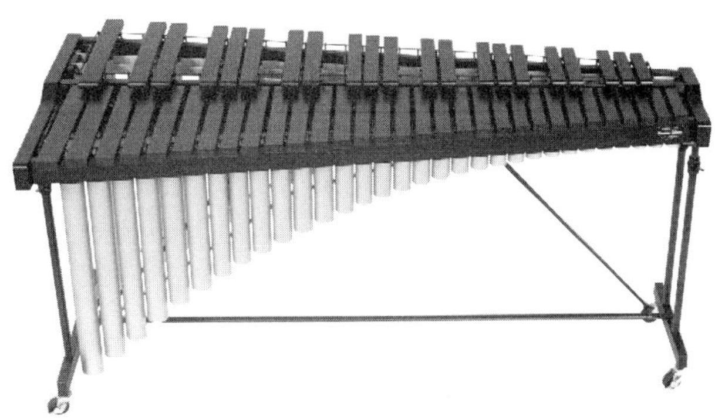

VIBRAPHONE

- Bars – metal alloy or aluminum, with a resonating tube below each bar
- Mallets – soft to medium cord covered
- Sounding pitch is the same as written pitch

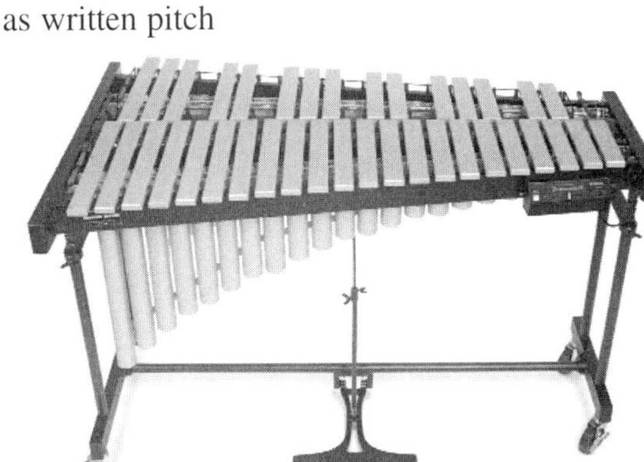

INDEX

A percussion index can be found or page 56b in the first section of this

TERMS

COMPOSERS

WORLD MUSIC

HOLIDAY MUSIC

NOTES

NOTES